CONTINUITY AND CHANGE IN VOLUNTARY ACTION

Patterns, trends and understandings

Rose Lindsey and John Mohan,
with Sarah Bulloch and Elizabeth Metcalfe

First published in Great Britain in 2019 by

Policy Press
University of Bristol
1-9 Old Park Hill
Bristol
BS2 8BB
UK
t: +44 (0)117 954 5940
pp-info@bristol.ac.uk
www.policypress.co.uk

North America office:
Policy Press
c/o The University of Chicago Press
1427 East 60th Street
Chicago, IL 60637, USA
t: +1 773 702 7700
f: +1 773-702-9756
sales@press.uchicago.edu
www.press.uchicago.edu

© Policy Press 2019

British Library Cataloguing in Publication Data
A catalogue record for this book is available from the British Library

Library of Congress Cataloging-in-Publication Data
A catalog record for this book has been requested

ISBN 978-1-4473-2483-6 hardcover
ISBN 978-1-4473-2484-3 paperback
ISBN 978-1-4473-2487-4 ePub
ISBN 978-1-4473-2488-1 Mobi
ISBN 978-1-4473-2486-7 epdf

The right of Rose Lindsey and John Mohan, with Sarah Bulloch and Liz Metcalfe to
be identified as authors of this work has been asserted by them in accordance with the
Copyright, Designs and Patents Act 1988.

Cover design by Qube Design Associates, Bristol
Printed and bound in Great Britain by CMP, Poole
Policy Press uses environmentally responsible print partners

Contents

List of figures and tables

Figures

Tables

Foreword

Pete Alcock

This is the third volume to appear in the Third Sector Research Series. Previous contributions have focused primarily on the organisational base of the sector, and this will continue in planned books on the third sector in the devolved administrations of the UK, on the geography of the sector, and on attempts to build the infrastructure of the third sector to support organisational development.

In this book the emphasis shifts to action by individuals – in many ways a defining feature of the third/voluntary sector. The extent, distribution, measurement and meanings of volunteering formed an important strand in the research of the Third Sector Research Centre (TSRC). These have also been issues of direct public concern, with great weight being attached, in particular during the UK Coalition government (2010–15), to trends in voluntary activity. Understanding volunteering is thus of central political, and academic, interest. The innovative approach embodied in this book mean that it will make a significant addition to the current body of literature on volunteering.

First, the authors have drawn on more than three decades of survey data. Despite variation in the approaches taken by these surveys, they demonstrate the long-term stability of volunteering rates. Second, recognising that there is considerable disagreement about how to define and measure voluntary action, the authors also examine contemporaneous qualitative evidence from individuals about the nature and meaning of their voluntary activities. This has been achieved through a long-term collaboration with the Mass Observation Archive, using qualitative material submitted by individuals in which they describe the nature and meaning of their voluntary activities, and discuss their attitudes to volunteering.

The result of this research is a rich mixed-methods study which offers important lessons, both positive and negative, about the nature of voluntary action. The quantitative research reveals that those seeking to raise levels of voluntary action should be more cautious in their claims regarding the extent to which it is possible to do so. The overall message here is that there has been stability in voluntary engagement, albeit with short-term fluctuations largely related to economic circumstances. The good news is that volunteering rates have not declined; the bad news is that despite generally rising prosperity, and increased levels of participation in higher education, neither have they risen.

The qualitative material presented here provides fascinating insights into the place of voluntary action in people's lives, and into their attitudes to voluntary engagement. Individuals have been tracked over time, using Mass Observation Project data, allowing the researchers to explore how writers' voluntary commitments originate from, and fit around, their other activities and relationships - such as home, church or workplace. It has also permitted the authors to develop a significant understanding of attitudes to voluntary action – although again there are cautionary notes here. Those who write for Mass Observation are active citizens by any definition, but they react adversely to unreflective calls for more volunteering, feel that their previous commitments have been taken for granted by governments, and are very cynical about being asked to do more, especially in a context of austerity.

This book provides a fascinating portrait of the enormous range of voluntary activities undertaken by individuals, revealing how their activities cannot be corralled into neat divisions between formal and informal volunteering. It also provides an evidence-based account of why some of the great expectations of voluntary initiative are unlikely to be realised without a fuller understanding of the place of volunteering in people's everyday lives.

Pete Alcock
Emeritus Professor of Social Policy and Administration and former Director
of the Third Sector Research Centre, University of Birmingham

Acknowledgements

This book would not have been possible without the enormous contributions of two groups of people, to whom we are greatly indebted. The first is the volunteer writers who respond, several times a year, to the directives issued by Mass Observation. The material they generate is a never-ending source of insights into life in contemporary Britain. It provides extraordinarily rich material for a study such as ours, greatly enhancing the picture of voluntary action from more conventional social research sources such as surveys. We are not sure what the Mass Observers would have made of this book but we dedicate it to them with gratitude for their efforts.

Second, this material is curated through the heroic efforts of the Mass Observation project staff at the The Keep, Brighton. Since 1981, the project has accumulated responses from several thousand individual volunteer writers and has meticulously catalogued them so that they can be used as a research resource. We are particularly grateful for all the support, over a number of years, of Jessica Scantlebury and Kirsty Pattrick, for what has become a long-standing collaboration sparked off by discussions at the Mass Observation 75th anniversary conference in 2012.

The project on which this book draws originated in joint work by Rose and John with Sarah Bulloch (TSRC, Southampton) and Ros Edwards (Sociology and Social Policy, Southampton) resulting in a successful bid for ESRC support which provided the resources to employ Liz Metcalfe as researcher on the project. Sarah and Ros contributed to the early development of the project, and co-authored methodological papers which are reflected in part of Chapter Three. Sarah carried out further work with Rose on attitudes to the Big Society which is reflected in Chapter Eight, and with John on the civic core, discussed in Chapter Five. Liz conducted extensive quantitative analyses which are reflected in Chapters Four and Seven. We are very happy to acknowledge these contributions to the project and to credit Sarah and Liz with co-authorship of the chapters referred to.

Various colleagues in the Third Sector Research Centre and elsewhere have also provided support and/or comments on this work. These include David Clifford, Adalbert Evers, Daiga Kamerade, Jeremy Kendall, Andrew McCulloch, Steve McKay and Rob MacMillan. We are especially indebted to Angela Ellis Paine, who read the entire first draft of the manuscript and provided characteristically insightful comments. Other TSRC colleagues who supported the work included

Rachel Cooper and Ellie Rivers. Transcription work on handwritten Mass Observation directives was conducted by Zoë Lindsey, Ben Allen and Bryony Kirkpatrick.

We are also grateful for the insights of our project advisory group, which included Jessica Scantlebury and Kirsty Pattrick from Mass Observation, Irene Hardill (Northumbria University), Julia Slay (New Economics Foundation) and Peter Smith (University of Southampton).

Findings from the project were presented at several conferences: the Voluntary Sector Studies Network (2014, 2017); the International Society for Third Sector Research (2014), the Association for Research on Nonprofits and Voluntary Action (ARNOVA) (2016); at the ESRC Research Methods Festivals in 2014 and 2016; and at the Mass Observation 75th and 80th Anniversary conferences (2012 and 2017) and separately at Mass Observation in 2013; we have benefited from the thoughtful comments of participants at all those conferences. .

Financial support for the project came from a number of sources: the ESRC's Secondary Data Analysis Initiative funded two separate projects (reference numbers ES/K003550/1, ES/L013819/1) and on MO data from 2012 through to 2015; the Barrow Cadbury Trust and the University of Birmingham have supported John Mohan's work as Director of TSRC; and John, Rose and Sarah initially collaborated through work on the Third Sector Research Centre, funded by ESRC, the Barrow Cadbury Trust and the Office for the Third Sector (ESRC reference ES/G028877/1).

We have acknowledged our debt to those who have written for Mass Observation but writing a book on this scale also has effects on others, so we conclude with our personal acknowledgements:

John: I would like to acknowledge the unprompted editorial advice and, much more importantly, the unstinting personal support of Ellie Rivers.

Rose: I would like to acknowledge my lovely dad, John Lindsey, and daughters Zoë Lindsey and Tilda Lindsey for their patience and support while I was writing this book. Thanks also to Zoë for regular walks around Southampton Common while chatting about the nature of voluntary action; and to Tilda who joined me at the kitchen table to write her essays, providing much appreciated writing companionship.

Rose Lindsey and John Mohan
December 2017

Notes on authors

Rose Lindsey has experience of working both in academia and in the voluntary sector. She is currently a Senior Research Fellow based in the Department of Sociology, Social Policy and Criminology at the University of Southampton. She has been the Chief Executive Officer of a domestic abuse charity and a trustee for several charities.

John Mohan is Professor of Social Policy, University of Birmingham, and Director of the Third Sector Research Centre. He has published extensively on contemporary and historical aspects of the third sector, with a particular recent focus on analyses of volunteering and the resources and characteristics of voluntary organisations.

Elizabeth Metcalfe was a research fellow in the Third Sector Research Centre, working on quantitative analyses of survey datasets for this project. She has subsequently moved to data scientist positions in the Office for National Statistics and the private sector.

Sarah Bulloch worked in the Third Sector Research Centre in the early stages of this project; from there she became research manager at Scope. She is currently a Teaching Fellow at the University of Surrey, and an associate of QDAS (Qualitative Data Analysis Services), specialising in mixed-methods approaches to research and teaching.

Acronyms

BHPS	British Household Panel Survey
BSAS	British Social Attitudes Survey
CLS	Community Life Survey
CPRS	Central Policy Review Staff
CS	Citizenship Survey
CSJ	Centre for Social Justice
DCLG	Department for Communities and Local Government
FPG	Family Policy Group
GHS	General Household Survey
ILO	International Labour Organisation
IPPR	Institute for Public Policy Research
ME	myalgic encephalomyelitis
MO	Mass Observation – the original project which ran from 1937–55
MOA	Mass Observation Archive
MOP	Mass Observation Project – ongoing writing panel set up in 1981
MSC	Manpower Services Commission
NCDS	National Child Development Study
NCVO	National Council for Voluntary Organisations
NHS	National Health Service
NSV	National Survey of Voluntary Activity – undertaken in 1981 and 1991
OTS	Office of the Third Sector
PSA	Public Service Agreement
PTA	Parent–Teacher Association
TSRC	Third Sector Research Centre
UK	United Kingdom
US	Understanding Society survey, replaced the BHPS in 2010/11
VFI	Volunteer Functions Inventory
WI	Women's Institute
WRVS	Women's Royal Voluntary Service

ONE

Introduction

'*I think it might surprise even the Prime Minister if a register were to be made of everything done voluntarily in this country. Certainly society would come to a juddering halt if all the volunteers, in every capacity however small, went on strike.*' (Mass Observation Project writer, Alice Dickens, responding to the 2012 '*Big Society*' directive)

'*I haven't got a clue what it* [the Big Society] *means. Nobody I've spoken to don't know either. If it's about our PM saying we're all in this together, it's a laugh.*' (Mass Observation Project writer, Gillian Reddy, responding to the 2012 '*Big Society*' directive)

'And it all starts in the family…those who set us on our way certainly knew none of the jargon phrases and would never have spoken of "informal caring networks" when they meant family and friends, relatives and neighbours.' (Margaret Thatcher, Speech to the Women's Royal Voluntary Service (WRVS), 1984)[1]

'Charitable giving is up, volunteering is up, and the Big Society is getting bigger.' (David Cameron, 2013)[2]

The Mass Observation Project (MOP) is an extraordinary resource for students of the behaviour and opinions of the British public. Individuals write for the project on a voluntary basis, and they do so in response to prompts, which allow them to develop a discussion of the subject in any way they wish. Those who write for MOP, often doing so over many years, are active citizens by any definition, and we begin and end this book by quoting their views on voluntary action. As our first (anonymised) writer for the MOP indicates, voluntary action is a crucial component of British society. But as the blunt response from our second writer implies, there is scepticism about the motives of political leaders calling for more engagement, and a lack of comprehension of what a policy to promote engagement might involve. This reflects a wider lack of understanding of the nature of voluntary action which is evident in both academic writing and non-academic discourse. Margaret Thatcher's view was that voluntary action was informal and local in character, deeply rooted in family and community. By implication, she would have had little truck with a complex social scientific enquiry into the subject, and some of her own ministers displayed an evidence-free approach to policy (Chapter Two). By the time David Cameron came to occupy 10 Downing Street, however, twists and turns in volunteering statistics were viewed as an index of the success, or otherwise, of government policy on voluntary action – though as we see in Chapter Four, there are conflicting interpretations of the trends.

Why has voluntary action become so politically important? One reason is that we expect so much of it: among many beneficial outcomes claimed for it, we might cite contributions to social cohesion and the production of social capital, providing individuals with the opportunity to gain skills which will enhance their employability, supporting the delivery of public services, and promoting civic engagement. A second reason is that in hard times governments are likely to expect more of citizens. Of course, David Cameron's Big Society initiative was the most visible sign of changes in Conservative political philosophy, and arguably the most sonorous call, from any of the recent administrations, for a change in levels of citizen engagement. Through a fusion of policies, exhortation and legislation, the 2010–15 Coalition government placed responsibility on individuals and communities to meet local needs through voluntary effort. Most recently, the current (December 2017) Prime Minister, Theresa May, has spoken of a 'shared society'[3] – but under any conceivable funding scenario, the 'perpetually moving frontier'[4] between public and private initiative will shift decisively back towards the latter.

The post-2010 period is not the first time in recent history that a British government has called for such a rebalancing of responsibilities. Chronologically, the starting point for this book, in policy terms, is 1979, with the election of Margaret Thatcher's first administration, heralding an era of privatisation and marketisation, accompanied by a constant search for public expenditure reductions, and reforms in the welfare state. While Thatcher's administrations were characterised as an era of a 'naive anti-statism' (Wistow, 1992), Thatcher's governments can be differentiated from their successors by their stress on rhetorical encouragement of voluntary action by *individuals*. This contrasts with the more formalised policies of the Labour governments (1997–2010), aimed at encouraging the development of voluntary *organisations* and constructing institutional structures for bringing the voluntary *sector* into public policy deliberation, as well as promoting voluntary action as a route to the generation of social capital (Kendall, 2003; 2009). The Thatcher and post-2010 Coalition and Conservative governments have in common a great stress on the importance of voluntary alternatives to the welfare state, and on the primacy of individual initiative. There are discourses of both virtue and necessity here: virtue, in the sense of restating traditional values of voluntary action; and necessity, in that substantial cuts in public funding require communities to develop their own solutions. This is why David Cameron, seeking a rhetorical cloak for austerity and also attempting to distinguish his party from its Thatcherite predecessors, invoked the virtues of the 'Big Society'. While there are differences in terms of political philosophies between the parties that have held power since 1979, one can also differentiate administrations in terms of whether they confined their support for voluntary action to rhetoric, endorsement and exhortation, or whether they sought to implement practical policies. Likewise, the language used has changed over time – terms in current usage, such as prosocial behaviour (associated with theories of 'nudging' and behavioural change: John et al, 2011) and 'social action' (Cabinet Office, 2015) (a much wider conception than volunteering) were simply not in evidence even ten years ago.

The principal features of these policy shifts and their implications for voluntary action and the voluntary sector are discussed in Chapter Two. An important question which as yet remains unanswered, however, is the extent to which there is stability or change in voluntary activity over the post-1979 period. How has voluntary action been defined and measured, and how do the results of such efforts resonate with the accounts given by individuals of their own participation and engagement? If there is underlying stability, for instance in the proportion of the population engaged, to what extent does that conceal a process of 'churning' – in other words, people moving in and out of voluntary commitments in response to changing personal circumstances? And what is known about the public's attitude towards and appetite for greater engagement? Is it realistic, for instance, to expect a step change in voluntarism? Are the public cynical about, or receptive to, calls for greater voluntary action?

These are the questions that motivated this book. We sought to investigate the subject through mixed methods, drawing on the extensive range of social surveys which have given consideration to volunteering in the UK since the early 1980s; and through the use of MOP writing, which offers rich qualitative insights into public attitudes and behaviours (Chapter Three). This material not only offered qualitative evidence that would considerably enrich any quantitative analyses, but also offered scope to track the behaviours and attitudes of individuals who had engaged with the MOP over a long time-period.

But, one might respond, why should we be so concerned to provide protracted academic appraisals of voluntary action by individuals? Such exercises, and the very process of academic debate about something that is both regarded as a private matter for individuals and treated uncritically as self-evidently beneficial, bring forth what we might characterise as 'anti-expert' reactions. Margaret Thatcher herself – a trained scientist – was not immune to this, as is clear from her scornful reference, in the epigraph to this chapter, to 'jargon phrases'. In proposing measures to increase volunteering and charitable giving the Cabinet Office (2011) explicitly said that engagement was a good in its own right: 'it does not matter how people give … or what they give'.

We do not think such dismissals are warranted. Analysing voluntary action is important if we are to form a realistic view of whether the expectations held of it will be fulfilled. We do need an understanding of what people do and how they do it. The capacity of communities to take over and run, through voluntary inputs, public services relinquished by the state, and the likelihood that individuals will receive direct support from friends and neighbours in the immediate community, involve two quite distinct forms of action (formal and informal volunteering respectively) and may have different consequences for the functioning of communities. A better understanding of the social patterning of voluntary activity can contribute to proposals to encourage more of it. To paraphrase Clarke (2014), communities do not always respond when they are summoned, and we need an understanding of why this is the case.

In this introductory chapter, we first place this study in the context of previous research on voluntary action and spell out the contribution that our work will make. In particular, we relate our work to academic understandings of volunteering and demonstrate its potential to illuminate key questions around the meaning of voluntary action to individuals, their motivations for engagement, and the opportunities and constraints that they face. Next, we describe the sources and methods we have used to provide a rich mixed-methods study of continuity and change in voluntary action; these include previously-untapped sources on the behaviour and attitudes of individuals. Finally, we outline the structure of the book.

How and why people volunteer: definition and measurement, motivations and meanings

Most social survey questions on the topic define voluntary action as help given, or work done, without remuneration that is of benefit to people beyond one's immediate family, albeit with much variation on this theme in terms of question phrasing, framing and sequencing. Such a definition might seem unproblematic, but there are extensive debates concerning: whether or not such approaches capture the full range of voluntary activity or whether they prioritise certain categories of action over others (Hustinx, 2001; Hustinx and Lammertyn, 2003); different explanatory and disciplinary 'paradigms' used in the analysis of voluntary action; and the meanings of voluntary action to individuals, and their motivations for undertaking it. Our approach, using rich qualitative material in which individuals describe and reflect on their volunteering activities, alongside analyses of survey data, adds much to these debates. It situates individual accounts of voluntary action in the context of the lifecourses of the individuals concerned, and the communities in which they live.

Definition and measurement

Extensive international and comparative research effort has gone into producing a consensus definition of voluntary action and a methodology for measuring it that can readily be deployed across the world. The International Labour Organisation (ILO) proposed a definition of volunteering as 'unpaid non-compulsory work; that is, time individuals give without pay to activities performed by an organisation or directly to individuals outside their own household' (ILO, 2011, 13). Note two features of this: volunteering is defined as 'work', and not as 'help', as is the case in many surveys; and the definition encompasses both formal volunteering through organisations, and informal volunteering (direct support for individuals). Compare the ILO definition with that used in the 1991 National Survey of Volunteering in the UK, a definition which was later given some formal status by the Home Office (2005b):

> Any activity that involves spending time, unpaid, doing something that aims to benefit the environment or someone (individuals or groups) other than, or in addition to, close relatives. (Lynn and Davis-Smith, 1992, 16)

5

This is almost identical, except that 'work' is replaced with the looser 'doing something' (see Staetsky and Mohan (2011) who summarise the definitions used in key British surveys over time). In various ways, questions have been asked about both formal and informal volunteering regularly since 1981.

Formal volunteering refers to actions undertaken through an organisational structure. Survey questions usually ask individuals to respond to a list of prompts about the kinds of formal activities they have carried out, and the types of organisation of which they are members. Informal voluntary action – sometimes referred to as 'direct volunteering' (Salamon et al, 2011) – refers to individual acts of assistance of a more spontaneous kind, given to other members of one's own community. We explore the balance between formal and informal volunteering in Chapter Five.

These debates are further complicated by the different terminologies used to measure voluntary action in surveys. For example, some surveys refer to unpaid *help*, whereas in others volunteering is characterised as unpaid work. It is known that individuals are more or less likely to recall certain elements of voluntary activity, depending on whether questions are posed in terms of unpaid work or unpaid help. Respondents do not necessarily possess a common, shared understanding of the distinction between unpaid work, and unpaid help, and therefore surveys can generate quite different results depending on the methods used (Tarling, 2000; Rooney et al, 2004; McCulloch, 2011) and the definition used. There are also variations between individuals in the accounts they give of voluntary action: what individuals themselves regard as volunteering does not always correspond in an unproblematic way to question prompts given in social surveys (Chapters Three and Four).

A further measurement challenge is capturing the depth of engagement in voluntary action. Recent literature (Hustinx, 2001; Hustinx and Lammertyn, 2003; Macduff, 2005) has spoken of short-term and one-off voluntary acts – 'episodic' volunteering, associated with reflexive and individualised approaches to voluntarism. This is something that our respondents also identify with – for example, through participation in occasional community events. It is also a feature of recent arguments by Sampson et al (2005), based on their longitudinal study of Chicago, that social action (particularly protest and campaigning activity) increasingly takes the form of one-off acts of mobilisation, rather than regular participation through formal organisational structures. Survey questions based on the number of hours committed to volunteering, or the frequency with which it occurs, may not necessarily pick up such participation.

What Sampson et al (2005) identify here is the malleability of notions of engagement. Whether accidentally or deliberately, there are echoes of this argument in current British discussions of a broader notion of 'social action', which appears to refer to a greater range of prosocial behaviours by individuals such as seeking to set up new services in their locality, or to campaign against their closure (Cabinet Office, 2015; DCMS, 2016) which is not constrained by survey definitions of formal and informal volunteering. However, it is not just episodic volunteering that gets elided by the way in which survey questions are framed. Without exhaustive and extensive questioning, surveys will always be constrained in their ability to represent the mix of activities that respondents undertake (Chapter Five), or their movement in and out of volunteering over time (Chapter Seven).

Paradigms of voluntary action

According to Lyons et al (1998) and Rochester et al (2010) three key paradigms — or analytical frameworks — for the analysis of voluntary action can be identified in academic debate: the dominant, civil society, and serious leisure paradigms. These three perspectives differentiate between voluntary acts in terms of motivation, organisational setting, field, and scope for agency on the part of the volunteer.

We begin with the 'dominant' paradigm. In the view of the aforementioned authors, this is an unduly narrow perspective on voluntary action. The dominant paradigm has the following characteristics. First, in terms of motivation, volunteering is merely presented as an altruistic act. Second, the areas in which voluntary action occurs are relatively narrow, namely the field of social welfare, to the exclusion of many other settings (recreational clubs and associations, or campaigning and advocacy groups) for voluntary action. Third, the organisational context is one in which volunteering is an activity that is managed through large, professionally structured organisations. Finally, these organisations confine the scope for agency on the part of volunteers, whose tasks are prespecified in advance; they are treated as an unpaid element of the workforce, who are to be managed.

They contrast this with the *civil society paradigm*. Here, the motivation is not altruism, but instead self-help or mutual aid, based on the ability of people to work together to meet shared needs. There is a much wider range of actions than purely delivering services: there is a focus on mutual support but also campaigning. The organisational context is likely to be volunteer-run organisations or self-help groups, not agencies with paid managerial personnel; and members are not brought in to play particular pre-specified roles. This leaves much greater scope for agency: those involved are as likely to be activists as volunteers: 'volunteers target people while activists target structures. The activist changes, while the volunteer maintains' (Musick and Wilson, 2008, 18).

The third paradigm is referred to as *serious leisure*: the systematic pursuit of a hobby or interest, which may be casual or more project-based (Stebbins, 2007). The motivation is intrinsic, not extrinsic: an enthusiasm for a specific form of involvement and commitment. It is particularly common in fields such as the arts, culture, sports and recreation. Volunteer roles can be as performer, practitioner, participant and/or administrator. The context may be large or small: an informal hobby group, or a formal cultural organisation.

How relevant are these characterisations of voluntary action to this book? These perspectives overlap, and critics of the dominant paradigm are surely right to emphasise the richness and multidimensional character of voluntary action. When exploring our qualitative source material, we find that our respondents (like those in similar qualitative investigations of engagement such as Brookfield et al, 2014) describe and characterise the voluntary action they undertake in ways which do not easily fall into one of the foregoing broad paradigms. If anything, what is striking is the reluctance of writers to exaggerate the significance of what they do, or to overemphasise its degree of formalisation (Chapters Four and Five); and voluntary action is first and foremost contextualised as part of their everyday lives.

Disciplinary perspectives on the interpretation of volunteering

Hustinx et al (2010) are wary of developing overarching theories of voluntary action because of the complexity of the topic, involving a range of acts in different contexts which have very different meanings to individuals, and because of the disciplinary range of perspectives on voluntary action. They differentiate between volunteering as altruism (whether pure or impure, in economic terminology, see Andreoni, 1990), a social phenomenon (involving relationships with others, including recipients of assistance, in which the question of social bonds and social solidarity is uppermost), a psychological phenomenon (a sustained or planned form of behaviour, which is influenced by personality traits), and actions informed by a sense of participation in an active democracy. We find many echoes of these arguments in the qualitative material from the MOP. Altruism might or might not be recognised by our respondents; we certainly find respondents characterising what they do as a social phenomenon, involving interaction with individuals; and, as to active, participatory democracy (Eliasoph, 2011; 2012) some respondents are vocal about the political dimensions of voluntary action (Chapters Five and Six).

A key question, though, which can be illuminated by the material upon which we draw in this study, concerns the individual motivations for and meanings attached to voluntary action. The question of why people spend their free time helping an organisation, for no financial reward, has been addressed by scholars using a variety of different theories, tools and perspectives. A rational choice, or economic, perspective predicts that volunteering will take place if, having weighed up the costs and benefits, an individual concludes that net benefits will occur. These include direct benefits to family or career, a 'warm glow' effect with consequential indirect impacts such as improved wellbeing, or the acquisition of skills to increase future wages (Rose-Ackerman, 1996; Andreoni, 1990; Sauer, 2015). As well as uncertainty as to whether these benefits accrue (Ellis Paine et al, 2013; De Wit et al, 2015), one might question whether volunteering can be reduced to this type of calculus.

Psychologists have moved beyond utility-maximising assumptions by emphasising the range of functions which can be fulfilled by volunteering (Clary et al, 1996). Functional analysis theories and tools include the 'Volunteer Functions Inventory' (VFI) (Clary et al, 1996), a model based on six different psychological functions/ motives that relate to *understanding* (personal growth by developing new skills and knowledge), *enhancement* (learning and gaining new skills and knowledge), *social* (integration with social groups), *career* (gaining experience that will benefit the volunteer's career) *protective* (therapeutic help for physical or psychological difficulties); and *values* (acting on values important to the self, such as altruistic or religious concerns). These functions include and encompass traditional volunteer rhetoric on motives such as 'reciprocity', and 'giving something back'. Psychologists using the VFI have argued that individuals will volunteer if they see volunteering as fulfilling one or more of these six functions (Clary et al, 1996). Nevertheless, apart from the *'values'* motive (acting on values that are important to the self, such as altruistic or religious concerns) these functions focus on volunteers' perceptions of the benefit that they themselves will gain from volunteering. Yet, Cnaan et al's (1996) work on public perceptions of volunteering shows that the higher the benefits or rewards to the person who is doing the helping (the volunteer), the less likely they will be considered by the public to be a volunteer. This focus on purity of motive is consistent with dominant public perceptions of volunteering as a form of help, a form of giving, or an act of altruism.

Context and lifecourse

Sociological theorists (Taylor, 2005; Hustinx et al, 2010) argue that research which focuses on the functions that volunteering serves for individuals, and the social resources possessed by those individuals, overlooks the contexts in which volunteering originates and takes place. Volunteering is inherently multi-dimensional and the study of individuals' motivations, personality traits, social and economic characteristics needs to be situated in the broader social, structural, cultural (and as we argue in this study), temporal environment of their lives. Accounts of volunteering will be limited if we fail to take account of context, and if we neglect lifecourse influences on participation. A functional approach also fails to recognise a broad range of motivations, which are rarely the subject of explicit consideration: researchers have not systematically explored the links between the type of activity carried out, the social characteristics of the volunteer, and the underlying motivations for action (Taylor, 2005, 122).

There are two key points here. First, we should consider volunteering as part of the 'total social organisation of labour' (Glucksmann, 2005): all forms of work and non-work, paid and unpaid are interconnected and have shifting boundaries (Chapter Five). Therefore, volunteering is not a discrete phenomenon which can be studied as separate and distinct from other forms of work and leisure, and the accounts given in this study emphasise this, particularly in relation to caring responsibilities. In their discussion of the content of voluntary action (Chapter Five), for example, we find that MOP writers frequently blend their accounts of volunteering with descriptions of the forms of caring activities in which they are simultaneously engaged.

An approach that presumes a singularity of motive sits uneasily with the complexity of the ways in which individuals become involved in voluntary action: with the complexity of motivations, both altruistic and self-interested, leisure and work (Chapter Six), which underpin individual actions; and with the complexity of individual biographies. In this book we argue that we may obtain greater insight from investigating different types of volunteering against the background of the personal and social circumstances of volunteers (Leat, 1983, 52).

A longitudinal perspective is crucial. Musick and Wilson (2008, 221–3) argue that what is missing is a longitudinal and/or retrospective understanding of patterns of volunteering, and an understanding of the individual volunteering lifecourse. Their exhaustive review of volunteering at various life stages covers numerous, mainly North American studies involving panel data on individuals and households, but it does not identify studies which have tracked, using qualitative methods, the lifecourses of individuals. In the UK the Neuberger Commission on the Future of Volunteering (2008) pointed out that people move in and out of volunteering-states. It is now possible to study such transitions, with some limitations, using quantitative longitudinal datasets (Chapters Three and Seven) but there are older antecedents.

A key British reference is Sherrott's (1983) study, *Fifty Volunteers*, which criticised work on volunteer motivation for paying little attention to the life-histories of the volunteers themselves. Sherrott selected his interviewees randomly from lists supplied by five different formal voluntary organisations. His respondents were able to generate timelines of voluntary activity (Hatch and Sherrott, 1983, 12–13) in which they estimated how long they had volunteered for the organisations through which they had been recruited, and also summarised volunteering for other organisations. Even within this small sample, there were notable differences between organisations in the age profile and level of engagement of volunteers. His intensive interviewing process repeatedly prompted interviewees to recall how they became involved and extracted a large range of statements of motive. Of course, there were selection biases arising from the different organisations studied (WRVS, youth services, Marriage Guidance, Age Concern and Citizens' Advice). Sherrott's work acknowledges this, and we know from other work on specific subsectors of voluntary action, such as large heritage organisations (Harflett, 2015) that volunteering demographics differ between organisational types. His respondents were also being asked to recall involvement that in some cases had taken place up to five decades previously. Nevertheless, this is a rich and compelling account, and its neglect by British researchers (at least based on citation evidence) is puzzling.

Davis-Smith and Gay (2005) conducted a qualitative investigation of the volunteering histories of adults who were around retirement age (though in practice they recruited several who were well over this age). They categorised them as lifelong, serial and trigger volunteers, depending on the nature and extent of engagement. Though not as focused on individual engagement biographies, Roberts and Devine (2004) also considered the influences of lifecourse events and personal circumstances in their smaller-scale study of the 'contingency' of participation. Hogg (2016) adopted Davis-Smith and Gay's typology in his study of 26 older volunteers – also recruited through organisations – but opted for describing the first category as 'constant' rather than 'lifelong' volunteers. The aim of the qualitative Pathways through Participation Project was 'to create a fuller picture of how people participate over their lifetimes' (Brodie et al, 2011, 5). The authors interviewed 101 participants in three English localities, and designed their study in an attempt to include a broad range of organisations and maximise demographic and social diversity among respondents. The authors were also interested in a wider range of types of participation. In-depth interviews were conducted with participants 'who reflected on their past and current experiences of participation' (p 6), and the motivations, opportunities and triggers for their participation. The study found that while some individuals' participation may be short-term across the whole of their life, or across portions of their life, the process of volunteering for many was dynamic, with engagement waxing and waning in relation to changing personal circumstances.

These studies have all relied on the ability of individuals to recall engagement, and trajectories of engagement, often some years after the fact. Hogg (2016, 174) acknowledges his respondents' inability to recall events from early adulthood as a clear limitation. To a degree this is true of our source, the MOP (Chapter Three), but with some important differences. Individuals are contributing contemporary and retrospective evidence in response to a number of different directives (sets of themed questions) over time, which means that they are prompted at intervals to recall elements of engagement, rather than attempting to do so at one sitting. They also have time to compose their own thoughts, rather than being taken through a particular interview script. Furthermore, we obtain information about individuals' volunteering behaviour from directives that are not explicitly concerned with the topic, permitting triangulation and corroboration. In further contrast, previous studies have not contextualised their qualitative findings against contemporaneous survey data in the way that we have done here. Our mixed-methods approach is novel in that it provides in-depth insights that corroborate and develop more recent cross-sectional understandings of formal and informal volunteering patterns, while also supplying further evidence of the complex dynamics of volunteering patterns across the individual lifecourse.

We provide insight into the contexts in which individuals report engagement, the circumstances which lead them to do so, and their perceptions of the meanings of voluntary engagement (Chapters Five and Six). In addition, the capacities of individuals to engage in voluntary action is clearly foregrounded in the qualitative material; with some individuals pointing out quite forcefully that they have very limited additional capacity to do more. We are also able to explore attitudes to volunteering, and the place of voluntary action in society, using responses to specific directives. Attitudinal perspectives come across strongly, for example, in the discussion of responses to The 'Big Society' directive, commissioned by the authors in 2012 (Chapter Eight). The MOP material also enables us to explore the kinds of satisfaction which people obtain from their actions, and their views about what they (and/or their organisation) can achieve (Chapter Six). We question if individuals see their voluntary actions in terms of a wider political frame of reference, for example, in the context of debates about the so-called 'Big Society'.

Sources and methods

How, then, did we design this project? Awareness of contestation over the meaning and measurement of voluntary action led us in the direction of a mixed-methods approach; concern for the analysis of continuity and change over time suggested longitudinal work. Ideally, we would have liked a continuous series of data on volunteering behaviour, and attitudes to voluntary action, over the whole of this time-period. In practice, life is not so simple, and we attempted to link together various sources in an innovative way (see Chapter Three).

The primary empirical focus being on individual behaviour and attitudes to voluntary action, we draw upon various cross-sectional social surveys which measure volunteering by individuals, covering most of the post-1979 period (such as the National Survey of Volunteering (NSV), and the British Social Attitudes survey (BSAS). Notwithstanding differences in survey methodology, we argue that there is sufficient continuity to provide a robust portrait of trends over time. The surveys also provide some information about questions of motive and meaning, and occasionally about attitudes to voluntary action.

When it comes to tracking longitudinal changes in volunteering behaviours over time, the quantitative landscape is sparser. British research has largely used cross-sectional surveys (Staetsky and Mohan, 2011; Bennett, 2013; Li, 2015) that have provided a picture of social and geographical variations in voluntary activity (Mohan and Bulloch, 2012; Mohan et al, 2006; Williams, 2003). To date, the longitudinal exceptions (Warde et al, 2003; Kamerade, 2011; McCulloch, 2014) are studies primarily concerned with involvement in associations, rather than with volunteering.

The principal relevant longitudinal surveys are the National Child Development Study (NCDS) and the British Household Panel Survey (BHPS) (renamed Understanding Society (US) on its expansion in 2009). The former, a study of individuals born in a selected week in 1958, asked useful questions about voluntary action when its respondents were aged 16, 23 and 50. We have not used it here for two main reasons: some of the data on volunteering are problematic, leading to challenges in measuring trajectories between youth and adulthood; what is more important is that the population of inference is limited to adults born at one point in time. However, important longitudinal work has been done on the survey by, among others: Laurence and Lim (2013) on the influence of labour market circumstances on participation; Bolton (2016) on connections between volunteering in early adulthood and political engagement; and Brookfield et al (forthcoming) on non-engagement, and on relationships between quantitative NCDS data and qualitative interview material. The BHPS, in contrast, has tracked many thousands of individuals continuously since the early 1990s, asking them questions about engagement in voluntary activity in alternate years from 1996 onwards, and this is our key source of quantitative longitudinal data.

Our qualitative longitudinal material is drawn from the resources generated by the MOP, run by the Mass Observation Archive (MOA) at the University of Sussex, an extraordinarily rich repository of qualitative data. We believe this project is the first to use MOP material in a longitudinal way to study the evolution of individual attitudes and behaviours on a specific topic, in a manner which combines the qualitative MOP data with quantitative material from surveys. Although Hinton has subsequently published his study of *Seven Lives from Mass Observation* (2016) his work ranges much more widely in its account of their lives, in contrast to our study of voluntary action.

The original Mass Observation (MO) initiative operated from 1937 until the mid-1950s, recording everyday life in Britain through the media of photography, film, written ethnographic observations, surveys, diaries and volunteer writers' responses to specific themes and questions put to them by the project's founders (Madge and Harrison, 1939). The findings of the original project provided the basis for some well-known publications, perhaps the most famous being Angus Calder's (1969) *The People's War*, and the published diaries of one of its volunteers, Nella Last (2006). MO material provided valuable input into debates about war-time and post-war public policy, and featured prominently in William Beveridge's report *Voluntary Action* (1948) and Beveridge and Wells' *The Evidence for Voluntary Action* (1949, 33–59).

The project ceased to operate after the mid-1950s;[5] subsequently its archives were brought to the University of Sussex under the care of the MOA (www.massobs.org.uk).

MO was relaunched in 1981, as the MOP, since when it has operated as a volunteer-writing project, recruiting volunteers who agree to receive and respond to themed questions or 'directives' that are sent to them three times a year. Their responses – usually several pages in length – provide a rich account of individuals' activities and attitudes, including insights into the changes and continuities in writer's lives, while retrospective writing illuminates their individual lifecourses. What is more important it that individual writers can be followed across time, *and across the portion of the lifecourse in which they are writing*; thus it represents a unique source of qualitative longitudinal data.

A mixed-methods approach has enabled us to take advantage of the joint strengths of quantitative and qualitative analyses to provide a rounded picture (Bryman, 2008, 91) of volunteering behaviours and attitudes to voluntarism. We have combined longitudinal qualitative and quantitative data, on volunteering behaviour and attitudes to voluntarism in the United Kingdom (UK) between 1981 and 2012. The timeframe we focus on encompasses the recessions of the 1980s and 1990s; a period of relative prosperity and an increase in investment in public services from the mid-1990s onwards; and the most recent recessions from 2008, which were accompanied by the implementation of austerity measures from 2010 (Timmins, 2001; Glennerster, 2007; Alcock 2011; Defty, 2011; Driver, 2011). The study seeks to place volunteering behaviour and attitudes to voluntarism in the context of these social and economic events.

Structure of the book

Chapter Two sets out the economic, social and political context against which governments have called, albeit in different ways, for a revival of voluntary action, and describes policies which have supported these calls. Chapter Three provides discussion of the key sources and methods we have used. For quantitative data, these are cross-sectional and longitudinal surveys of individuals. The former include the NSV, the General Household Survey (GHS), the BSAS, and the Citizenship Surveys (CS). Our principal longitudinal source is the BHPS/US. Our qualitative data is drawn from the MOP, and we explain the importance and uniqueness of this source. The chapter also considers the challenges associated with attempts to analyse these sources in parallel.

In the subsequent substantive chapters, we use the academic literature to explore the many ways in which individuals engage in different types of voluntary action. In each of the five substantive chapters, survey data provide one perspective, but we juxtapose quantitative findings with the accounts given by individuals. First, then, Chapter Four analyses trends in voluntary action and in the voluntary sector. Survey data provides a quantitative overview of volunteering behaviour, including: cross-sectional portraits of the levels of volunteering in the population, the mix between formal and informal volunteering, and changes in the level and frequency of these over time. We also draw on the qualitative material from the MOP to problematise the quantitative material: for example, would the respondents to MOP directives characterise themselves as volunteers, in the terms given by social surveys? We also consider the relationship between aggregate trends in volunteering rates, and wider developments in the voluntary sector. It is notable, for example, that this period was characterised by an expansion in the resources available to the voluntary sector, yet also by relative stability in levels of volunteering and charitable giving.

The content and context of volunteering behaviour is the subject of Chapter Five. Headline figures (for example, rates of voluntary action) are made up of many different commitments to different types of voluntary activity. Here, we look at the insights provided by individual narratives of volunteering through the MOP material, which include descriptions of the kinds of activities which people carry out (for example, formal volunteering through organisations versus informal acts of neighbourliness and help). We note in particular, the entry points into voluntary activity – some of which draw on class-based social networks and connections, while others simply reflect being drawn into voluntary action through children, supporting them in various ways (school, sport and other extra-curricular activities). The perspective provided by the MOP writers is contrasted with the analyses of formal and informal volunteering available through survey data, including evidence on the type of actions described as volunteering.

Chapter Six is about why people volunteer – and here we rely to a greater extent than elsewhere on the MOP material, because of the limitations of survey-based approaches to this subject. We emphasise discussions by the MOP writers of the complex motivations and barriers relating to volunteering across the lifecourse. We explore questions such as: accounts given of individuals' routes into volunteering (children, social networks, work, church); the trigger points identified by individuals (being asked, identifying an unmet need, needing to belong to a community, wanting work experience, and so on); trigger points for deciding *not* to volunteer (for example, changing economic circumstances); and perceptions of the benefits of volunteering to those engaged in it.

In Chapter Seven, attention turns to longitudinal perspectives. We show how people move into and out of volunteering 'states' over time – both quantitatively and qualitatively. Tracking people through 15 years of the BHPS/US, and following serial responders to MOP directives, we offer novel insights into the nature of people's volunteering through the lifecourse. This includes the age and point in their lifecourse at which MOP writers begin to volunteer; the patterns of volunteering across the lifecourse – for example some are continuous volunteers who swap one type of volunteering for another; and sequences of transitions in and out of volunteering as revealed through survey data.

Chapter Eight shifts the focus to attitudinal questions about the respective roles of voluntary action and the state. Survey evidence on attitudes includes a broadly consistent time series from the BSAS about attitudes to poverty and the role of the state. However, questions on the role of charity and voluntary action, or on the respective role of voluntary organisations and the state in delivering public services, are asked rather less frequently. We present relevant attitudinal data where it is available, but the bulk of the chapter is a consideration of detailed responses from MOP writers to directives issued in 1996 (*Unpaid Work*) and 2012 (*The 'Big Society'*). These responses provoke considerable thought about the appropriate place for, and contribution of, voluntary action. Finally, we consider reactions to our own commissioned directive on the 'Big Society', providing insight into the reception of the Coalition Prime Minister's ideas. This is unusual, as it illuminates how individuals react to a quite specific circumstance, namely whether or not they have capacity to increase their levels of voluntary action.

A concluding chapter sums up the key messages of the book in relation to: levels of engagement in and trajectories in and out of volunteering; individual and community capacity for voluntary action; motivations for and barriers to volunteering; and attitudes to the role of the state and voluntarism in responding to need. We consider the wider implications of this study for policy and practice: is volunteering genuinely a renewable resource, as the International Labour Organisation (ILO, 2011, 1) has suggested? And, bearing in mind that the economic circumstances confronting the UK are now very different to those in which many of the MOP writers grew up, what sort of framework might be necessary to create the conditions in which people have the resources to engage as they would wish in their communities?

Notes

[1] Margaret Thatcher, speech to the Women's Royal Voluntary Service National Conference ('Facing the new challenge'), 19 January 1981, www.margaretthatcher.org/document/104551
[2] H.C. Deb., v. 558, 13.2.13, c. 858 (Cameron)
[3] Theresa May, The shared society: Prime Minister's speech at the Charity Commission annual meeting, January 2017, www.gov.uk/government/speeches/the-shared-society-prime-ministers-speech-at-the-charity-commission-annual-meeting
[4] H.L. Deb., v. 163, 5 June 1949, c. 95.
[5] The dates and manner of the ending of the original MO project was a complicated and contested affair, see Hinton, 2013

TWO

The changing policy environment for voluntary action from 1979

Introduction

Mass Observation (MO) was originally set up in 1937, becoming established during the Second World War, a period which witnessed a substantial extension of state intervention in the provision of welfare services. MO's work contributed greatly to the understanding of public attitudes during the period of wartime planning for the welfare state. For several subsequent decades a broadly-shared consensus on welfare held sway, associated with the primacy of public financing and provision of key elements of the welfare state, with voluntary initiatives by citizens playing a relatively residual part in the welfare mix. Of course, voluntarism never went away in the post-war period; voluntary effort and voluntary organisations continued to have articulate supporters, who made the case for more pluralist arrangements for the delivery of welfare services. Prior to 1979, however, few people outside right-wing thinktanks would have proposed that Beveridge's 'perpetually moving frontier' between statutory and voluntary sectors would shift substantially back in the direction of the latter. Arguably, nearly four decades after the Conservatives were returned to power in 1979, the shift has been as much one of rhetoric and style as of substance.

The advent of Margaret Thatcher's Conservative administration, committed to rolling back the state, raised the possibility that government policy might open up much more scope for greater reliance on voluntary organisations and voluntary action. In this chapter we therefore consider subsequent key changes in the policy landscape. Discussion of the development of social policy under the governments of Margaret Thatcher and John Major also provides opportunities to identify parallels with the post-2010 administrations led by David Cameron and Theresa May as well as continuities and discontinuities between those governments and those led by Tony Blair and Gordon Brown. All post-1979 Prime Ministers proclaimed their support, at various times and in different ways, either for voluntary action per se, for initiatives designed to enhance the scope for voluntary action, and for non-state provision of public services, although the means through which they pursued those objectives varied.

In the introductory chapter, referencing Kendall (2003; 2009), we noted that policy in relation to voluntarism in recent decades has tended towards measures targeted at voluntary action by *individuals*, initiatives to encourage the development of voluntary *organisations*, and the institutionalisation of mechanisms for bringing the voluntary *sector* into public policy deliberation. The underlying motivations could also vary, depending on the problem to which voluntarism has been seen as the solution – this might be civil renewal and democratic engagement, youth unemployment, or raising productivity in public services. Following from this, practical steps taken by government might range from the expression of hortatory pro-voluntarist sentiments, through strategic efforts to address problems of capacity on the part of voluntary organisations, to highly targeted initiatives aimed at engaging specific groups of individuals in voluntary action.

In reviewing the development of policy, this chapter is organised chronologically, and it emphasises the continuities between the Thatcher and post-2010 administrations, with the Labour government standing between them. The material sets the scene for substantive chapters in which we trace the extent to which there were changes in patterns of individual behaviour, and also in attitudes to voluntary action, over this period.

'A crescendo of political rhetoric': the Conservative governments, 1979–97

Margaret Thatcher's government came into office making statements about the need to reduce public expenditure while stressing the importance of voluntary effort. In an early post-election speech on 'the renewal of Britain', Thatcher emphasised the need to reinvigorate 'personal responsibility and the sense of responsibility to family, neighbourhood and community', which had been eroded by collectivism. She argued that charity was a 'personal quality', that 'public compassion, state philanthropy and institutionalised charity could never be enough', and that there was no adequate substitute for genuine caring for one another on the part of families, friends and neighbours.[1] Thatcher provided further eulogies to individual voluntary action when addressing the Women's Royal Voluntary Service (WRVS) in 1981.[2] She argued that the 'only effective way to reach all those who need help was through the voluntary service of millions of individuals who do what they can because they want to'. What she described as the 'volunteer movement' – note, not a movement of voluntary organisations – was 'at the heart of all our social welfare provision'; statutory services were 'the supportive ones, underpinning where necessary, filling the gaps and helping the helpers'. The real heroes were individual volunteers and small community-based groups, often local and spontaneous, which could be given continuity and support by the bigger voluntary organisations. The argument clearly foreshadowed a similar case made for the responsiveness of charity to social needs by the Conservative think tank, the Centre for Social Justice, over three decades later (CSJ, 2014). In an anticipation of what David Cameron later characterised as the 'kaleidoscope' of social action (see below), there was an acknowledgement that variety was one of the glories of the voluntary movement, and that this was expressed most vigorously through small-scale and local activity.

Critiquing the policies of Thatcher's governments, Brenton stressed Thatcher's rhetorical emphasis on a 'refinement of focus down to the primary supports of family and locality' (Brenton, 1985a, 143). Discussions of the scope of voluntary action by individuals or within communities were evidence-free. For example, Patrick Jenkin, Secretary of State for Social Services, had airily asserted that social service budget cuts could be absorbed because there would be an increase in voluntary effort, but was unable to back up his assertion (Brenton, 1985a, 60–1). However, authoritative results from government-commissioned work led by Philip Abrams suggested the infrastructural importance of well-financed professional social services: informal care needed 'not a safety net, but a springboard' if it was to be most effective (Abrams et al, 1989).

Margaret Thatcher's enthusiasm for voluntary action did not, however, translate into systematic policy initiatives to support voluntary action by individuals. This was not for want of advocacy – for example by prominent individuals such as Alec Dickson, the founder of Community Service Volunteers, of the potential role of voluntary organisations in combating youth unemployment.[3] Outside Parliament, Conservative think tanks advocated a return of welfare services to private and voluntary ownership, and greater involvement of volunteers in public services, arguing in Hayekian terms that spontaneous and voluntary choices by individuals, in the form of donations of time or money, always gave better results than political direction (for example, Harris and Seldon, 1979). Although these proposals appeared from the right of the political spectrum, there was also a sense that their advocates were swimming with the social tide in advocating non-state alternatives: reduced deference, the experience of post-1960s community action and frustrations with top–down planning (Power, 2012) were associated with an emerging welfare pluralist philosophy (Brenton, 1985a, 156–72; Gladstone, 1979; Hatch, 1980).

How were such views translated into policy discussions? Brenton (1985a) remains the most incisive commentary on the early Thatcher period but recent documentary releases at the National Archives allow further insight into key internal debates in the early 1980s. The Central Policy Review Staff (CPRS), the 'think-tank' at the heart of government, was charged with 'thinking the unthinkable' (Blackstone and Plowden, 1988). However, even the radical options for the welfare state considered in a famous CPRS paper in 1982 show no evidence of discussion of the potential contribution of the voluntary sector.[4] For example, there does not appear to have been an assessment of whether savings in expenditure could have been achieved through promoting voluntary action. This can be contrasted with subsequent Labour emphases – for example, Treasury-led studies of the contribution that volunteers might make to public service productivity (HM Treasury, 2002). In the CPRS papers, there is no reference to voluntary action by individuals and the only discussion of shifting the balance between the individual and the state was in relation to health insurance.

The Family Policy Group (FPG), led by Ferdinand Mount, gave more consideration to the scope for voluntary alternatives to state provision. The focus of the group on 'renewing the values of society' echoed Thatcher's determination to reverse economic decline. The particular concern was that the decline of the family had led to social breakdown, so the FPG sought to identify ways of supporting traditional families.[5] By late 1982, an emerging theme was 'meeting social needs through voluntary action'. These discussions also talked of 'loosening some shackles' on voluntary initiatives, such as enabling communities to raise funds for local schools and hospitals. However, there were no concerted moves to transfer public services to charities or the voluntary sector, leading Mount to brief Thatcher that the group's discussions 'were ducking a question we have not really asked – namely, why don't we let volunteers take over some of the welfare services?' However, the Cabinet Committee which had received papers on the voluntary sector and on charitable giving contented itself with endorsing generalised intentions to 'divert more of our planned expenditure to the voluntary sector' and to support voluntary organisations to develop their capacity to provide public services. The only direct reference to voluntary action in the group's papers seems to have been identification of the potential of student volunteering and of business engagement in communities.[6]

While Brenton (1985b, 177) describes a 'crescendo of political rhetoric' in favour of voluntarism from 1979 onwards, there was relatively little evidence of substantial changes in policy. There were some specific legislative measures, such as an expansion of fundraising for health authorities following the 1980 Health Services Act, which empowered health authorities to organise charitable appeals themselves. This led to a number of initiatives, some very high profile indeed, such as the 'Wishing Well' appeal for Great Ormond Street Children's Hospital; these certainly engaged many individuals in vigorous fundraising efforts (Moore, 2008), but nevertheless had negative effects in terms of competition for resources and distortion of priorities (Mohan and Gorsky, 2001). As well as charitable fundraising, opportunities were opened up for voluntary organisations through policies to promote care in the community rather than in long-stay institutions, and through the opening up of NHS and local government health and welfare services to greater competition.

Outside the NHS, despite the vigorous rhetoric of Ministers, the existing statutory dominance of personal social services remained entrenched. Although some large national voluntary organisations depended heavily on public funding in the 1970s (for example, Unell, 1979; Wolfenden Committee, 1978) and some organisations continued to receive substantial portions of their income from central government through the Thatcher years (Kramer, 1990), the sums involved were minuscule, when compared to the budgets of statutory authorities.

Under Thatcher's governments, voluntary organisations were also drawn into important policy issues such as the management of unemployment, through the Manpower Services Commission (MSC), and the tackling of urban decay. Programmes were set up to provide temporary employment opportunities on projects designed to provide community benefits, to offer work experience for disadvantaged young people, or to support the unemployed to carry out unpaid work in their communities. These included Opportunities for Volunteering, which facilitated voluntary activity by the unemployed in the health and social services fields and was to become the longest-running government-funded programme of its kind, and the Voluntary Projects Programmes, with a focus on the long-term unemployed.

The Thatcher government's policies towards voluntary action have been characterised as an untidy melange of 'official ad-hoccery and political image management' (Brenton, 1985a, 100), and inconsistency (6 and Kendall, 1997). Perhaps one exception was the growth of the housing association movement, which gathered pace, accounting for three quarters of government funding for the voluntary sector by the early 1990s (6 and Kendall, 1997). As a result of this growth, Power (2012, 55) argues that there is now no serious disagreement about the value and appropriateness of such third sector ownership in the housing field.

While the 1983 FPG discussions had made some reference to the need for investment, there was no sign of the institutionalisation of support for the third sector that became such a feature of policy under new Labour (see the next section in this chapter) – in other words, central investments in policy, research, consultation and capacity-building – and certainly none of the target setting and centralised management characteristic of those administrations. Indeed, there was no sense, in government or ministerial statements or policy initiatives, that the government conceived of the voluntary sector *as* a sector. Instead, the radical Right, and the Thatcher governments, prioritised informal social action by individuals, believing that large, professionalised and independent organisations represented an alternative social and political power base (Brenton, 1985a; Lawrence, 1983). The FPG papers were aware of the danger that 'government finance would turn voluntary organisations from their traditional role into protest groups run by "professional volunteers". Genuine voluntary action did not always need state subsidy'.[7]

An enduring challenge, then as now, was the funding of residential care. The Conservatives initially transferred much of the costs of this to the social security budget, but the spiralling costs of this led, ultimately, to a decision to make local authority social services departments the lead agency, which was perceived as an effort to pass this financial buck from central to local government (Lewis and Glennerster, 1996). With a growing elderly population, and no enduring cross-party consensus on ways out of the funding impasse, this remains a highly contentious political issue. It is also one which poses very real challenges to individuals. Margaret Thatcher's speeches, quoted above, pointed to the expectations that individuals will be the first port of call in supporting relatives in need of care. Our Mass Observation Project (MOP) writers, as we see in Chapters Four and Five, take her at her word, prioritising such commitments in their responses to questions about unpaid work and voluntary activity, while in Chapter Eight they describe the failings of the existing social care system and the burdens that it imposes on them.

Given Thatcher's emphasis on the reversal of Britain's decline and the need to revive a tradition of voluntary action, the absence of many positive policy steps to support voluntary action by individuals might appear surprising. One might argue that the government's attention in its early years was absorbed by the need to reverse economic decline, tackle inflation, weaken and defeat the trade unions, and the Falklands war. The austere public funding climate also militated against substantial initiative. On the other hand, the relatively small-scale and ad hoc initiatives that took place might be read as the government playing a long game, building up slowly towards, and encouraging receptivity to, radical policy innovation (Brenton, 1985a, 219). Over the years, such initiatives made the expansion of voluntary organisations look like a natural, and non-controversial, process. Hence Brenton's prescient argument that a government that is interested in establishing hegemony might 'trade off ideological purity' in the short term in exchange for a future advantage in gaining support for its policies' (Brenton, 1985b, 176). The 'loosening shackles' described in the FPG and the absence of a blueprint or top-down plan may be thought not so far removed from the subsequent 'Big Society' philosophy of David Cameron. Voluntary action was supported because it offered the possibility of privatising parts of the welfare state in a non-market form (Brenton, 1985a, 143) with the added virtue of promoting an array of Conservative virtues; in the process, however, communities were thrown back on their own resources. Yet, in contrast to the post-2010 period, voluntary sector providers of public services did not face the wholesale commercialisation of the environment in which they were to operate.

In an attempt to put at least some distance between his administration and those of Margaret Thatcher, the rhetorical figure of the 'active citizen' was deployed by Prime Minister John Major (1990–97). The idea was that the beneficiaries of the government's policies should commit to active engagement in their communities, but it failed to gain traction with the public. As Ignatieff (1989) put it, 'society was too riven by inequality to be sewn back together by rhetorical flannel'. Nevertheless, Major's government's 'Make a Difference' programme was described by Rochester et al (2010, 89–90) as the 'most ambitious and innovative' recent UK government initiative to support volunteering, because it saw volunteering as a vehicle for engagement, rather than merely delivering services, made a commitment to breaking down social divisions in voluntary action, and was characterised as a 'comprehensive, holistic and volunteer-centred blueprint for action' (Zimmeck, 2010, 91). Sheard (1995) connects the more expansive emphasis of this initiative to improvements in the state of the economy – with falling unemployment, there was less of a focus on finding productive things for workless people to do. However, the UK-wide strategy from the Make a Difference team was published in June 1995, less than two years before the Major government was defeated at the

1997 election, leaving little time for Make a Difference to – as it were – make a difference, and the funds committed to it were less than a tenth of what had originally been envisaged.

The 18 years of Conservative government from 1979 thus witnessed a fair amount of Prime Ministerial rhetoric, emphasising voluntary action by individuals. Voluntary organisations became involved in crisis management – particularly in relation to regeneration of deprived areas and youth unemployment – while ideological distaste for local authorities was associated with the encouragement of the nascent housing association movement. Policy towards volunteering was, however, seen as 'low-key, piecemeal and ad hoc' (Kendall, 2003, 46) with no sustained commitment to, or engagement with, the voluntary sector. Only in the later years, under John Major's government, seeking a new balance between citizen and state, was there a clear statement of policies aimed at supporting volunteering.

New Labour and hyperactive mainstreaming

The period of office of the Blair and Brown governments witnessed the development of a broader frame of reference within which to refer to voluntary action and voluntary organisations, namely that of the 'third sector', which encompassed not just voluntary and community organisations and charities, but also social enterprises, cooperatives and mutuals. While the Labour party's historic hostility to voluntary action has been overestimated (Deakin and Davis-Smith, 2011), Labour had begun to reconsider its approach to the voluntary sector and voluntary action while in opposition. Moves towards a proactive policy towards the third sector had great advantages: by being explicitly neither state nor market, the third sector could offer a genuine alternative provider base for public services, while Labour's shift in approach allowed the party to distance itself from adversarial politics as well as from its own heritage of centralised, top-down policies. Indeed the Labour leader, Tony Blair, saw the opportunity to connect social progress with the scale of voluntary action: all successful societies, he argued, displayed high levels of private initiative (Blair, 1999). His governments also, however, made determined efforts to introduce new providers of public services, including both commercial and non-profit organisations, while market forces held greater sway in determining the fortunes and survival of individual provider units in the public sector.

Thus the Labour governments saw a quite distinctive period of policy-making, characterised by Jeremy Kendall (2009) as the 'hyperactive mainstreaming' of the third sector into public policy. Instead of third sector policy being organised on vertical, departmental lines, there was a systematic effort to promote horizontal policy initiatives, across the whole of government. Opinions differ on the extent to which Labour's pro-voluntarism marked a decisive break from previous Labour governments (Alcock, 2011; Deakin and Davis-Smith, 2011; Zimmeck, 2010). Here we comment on the ways in which voluntary action and the voluntary sector came to occupy such a prominent place in their policies.

The development of 'third way' politics (Blair, 1998; Giddens, 1998) combined with the emphasis in public policy that what mattered was what worked (Barber, 2008) created space for the third sector to offer an alternative to state or market provision. Labour's thinking drew upon ideas developed by various supportive thinktanks (for example, Demos, the New Economics Foundation, and the Institute for Public Policy Research (IPPR)), which had a focus on costless redistribution, the formation of social capital as a route towards solving social problems, social innovation and reshaping the relationship between citizen and state. Both Blair and Brown emphasised the importance of identifying a *sector*, in contrast to the Thatcherite stress on social action by individuals. This was translated into policy by high-level reviews on the role that the sector could play in public service delivery (HM Treasury, 2002) and in social and economic regeneration. For Alcock and Kendall (2011), these developments helped create a 'decontested space' for voluntary action, while Alcock (2011) developed the notion that there had emerged 'a strategic unity' among a range of key third sector stakeholders. In contrast to the Thatcher period, there were substantial strategic initiatives, encompassing substantial institutional change, investment in capacity building, and partnership working (Kendall, 2009, 73–7; Rochester et al, 2010, 90–7).

Institutional change included the restructuring of existing units within government departments, to give effect to Labour's commitment to the sector, culminating in the creation of the Office of the Third Sector (OTS) within the Cabinet Office. Capacity building and investment in the third sector (especially expanding the ability of organisations to bid for public service contracts) became a significant concern for government following the recommendations of the Commission on the Future of the Voluntary Sector (1996) (commonly known as the Deakin Commission), which informed much of the new Labour government's policies. There was a perception that not all voluntary organisations were well placed to engage with government and compete for public service contracts. The result was the 'Compact' between government and the voluntary sector, a proactive formalisation of relationships, designed to promote good practices in contracting for public services to ensure that, as far as possible, voluntary organisations were competing on a level playing field (in relation to volunteering, for example, there was an acknowledgement that the costs of involving volunteers in public service delivery represented a legitimate expense for third sector organisations).

Significant investments in third sector organisational development in England followed from the Treasury-led cross-cutting Review of Public Expenditure in 2002. Several funding streams were established, which directly supported individual organisations in their attempts to bid for public service contracts. Support was also provided for local voluntary infrastructure organisations such as Councils for Voluntary Service. In parallel, though independent of government, the Big Lottery Fund also invested significantly in such areas.

Third, partnership working between governments and the sector became increasingly important. This was partly driven by the emphasis on third sector provision of public services, but it was also part of a wider civil renewal agenda, in which voluntary and community organisations could promote citizenship and re-establish a sense of community. Inspired in some measure by the work of Robert Putnam (2000), a forceful advocate of efforts designed to strengthen social capital, policies were implemented with a view to raising levels of engagement in communities. These were mainstreamed into broader programmes such as urban regeneration initiatives (for example, the New Deal for Communities; see Lawless et al, 2010), the assumption being that raising levels of social capital would in some measure compensate for material deficiencies in the resources available to communities. This view has been criticised (McCulloch et al, 2012) on the grounds that while there are certainly positive associations between voluntary activity and social capital, these largely disappear once controls are introduced for neighbourhood socioeconomic characteristics.

What was actually done in terms of the promotion of volunteering, and how did Labour's policies differ from those of their predecessors? One novelty was the use of technology to enable volunteering, both in terms of connecting potential volunteers with volunteering objectives, and in terms of online, virtual or 'micro' volunteering. How much impact the latter have is still uncertain: total hours committed to voluntary action have barely altered, suggesting little discernible impact (ONS, 2017) although these episodic forms of engagement are not always easily identified in surveys. Another novelty was the specific targeting of demographic and social groups believed to be under-represented in the volunteering population. This included the creation of new organisations for developing volunteering programmes (probably the most high-profile of which was the Russell Commission Implementation Body, charged with increasing the engagement of young people in volunteering, otherwise known simply as v (now vInspired)). Zimmeck lists at least 14 such central initiatives (2010, 91–2). The government instituted extensive mechanisms for involving and consulting peak bodies in the voluntary sector.

These policies embodied tensions. Some saw the emphases on service delivery and civil renewal as competing, not complementary, and as threatening a bifurcation between well-resourced service delivery organisations, and smaller, less well-established community groups. Different frameworks underpinned Labour's strategies and policies – Kendall (2009), for instance, identifies ideologies of consumerism, civil revivalism and democratic renewal. In the first of these, the third sector was seen as a source of improved performance and as offering a challenge to the public sector, so that the wider public goods produced by voluntary action were given less prominence. As an example, he suggests that provision of resources for capacity building, to enable third sector organisations to bid for public service contracts, was driven by Treasury imperatives to promote competition and choice. The agenda of 'civil order renewal', suggests Kendall, sought to support the sector as a vehicle for 'elaborating traditional citizenship', and was accompanied by an emphasis on targets for volunteering, and for expenditure on the sector, as well as by an interest in '"orderly" associations, such as cadet forces and uniformed brigades'. Finally, a strand of Labour party thinking emphasised 'democratic life renewal', stressing local empowerment, understood as being built around collective communication and deliberative processes (Kendall, 2009, 88–9). The tensions between these frameworks were not satisfactorily resolved (Alcock et al, 2012, 351).

Labour's policies were also not without their critics. Zimmeck, for example, identifies the gradual supplanting of broad pro-volunteering objectives by an instrumental focus on service delivery and the renewal of civil order (2010, 95–7). Whereas Labour's spending review of 2000 built upon the Conservatives' Make a Difference campaign through a broad set of proposals for supporting volunteering, the corresponding document in 2007 rather constrained the role of volunteering and voluntary action to one of support for public service delivery (HM Treasury, 2007). Thus Zimmeck argues that towards the end of their term of office, Labour saw the third sector in proportion to its ability to deliver on the government's particular and evolving agenda (2010, 97).

Zimmeck also criticises the heavily target-driven rhetoric adopted by Labour. For instance, a succession of Public Service Agreement (PSA) targets were set, giving government departments (mainly the Home Office, but also the Department for Communities and Local Government (DCLG)) the challenge of raising overall levels of voluntary activity. Targets also extended to specific demographic groups, and were part of the performance management regime for local authorities (DCLG, 2008). The extent to which government, and even more so local government, can actually influence levels of volunteering would be called into question by the qualitative evidence from our MOP writers regarding the ways in which they became involved in volunteering and their trajectories through it (Chapters Five to Seven). The more general point here, however, is that volunteering became caught up in Labour's top-down management.

The Labour governments were also criticised for adherence to the 'dominant paradigm' in their volunteering initiatives, in which disproportionate attention is given to formal and measurable acts of engagement in organisational settings (Rochester, 2013). Williams (2003) argues that the Labour government prioritised the nurturing of voluntary organisations (a 'third sector' approach) and the encouragement of formal volunteering, rather than the cultivation of informal volunteering (which he terms a 'fourth sector' approach). Is it reasonable to criticise a government for failing to prioritise informal voluntary action? It is not obvious what can be done to persuade individuals to engage in more informal, neighbourly acts, which are inherently not susceptible to public policy initiatives (other than, perhaps, those to do with the physical layout of streets to facilitate encounters between neighbours (see Jacobs, 1961)).

Labour certainly succeeded in establishing a policy consensus on the expanded role of the third sector in public service delivery. Significant elements of the third sector were able to accommodate their own differences under the banner of a 'strategic unity' (Alcock, 2011) in a context in which unprecedented levels of public funding contributed to significant expansion in the resources available to the sector (Chapter Three). Voluntary action, and the third sector, were advocated in relation to a large range of possible objectives and policy priorities. That said, Labour's approach was also centralised and target-driven, while the volume of public funds channelled to some charities provoked strong criticisms from the right about politicisation and the associated lack of independence (Seddon, 2007).

The Big Society, localism and the kaleidoscope of voluntary action

Rhetoric in the 2010 General Election campaign from all major political parties suggested broad agreement on the importance of the third sector and the need for a proactive engagement with government. The distinctive feature of the Conservative manifesto, however, was that it envisaged a substantial expansion in the contribution of voluntary effort to the welfare mix while simultaneously proposing very substantial reductions in public expenditure, which were to fall particularly heavily on local government (Taylor-Gooby, 2012; Taylor-Gooby and Stoker, 2011). Rhetorically, this was presented as the rolling-back of an overextended state and the expansion of scope for voluntary action, which formed the centrepiece of David Cameron's 'Big Society' proposals – which appeared, initially at least, to be *the* flagship domestic initiative of the government. In Cameron's view, Britain had become a 'broken society', as a result of excessive, top-down state intervention.[8] To repair the damage, the government sought to take power away from politicians and give it to people. In a speech to NCVO in 2006, Cameron had envisaged a shift 'from state welfare to social welfare'. He optimistically characterised the 'map of social action' as a 'vibrant kaleidoscope of institutions and organisations, competing and combining, developing effective responses to social needs'.[9] This Burkean vision of 'little platoons' combined elements of public sector reform, community empowerment and philanthropic action. From this perspective, responsibility for providing public goods is best devolved to communities; individuals and businesses are to be encouraged to make greater contributions to their communities; and social action and social enterprise are to be strongly supported. As is well-known, the rhetoric of the 'Big Society' did not last long, but the underlying policies – especially around public service reform, localism and social action – remain in place.

In a manner analogous to the development of 'third way' thinking under Tony Blair and 'New Labour', Cameron attempted to distinguish his own party not only from Labour, but from its Thatcherite predecessors (Ware, 2012). Perhaps like 'third way' thinking, the notion of a Big Society drew on a heterogeneous range of traditions of political thought (Blond, 2010; Norman, 2010). While this raises difficulties for those who would pigeon-hole post-2010 policies simply as neoliberalism in a new guise, it also meant that the ideas were open to criticism for vagueness and lack of rigour (see Raban, 2010).

Cameron insisted that the Big Society was his 'passion', but had trouble explaining to a wider audience about what, exactly, he was passionate.

Alan Ware (2012, 85) interpreted the 'Big Society' rhetoric as a strategy by the Conservative party to distance itself from the Thatcher-led governments of the 1980s, which had systematically weakened the powers of intermediate organisations, such as local government and trade unions, which provided some degree of protection for individuals and communities against encroachment by the state or the market. Rhetorical support for voluntarism allowed David Cameron to reassure the electorate that there were intermediate institutions standing between individuals and large-scale economic and political forces, safe in the knowledge that small-scale community organisations would never be a serious source of countervailing power against the rolling-out of pro-market policies.

In contrast to Labour, the emphasis was on bottom-up, rather than top-down policies. Whereas the Blair and Brown governments proposed targets, the post-2010 governments have used the tools of competition, choice, payment by results and transparency, which they argue will lead to a radical shift of power away from the centre. Individual action has been central to this vision; according to Greg Clark (Minister for Decentralisation, 2010–12) there were three essential elements in the Coalition government's policies: 'The first is about what the state can do for us. The second is about what we can do for ourselves. And the third is about what we can do for others.'[10] Three key elements were opening up public services, community empowerment and social action. We begin with the latter.

First, there has been a desire to foster a climate of social responsibility, to stimulate increased levels of engagement, and to enable people to come together to improve their communities and help one another. Policy was framed in relation to a broader concept of *social action*, rather than just volunteering. Social action was defined (Cabinet Office, 2015) as something which: can be carried out by individuals or groups; is not mandated, and is not-for-profit; is done for the good of others; and is done in order to bring about social change and/or to produce social value. This blurs existing divisions in the volunteering literature (for example, between formal and informal volunteering) while also raising further definitional challenges (how do we know the answers to the questions about the orientation of the actions described?). Much faith was placed in behavioural change and the phenomenon of 'nudging' people to engage in prosocial behaviours such as volunteering and charitable giving (John et al, 2011). There was also much interest in innovative methods for giving money and time. An example was the

Giving White Paper (Cabinet Office, 2011), a description of various relatively small-scale and novel initiatives through which people could give more, or could give in different ways – for example, 'slivers of time', through which people might engage in prosocial behaviours, even while doing something else (examples given in the paper were somewhat underwhelming, such as the notion that charity trustees could read committee papers while commuting). The White Paper contained no normative or aspirational targets about levels of volunteering or charitable giving, simply stating that 'it doesn't matter how people give...or what they give'. Nudging of course implies relatively small-scale change, and whether modifications to the choice architecture facing individuals can achieve substantial change in levels of engagement has been questioned (John et al, 2011). In a further attempt to mobilise and promote voluntary initiative, the Coalition government established the Centre for Social Action Innovation Fund in 2013, in partnership with the charity NESTA, to get volunteers involved in tackling complex social problems, in areas consistent with government priorities (supporting people to age well and live independently, improving health outcomes, supporting young people, stronger and safer communities, and contributing to prosperity).[11]

Resting on the belief that volunteering promotes social mixing and social integration, significant funding was also provided for the National Citizen Service scheme. This is a programme designed to give 16-year-olds an opportunity to develop the skills for active and responsible citizenship, principally through undertaking 30 hours of social action during the programme. The intention was to encourage young people to increase involvement in such action, and enable them to mix with people from different backgrounds. The programme has been criticised for its high cost in comparison with other forms of youth social action, such as scouting (Committee of Public Accounts, 2017). If one wanted a comparison with the Thatcher years, recall her government's insistence on the economic logic of closures of industrial plants and coal mines in the 1980s, regardless of extensive demonstrations that the social and economic costs for communities greatly exceeded the savings generated to taxpayers. Now, social returns can, it seems, justify expenditures of hundreds of millions of pounds on an initiative in youth volunteering.

In addition the Coalition administration provided resources for the training of up to 5,000 community organisers (albeit with the rider that they would need to raise funds in order to keep going, once the initial funding has run out) and for the creation of neighbourhood groups across the UK, especially in the most deprived areas. The former was an idea imported from the USA, and raised some eyebrows when it was announced, because in its original formulation led by Saul Alinsky, it was very much associated with training community representatives to make claims against the state (Taylor, 2011). The creation of neighbourhood groups was also supported by the Coalition government-funded Community First programme, and by other initiatives from the major funder of voluntary activity, the Big Lottery Fund, which has made small-scale awards (through its 'Big Local Trust' initiative) to communities which are in need, or which have not previously had much funding from major lottery distributors or other regeneration initiatives.

Involvement in *public service markets* is a further way in which the post-2010 governments have promoted opportunities for voluntary organisations. Commissioners of services were encouraged to take account of social, economic and environmental wellbeing, and not just price considerations, in placing contracts (Teasdale et al, 2012). On the other hand, public service procurement has been opened up to any qualified providers, driven by a desire both to break up monopolies, and to improve outcomes. A highly visible and often controversial element was the introduction of 'free schools', developed through the voluntary initiative of parents. Whether such initiatives have drawn committed and skilled people away from other voluntary organisations in their communities is not known as yet. There has also been direct support for the rights of public sector workers to form employee-owned mutual organisations and cooperatives and to bid to take over the services they deliver (albeit against the background of a heavily market-driven approach to the placement of contracts for public services). It is arguable that these processes of competition are not new, and that they date back to reforms of health and community care services introduced in 1989. What is new is the scale of the process of opening up public services to competition – with contracts which can be worth hundreds of millions of pounds being placed for substantial elements of NHS provision. Despite occasional criticisms of the concentration of public funding in small numbers of large national charities, the reality is that public service markets are overwhelmingly dominated by a small number of commercial suppliers (Civil Exchange, 2014, 29–30), with voluntary organisations, especially those which are small and largely volunteer-led, being marginalised.

A third stream is *community empowerment*. Citizens and community groups were given a number of rights in relation to community assets and community planning, under the auspices of the 2011 Localism Act. For instance, community groups have a right to bid to take over community assets, and to challenge the local authority to take over public services.

There is no blueprint in this system, and in that sense no targets against which performance or success can be measured. The independent think tank, Civil Exchange, produced a series of 'Big Society Audits', which have highlighted elements of progress (for example, growth in communities taking control of local assets – some of which have been transferred from public sector ownership), but a mixed picture in other areas, particularly in relation to public service delivery.[12] Volunteering levels, potentially a key index of the success of this strategy, are considered in Chapter Four.

Relationships between government and the voluntary sector since 2010 have been by no means always harmonious. Consultative structures, infrastructural support provided by government and partnership arrangements have been scaled back, if not removed altogether; organisations therefore have no guaranteed place at the policy table, although some prominent individuals have been favoured with significant roles in leading enquiries. The opportunity has regularly been taken by Conservative MPs and Conservative supporters to criticise voluntary organisations on the grounds of their allegedly politicised campaigning activities, their reliance on public funding, and the high salaries paid to senior staff. The government went so far as to propose the introduction of a clause into public service contracts whereby charities would be required to agree not to carry out a range of activities which were regarded as lobbying the government. Described as a 'gagging clause', this was eventually withdrawn. So for all the supportive rhetoric – most recently the 'shared society' vision of Theresa May, the current Prime Minister[13] – these are not easy times for voluntary organisations.

Conclusions

What continuities, discontinuities, consistencies and inconsistencies do we find in government policy towards the voluntary sector and voluntary action over this time period?

Voluntary action is a field in which rhetoric, endorsement and exhortation may be as significant as legislation and specific policies. The major political parties have steadily increased the space allocated to consideration of voluntary action and the third sector in their political manifestos (Kendall, 2003, chapter 6), but whether this amounts to anything more than discursive attempts at differentiation of parties from previous sins of omission is debatable. Returning to the distinction made in Chapter One – that policies might focus on voluntary action by *individuals*, supporting the development of voluntary *organisations*, and institutionalising the involvement of the voluntary *sector* in public policy more generally – the following points can be made.

In relation to voluntary action by *individuals*, we see strong rhetorical support from all governments, but Thatcher's speeches about the unsung heroes in communities who provide the bedrock upon which the state builds seem rather understated in comparison to Blair's association between high levels of voluntary action and successful societies, or Cameron's statement that the Big Society was his 'passion'. We can clearly contrast the governments, however, in terms of policy. The Thatcher governments did relatively little to promote volunteering by individuals, but it is interesting to speculate what a post-1997 government led by John Major might have done. It is easy to characterise the Blair and Brown governments as top-down and centralised (was it ever a good idea to have volunteering targets for local authorities?), but they did at least focus attention not just on aggregate rates of volunteering, but also on specific underrepresented groups. While ostensibly non-directive – see the 2011 *Giving White Paper*'s statements, with their indifference as to the kind of voluntary action individuals undertake – the post-2010 governments do actually have a clear vision of what sort of voluntary action they wish to prioritise: uniformed groups, service by young people, high-profile projects such as Citizens' Service, and small-scale community organising.

When it comes to policy to support the development of voluntary *organisations*, there are clear differences between governments. The Thatcher and Major governments drew voluntary organisations into policy issues such as the management of unemployment, created some opportunities for involvement in community care, and actively encouraged the transfer of housing to voluntary ownership. But this was policy within particular vertical fields of activity, and it largely took the existing infrastructure of voluntary action as given. Labour had a strong and consistent view that investment was needed to build up the capacities in voluntary organisations, and to support the infrastructure for voluntary action. The Labour governments (1997–2010) also initiated alternatives to statutory provision, for example, in education. The removal of NHS hospitals from direct lines of accountability to the Secretary of State for Health, as well as the creation of mutuals in the public services, can also be seen as part of this process. The post-2010 governments have drawn back from such strategic initiatives, instead simply opening up the public services to market forces and letting the market fall where it will. While the governments have presented this as an opportunity, the third sector remains at the margins of public service markets. Voluntary organisations are critical of the marketised environment in which they operate, see few benefits from it, and are concerned about whether operating in a quasi-commercial manner compromises their ability to meet the needs of their clients (Kendall et al, forthcoming).

Finally, there are clear differences between the different governments in power between 1979 and 2017, in terms of policy towards the voluntary *sector*. It is arguable that when Thatcher was in power, there was no sense of the voluntary sector as a collectivity, interest group or power base. The idea of a *sector* came later: it had been 'invented by committee' (6 and Leat, 1997). Under Labour, discourses of partnership, a more directive policy regime and a systematic attempt at the inclusion of the peak organisations in the voluntary sector in policy consultation, all suggest that the sector had been institutionalised. Looking back from 2017, the position is now very different, with high-level inclusion in policy debate being confined to the nomination of selected individuals from peak voluntary organisations to chair task forces. It is true that austerity put paid to funding for various forms of strategic support, capacity building and consultation. While government ministers have been broadly supportive of the sector, however, junior MPs have not been slow to criticise charities on a number of fronts, aided by a Conservative-dominated media keen to represent the voluntary sector as an oppositional, and threatening, power base. The post-2010 governments therefore have no conception of the sector *qua* sector; what they offer, instead, is simply the opportunity for voluntary organisations to participate in markets.

The period we are studying, therefore, has witnessed significant policy change in relation to voluntary action and the voluntary sector. In the substantive chapters of this book we consider evidence as to how these policy changes have worked out – for example, in terms of levels of volunteering. We also consider whether these changes register in the public's minds, for example in terms of their attitudes to and trust in voluntary organisations, or their beliefs about the relative roles of statutory and voluntary agencies in meeting social needs. Before we address those subjects, we describe the principal data sources upon which this study draws.

Notes

[1] Margaret Thatcher, speech to the Conservative Political Centre summer school, ('The Renewal of Britain'), 6 July 1979, www.margaretthatcher.org/document/104107

2   Margaret Thatcher, speech to the Women's Royal Voluntary Service ('Facing the new challenge'), 19 January 1981, www.margaretthatcher.org/document/104551

3   TNA PREM 19 / 369, 'Prime Minister's meeting with representatives of the Community Service Volunteers to discuss youth unemployment'.

4   TNA CAB 184/556, CAB 184/628, Central Policy Review Staff (CPRS), 'Long-term public expenditure options'.

5   TNA CAB 184 / 563, Family Policy Group.

6   TNA PREM 19 / 1788, Ferdinand Mount to Margaret Thatcher, 19.4.83; TNA CAB 184 / 650 'Voluntary action to meet social needs: a general strategy', FPG (83) 13; 'Encouraging private giving to the voluntary sector', FPG (83)14.

7   TNA CAB 184/650, note by Tim Flesher, Margaret Thatcher's private secretary, 9 February 1983.

8   David Cameron, 'Fixing our broken society', speech in the Glasgow East by-election campaign, 7 July 2008, http://conservativehome.blogs.com/torydiary/files/fixing_our_broken_society.pdf

9   David Cameron, 'From state welfare to social welfare', speech to NCVO, 14 December 2006, https://conservative-speeches.sayit.mysociety.org/speech/599920

10   Greg Clark MP, speech to Policy Exchange: 'Growing the big society', 27 July 2010, http://webarchive.nationalarchives.gov.uk/20120919132719/http://www.communities.gov.uk/speeches/corporate/growingbigsociety

11   www.gov.uk/centre-for-social-action

12   Third Sector, 'Big society in need of a "radical review", says think tank', www.thirdsector.co.uk/go/news/article/1224144/big-society-need-radical-review-says-think-tank/

13   Theresa May, Prime Minister's speech at the Charity Commission annual meeting ('The shared society'), 8 January 2017, www.gov.uk/government/speeches/the-shared-society-prime-ministers-speech-at-the-charity-commission-annual-meeting

THREE

Data: sources and definitions

Introduction

In this chapter we describe the secondary quantitative and qualitative data that we have used in this study. Our quantitative data are drawn from a range of robust and authoritative cross-sectional and longitudinal studies, and are complemented by rich longitudinal qualitative data from the Mass Observation Project (MOP). We consider the ways in which volunteering and community engagement are conceived of and measured, and the challenges posed for analysts by the particular nature of these two types of source. Each dataset has different definitions of voluntary action; we reflect on these definitions, and on how they may influence the responses given by participants. We describe the ways in which we sampled from each source, and consider the question of representativeness. A further section then considers the possibilities for, and challenges associated with, simultaneous usage of the MOP and social survey datasets.

Collectively the data sources constitute a considerable resource for exploring change in voluntary action in the UK over a long period of time. In practice, most of the quantitative datasets used relate to England, or to England and Wales (see discussion below), while nearly all the MOP writers sampled live in England, with a small number living elsewhere in the UK.[1] Within the longitudinal datasets, tracking of individuals is possible for considerable periods of time – at least a decade, in the case of the British Household Panel Survey (BHPS), while the MOP material likewise permits us to follow individuals through extensive parts of their lives. The juxtaposition of the qualitative and quantitative material is also novel, with the qualitative data from MOP adding considerable depth to the survey data, while the latter provides context for the former. While no individual dataset has tracked individuals or measured volunteering in an identical manner throughout the period of our study, there is sufficient consistency within datasets, and in the overlaps between the periods for which individual surveys are available, to justify using the various sources to analyse continuity and change in voluntary action from the early years of the Thatcher government (the first survey dataset we use is for 1981) through to the Conservative government of Theresa May (although the last MOP directive we have used for this study was issued in 2012).

In describing the sources we have used, we consider the following points. First, how is voluntary action defined and measured, and with what consistency, across surveys? And what kinds of activity count as voluntary action? Second, how does the available evidence allow us to investigate whether the accounts of volunteering provided by individuals correspond to the three 'paradigms' of voluntary action identified by Rochester et al (2010)? In particular, can we identify in detail the nature of the voluntary activities that individuals carry out? Third, drawing principally on the qualitative material provided by MOP respondents, can we add further insight into volunteering behaviours by providing accounts of writers' motivations for voluntary action, and of the meanings attached to such action by individuals? These issues are presented in different ways by our different data sources, and a key novel feature of our work is the attempt we make to bring these data into relation with one another (see also Lindsey et al, 2015).

Quantitative data: longitudinal and cross-sectional studies of voluntary action

No individual survey of voluntary action covers the whole of the period in which we are interested. The topic has been approached through a number of separate cross-sectional and longitudinal surveys which differ in their approach and, therefore, in the estimates of voluntary action which they provide. The discussion relates to data derived from surveys of volunteering in England (see discussion of spatial coverage of surveys below).

The earliest relevant surveys used are the General Household Survey (GHS)[2] (1982 and 1987) and the National Surveys of Voluntary Activity (NSV)[3] (undertaken in 1981 and 1991 (Humble, 1982; Lynn and Davis-Smith, 1992). These surveys asked about individual voluntary action in the sense of an activity that 'involves spending time, unpaid, doing something which aims to benefit someone (individuals or groups) other than or in addition to close relatives, or to benefit the environment' (Lynn and Davis-Smith, 1992, 16). In the GHS individuals were asked directly about their 'voluntary work' and presented with a list of potential types of organisations through which they might do it. In the NSVs, as is common practice in other subsequent surveys (such as the Citizenship Survey (CS)), respondents were led to reflect on the topic of voluntary action through questions which prompted them to recall a range of activities in which they had been engaged in their spare time. Terms such as 'voluntary work' and 'volunteering' were avoided, quite deliberately (Lynn and Davis-Smith, 1992, 16; Humble, 1982, 4). As a result of the extensive range of prompts offered in the NSVs, estimates of volunteering from that source (including those from the 2007 *Helping Out* survey (Low et al, 2007) which followed the same methodology)[4] are the highest reported in the UK (see Chapter Four).

The annual cross-sectional CS,[5] also known as the Communities Study, was introduced in 2001 – partly as a result of Labour's desire to set targets for and monitor voluntary activity (Chapter Two) – and continued until 2011. Its core sample size was typically 9,000–10,000. The survey had a section of questions entitled 'Volunteering'. These questions were accompanied by a series of prompts, inviting respondents to consider whether they had provided active 'unpaid help' to groups, clubs or organisations ('formal volunteering'). Prompts also accompanied a separate question about unpaid help 'for someone who is not a relative' ('informal volunteering'). The manner in which these questions are defined and categorised clearly defines volunteering as unpaid help to individuals in either organisational or non-organisational contexts (formal and informal volunteering). The survey did not ask questions about caring responsibilities or activities (other than one question about whether there was a co-resident who required care in some shape or form). The section on volunteering was followed immediately by a section on 'Civic Renewal' which mapped the involvement of participants in community roles of responsibility, such as being a school governor or a magistrate. The Coalition government cancelled the CS in 2011, but commissioned the Community Life Survey (CLS) from 2012. This asks broadly the same questions on volunteering as the CS. It now also includes questions on 'social action', which ask whether participants have been involved in 'helping out', for example, in trying to set up or stop the closure of, a local service or amenity. Combining these surveys gives us a 15-year series of data, though analytical possibilities offered by the CS are more limited due to the smaller sample (with around 2,200–3,000 respondents, this is now one-quarter of the size of the CS). We have used the CS to provide additional cross-sectional insights into the proportions of people volunteering and the intensity of their contributions (see Chapters Four and Five). There have been recent changes to the CLS which affect the comparability of estimates derived from it for 2016–17.[6]

The principal longitudinal source is the BHPS.[7] The BHPS tracked the same 5,500 households, initially comprising 10,300 individuals aged 16+, between 1991 and 2008.[8] It was replaced by the Understanding Society (US) survey in 2011, when more than 80 per cent of the BHPS panel continued to participate in US. Although there is some variation in the questions asked, when analysed together the two constitute one longitudinal panel survey.

The BHPS included questions on voluntary action on alternate years between 1996 and 2008, and the US survey included voluntary action questions in 2011, allowing us to track individual participants' responses at eight different points in time (at the time we conducted the analysis described in Chapter Seven, only the 2011 US data were available). In the context of a module about 'the things people do in their leisure time', respondents were presented with ten options. One of these was whether they 'do unpaid voluntary work', and it asked them to indicate the frequency with which they did so.[9] This way of framing the question treats voluntary activity explicitly as a form of leisure, invoking a definitional paradigm that fits with Stebbins' (2007) and Rochester et al's (2010) category of 'serious leisure' (p 13). Therefore, if volunteers had perceived their own involvement as a form of *work*, they may have been less inclined to mention it in response to a question about *leisure* (Staetsky and Mohan, 2011, 7). There were no questions about the organisational context in which volunteering takes place, and we cannot establish whether the respondents were referring to 'formal' volunteering (through organisations) or 'informal' volunteering (activity that does not take place through an institutional structure). No prompts were provided to respondents as to what was meant by 'unpaid voluntary work' and so the survey relied on the participants' own judgement and understanding. For all these reasons, reported rates of volunteering derived from the BHPS are considerably lower than those obtained from studies which explore the giving of 'help' to organisations and which provide fuller guidance to respondents in the form of lists of activities from which to choose (such as Low et al, 2007).

Although the BHPS did not inquire about informal volunteering, it did ask whether respondents 'provide some regular service or help for any sick, disabled or elderly person' who was not co-resident with the respondent. The reference to 'regular service' suggests a firm commitment to this voluntary contribution. The survey also provided categories of beneficiaries which enabled respondents to specify whether these were close or distant relatives, 'friends and neighbours' or clients of voluntary organisations. Therefore, it is possible to use this question to distinguish between those who had been providing unpaid care to relatives who do not live with them, and those who had been providing support to non-relatives in the community. The data suggest that around 10 per cent of the population were engaged in providing such help, but the proportion was much lower (around 2 per cent) when support given to relatives was excluded. We cannot therefore assume that this question is equivalent to the CS measure of *informal volunteering*, since it specifically restricts coverage to help given to 'sick, disabled or elderly persons' (whereas informal volunteering might refer to help given to anyone in the community). Instead, we might view this activity as informal care. As we show when discussing material provided by MOP's respondents, such support for non-relatives and relatives does feature strongly in their accounts of unpaid work (see Chapters Five and Eight; see also Wheatley et al, 2017).

In 2010/11 the BHPS was incorporated into the US panel survey. There have been further volunteering questions (in alternate waves from 2011). Only the first (2011) wave data was available at the time of undertaking the analysis for this book and we note that the questions on volunteering were slightly modified, thus affecting our ability to compare responses to those given within the BHPS. We have, however, incorporated the 2011 data, given that our last MOP directive was issued in 2012. The BHPS/US provides a narrow definition of volunteering, in comparison to the much broader range of options offered by other survey instruments, such as the CS, which potentially confuses the respondent by conflating leisure activity with unpaid work. The BHPS enables us to follow individuals across time, illuminating the dynamic and fluid elements of volunteering trajectories (Chapter Seven), as also exemplified by other work (McCulloch, 2014; Tabassum et al, 2016; Geyne Rajme and Smith, 2011).

Finally, the British Social Attitudes Survey (BSAS) has been conducted annually since 1983. More than 3,000 people aged 18+, who are representative of the population of Britain,[10] are chosen at random to take part each year. The BSAS measures continuity and change in attitudes about 'what it is like to live in Britain and how… Britain is run'.[11] This provides contextual data on how public attitudes to welfare and the role of the state have changed over time within the British population, and whether these changes relate to external political, economic and social events. The BSAS offers: consistent data on attitudes to the welfare state over time; occasional insights into public opinion regarding volunteering and the role of the voluntary sector (for example, the merits of charitable versus state provision of some services (Mohan and Breeze, 2016, chapter 1)); and some questions on voluntary action by individuals.

In short, approaches to the measurement of volunteering during the period covered by our study reflect variations in definitions which influence the responses given by participants, and thus individual and collective understanding of voluntary action. Distinctions between informal and formal volunteering, and between unpaid help and unpaid work, appear to be the key sources of variation. The quantitative survey data covers nearly all the time-period of our study, but questions have been asked using different survey instruments while even within the same surveys we find variations in question phrasing and sequencing. As a result, no individual survey covers the whole period of our study. However, we can still draw broad conclusions about aggregate patterns over time, and we also track a subset of individuals from the BHPS consistently for the 15-year period from 1996 to 2011.

One final point to note concerns spatial units. The key national surveys used have varied in their coverage. The 1981 NSV covered mainland Britain; the 1991 NSV covered England and Wales but it is impossible to separate the two countries in the data; the 2006–07 *Helping Out* study, the successor to the NSVs, covered England only. The GHS focused on mainland Britain and it is possible to identify Wales and Scotland separately. The CS was for England and Wales but its successor, the CLS, relates only to England. The BHPS initially covered England, Wales and Scotland, and it is possible to separate out respondents from these different geographic areas. By and large the data in the tables relate to England, but occasionally, where comparisons have been drawn between some surveys (for example, comparing the 1991 NSV with the later CSs) we have presented data for England and Wales. We identify the spatial units used in the respective tables. As shown in previous analyses (Mohan et al, 2006) variations in rates of engagement between the constituent countries of the UK are very small, once allowance is made for the social composition of their populations.

Qualitative data sources: Mass Observation Project

Since the re-launch of the MOP in 1981, a panel of self-selected volunteer writers has generated many thousands of responses to individual 'directives' – sets of themed questions on different topics that are issued to writers three times a year. The directives are devised by the Mass Observation Archive (MOA), which runs the MOP and curates the archival material in its care, but are also commissioned by individuals or organisations. The size of the writing panel has fluctuated over time. In the 1980s it was not unusual for the MOP to receive over 600 responses to some directives; but in the past ten years, typical numbers have been of the order of 200. Responses can be up to 20 pages in length – representing a considerable body of textual material. Academics have tended to use this material cross-sectionally or thematically, focusing on responses to a given theme at given points in time (see for example, Deakin and Davis-Smith, 2011; Kushner, 2004; Parsons, 2013; Savage, 2010; Sheridan et al, 2000).

Discussions with MOA staff made us aware that many MOP volunteers have had a longstanding involvement in the project. Our expectation was, therefore, that we would find the same individual responding to a number of topics over time, providing an opportunity for longitudinal analysis. Following these people over time would, we thought, enable us to show connections between changes and continuities in people's lives, and the extent and character of their volunteering (see Appendix). We believe that ours is the first research project to use the post-1981 MOP material as a longitudinal qualitative data source to investigate a specific topic, and to compare and contrast the findings with material from social surveys. This is different from the approach taken by Hinton (2016) who has focused on seven MOP writers to produce wide-ranging biographical accounts of their lives. We identified 15 relevant directives (see Table 3.1) on the basis that they all had direct or indirect relevance to voluntary action by individuals. Writers were asked to discuss: helping friends, neighbours and relatives; unemployment; paid work; unpaid work; membership of organisations; social divisions; British values; where they live; being part of research; the 2008 economic crisis; their involvement in MOP; belonging; and the 'Big Society' (see Table 3.1). Later in the study we also drew on an additional directive that identified key events in writers' lives. Some of these directives – for example the 1984 *Relatives, Friends and Neighbours* directive – were timely in relation to then-current policy debates, such as Thatcher's own emphasis on the family. They also have continued relevance today, however, at a time when more is being asked of individuals.

Like social surveys, the MOP directives act as research instruments. The individuals who respond to directives are encouraged to write in freeform and are able to choose whether or not they wish to respond in part or in full to these questions (see Sheridan, 1993, for discussion of writing practice). We first illustrate the questions posed to writers in our selected directives.

Directives on voluntary action and associational membership[12]

Four key MOP directives – *Membership of Voluntary Organisations* (1990), *Unpaid Work* (1996), a *Special Questionnaire* on *Taking Part in the Mass Observation Project* (2010) and *The 'Big Society'* (2012) – relate specifically to voluntarism and ask writers about their voluntary activities. We included the directive on associational membership because we anticipated, correctly as it turned out, that individuals would describe not just membership of, but also their contributions to, organisations.

Membership of Voluntary Organisations (1990)

This directive, which was written by the MOP team, asked:

> Please list everything you belong to, from the local darts team to OXFAM, from your trade union to your babysitting club. You should include local clubs, self-help groups, national & international associations, charitable organisations, pressure groups, religious groups, writers' circles, witches' covens, political parties, special interest groups, professional organisations, campaigns, discussion groups, coffee morning networks, motoring organisations, sports clubs, social clubs. If in doubt, list it.
>
> Please make sure you explain what's on your list (e.g. don't just put initials). You could use the list above for headings. Please indicate how active you are in the organisation and if you hold office.

In short, this directive asked for a list of contemporary memberships, as of 1990, of voluntary organisations and the level of writers' involvement in these organisations. It has some resonance with the BHPS question described above, first asked in 1996, which contextualises formal volunteering as part of leisure, and potentially mixes passive membership with active engagement and involvement. The focus was on formal associations, so this directive was unlikely to pick up less formalised activities. Note, in addition, that it specifically requested information on the *extent* of commitment by individuals.

When considering the responses we looked for a clear indication that the writer had taken an active role in the organisation, and whether we could interpret their roles as voluntary action of a formal nature, provided to a group or organisation. Our analyses and findings were thus subjected to a three-way definitional filtering process: through the directive/research instrument written by the commissioner; through the interpretation of the writer; and through the interpretation of the researcher. We used the material both to estimate proportions of respondents involved in organisations, and to characterise the content of their involvement (see Chapters Four and Five).

Unpaid Work (1996)

This directive was commissioned by a post-graduate researcher at the University of Sussex, but we have been unable to trace any thesis or publication on the topic by the author. It opened with the following statement:

> Your Own Experience:
>   Everyone who participates in Mass-Observation already does this, but we are interested to find out to find out about anything else you do in a voluntary capacity.

The directive then asked writers to describe any unpaid work that they were undertaking, how much they did, why they started doing it, and for how long they had been doing it. The directive provided guidance as to what types of activities counted as unpaid work, and incorporated a range of different terminologies for unpaid work, such as 'voluntary capacity', 'volunteer', 'volunteering' and 'unpaid work for community benefit', into its text. Unlike the 1990 directive, voluntarism was contextualised as *regular work* not leisure, and a distinction was made between formal volunteering 'whether or not it is arranged through an organisation' and informal volunteering 'whether you arrange it yourself informally (such as doing shopping regularly for an elderly neighbour)'. Such a definition is broadly consistent with what we find from social surveys, but it does rely upon individuals to recognise what they do as unpaid work.

The directive also asked:

> If you don't do any unpaid work for community benefit (other than your M-O work) please say why. Or if you used to do unpaid work but have stopped, please let us know about this.

MOP Special Questionnaire (2010)

In the 1996 *Unpaid Work* directive the suggestion was made to MOP writers that their writing was a form of voluntarism, so we have also treated MOP writing as a form of volunteering. The 2010 *MOP Special Questionnaire* directive asked writers: why they became involved in the MOP; the directives which they most engaged with; whether they do other writing similar to MO; the benefits they derive from involvement; and what might stop them from writing in the future.

The 'Big Society' (2012)

This directive was commissioned by ourselves (Lindsey and Bulloch, 2013). First, writers were asked to give their immediate thoughts when they thought of the term the 'Big Society'. Then, in a section entitled 'Voluntary Work' the directive asked:

> Do you do any voluntary work? Or perhaps you help someone out in an informal way? Please describe the work that you do. How did you find out about this opportunity? How long have you been doing it? How is the voluntary work you do arranged (e.g. is it through a formal organisation, or is it done informally through groups of friends and neighbours?) Why do you do it? How does volunteering make you feel?
>
> Do you feel you could do more voluntary work? Or do you think that you are doing the maximum that you can?

When placed in the context of the 1990 and 1996 directives on voluntarism, the terms used – 'voluntary work', 'helping someone out in an informal way' and 'volunteering' – constructed voluntary acts both as a form of work, and a form of help, while also leaving it to the writers to determine what they think counts. The intention was to pick up a broad spectrum of voluntary activity, and responses included activities that resembled formal and informal volunteering as well as leisure-based commitments. In the substantive chapters we reflect on the consistency between these relatively unstructured accounts, and the more formalised and constrained responses to survey questions.

Using other directives

Our consideration of the wording of the MOP directives on voluntarism suggests how these directives may have shaped respondents' definition and conceptualisation of volunteering. However, we cannot identify whether the wording of the directives has produced negative responses, with writers discounting particular activities as not constituting volunteering. For example, some writers do not discuss informal volunteering, but we do not know whether this is this because they do not contribute in this way, or simply because they have not written about it. Therefore, we sampled additional directives which potentially promised insights into activities that academic researchers might have described as volunteering, but which the writers might not. These included:

Relatives, Friends and Neighbours (1984)

This directive asked writers to discuss the strength of kinship ties, their expectations of friends, relatives and near-neighbours, and the sorts of relationships and exchanges of favours in which they were involved.

Where You Live (1995)

Writers were asked to describe the locality in which they were living at the time of writing; we thought that this directive would complement insights provided by the directives on *Relatives, Friends, and Neighbours* (1984), *Belonging* (2010), and *The 'Big Society'* (2012), particularly in relation to involvement in community activities, community spirit and locality.

Being Part of Research (2004)

The interest here was in whether writers had been personally involved in research, either carrying out research activities themselves, whether as part of their occupation or for their own interest, or being part of research projects.

Core British Values (2006)

This directive asked general questions on whether schoolchildren should receive instruction in core British values, and what those values might be. Interestingly, and despite the evidence of relatively high levels of voluntary action in the UK in comparison with other countries, we found very little evidence that writers' conceptualisation of core British values encompassed voluntary action.

Belonging (2010)

This directive explored writers' sense of belonging to groups or communities, echoing some of the questions in the directives on *Where You Live* (1995), and *The 'Big Society'* (2012). The directive envisaged that individuals might experience a sense of belonging in relation to 'individual people, a group or a community of people, a place, a culture or a nation', so that, in principle, a voluntary organisation might be a setting through which individuals experienced belonging. The directive also expressed interest in how changes in employment, residential location, or social networks had affected feelings of belonging.

Directives that shed light on how writers balance work and voluntarism

We were interested in how writers had combined their everyday activities and commitments with their voluntary contributions of work, help or care. We sampled four directives related to work or lack of work: *Unemployment* (1981), *Work* (1983), *Doing a Job* (1997) and *A Working Day* (2010). We also looked at writers' responses to the *Your Life Line* (2008) directive, which asked writers to chronologically draw, list or write about significant life events. Responses to these directives enabled us to map writers' working biographies and how these fit alongside their volunteering and personal histories. They provided insights into what writers thought about their mix of work and volunteering activities, which we discuss in our chapters on volunteering trajectories and motivation (see Chapters Six and Seven).

As well as gathering demographic information supplied by writers in their responses to different directives, we also analysed directives which provided insights into the demographic characteristics and economic circumstances of the MOP writers. These include the 1990 *Social Divisions* directive, which asked writers to discuss their social class; the 2008 *World Financial Crisis* directive, which asked writers to discuss how the financial crisis had affected them; and the 2010 *MOP Special Questionnaire* (mentioned earlier) which collected demographic information on writers. Combining this data on work histories, finance, occupation and other demographic characteristics has enabled us to gain a deeper understanding of how the characteristics of our selected 38 writers compare with the broader British population and the population of active volunteers represented in our analyses of survey data.

Analytical decisions: selection and analysis of individual writers and survey respondents

Survey data

The CS and CLS, the BSAS, the GHS and the NSVs were all designed to accumulate representative samples of the population at the time of the survey. In relation to our key longitudinal source, the BHPS, two options were possible and the choice between them affects comparisons over time. One was to include all survey respondents, treating each year as a cross-sectional snapshot of volunteering behaviour (which we do in Chapter Four). The second was to focus on people who had volunteered between 1996 and 2011, to allow exploration of how people transitioned in and out of volunteering between waves of the survey. To reduce the impact of missing responses within the dataset, we sampled individuals who had responded to the volunteering question every year between 1996 and 2011 (serial responders), and who stated that they had volunteered at least once between 1996 and 2011 (serial volunteers). As discussed below when we consider the process of bringing our source materials together, this sample had strong similarities with the MOP writers, meaning that these two sources were compatible, facilitating comparisons between qualitative and quantitative material within this particular timeframe. For example, in our consideration of volunteering trajectories over time (Chapter Seven), we have identified strong similarities between long-term volunteers identified through the BHPS, and those of serial respondents in the MOP.

Because the BHPS only asked questions on volunteering behaviour every other year starting from 1996, we could only consider the 1996–2011 period, which represents half the portion of the lifecourse being analysed in the qualitative data (which potentially covers the early 1980s through to 2012, when we issued our 'Big Society' directive, but also potentially includes retrospective material on some writers' voluntary action prior to 1981). This timeframe presented difficulties when comparing this sample with the MOP data. If a BHPS participant had been regularly volunteering between 1979 and 1995, but had then ceased to do so, we would have no knowledge of their volunteering across the earlier portion of their lifecourse. Such a respondent would simply be perceived as a non-volunteer from 1996, and would not have been included in our 1996–2011 sample of those who had volunteered at least once. This absence of evidence limited some of the scope for comparisons between the BHPS/US volunteer sample and the MOP writers.

Mass Observation Project: Choosing writers and analysing texts

In this section, we consider the main issues we encountered in choosing a sample of writers for this study, and in analysing their responses to the different directives described above (for more details see Lindsey and Bulloch, 2014; Lindsey et al, 2015). The MOP writing panel has varied in size between the early 1980s and the present day. The archive hosted up to 1,000 volunteer writers in its early days, when the MOA accepted all volunteers offering to write. The panel has since shrunk, and currently hosts approximately 450 writers. Almost 4,000 distinct writers have contributed at least one response since 1981. Not all writers registered with the MOP respond to every directive, meaning that there are people who have been associated with the archive for a long time but have gaps in their contributions.

One of the key issues that required consideration was the extent to which the MOP panel of volunteer writers can be said to provide information from a representative cross-section of the population. The 'representativeness', or otherwise, of MOP respondents has attracted scholarly attention (see, for example, Pahl, 2011; Pollen, 2013; Savage, 2011). We have analysed the characteristics of the entire MOP panel for a recent collaborative research project, which has generated a searchable database, through which users of the archive can structure their searches for respondents – for example, by selecting only people from particular demographic groups, birth cohorts, or geographical areas.[13] Basic demographic information suggests that when compared to the population of the UK, the panel of MOP writers are more likely to be female than male; more likely to be middle-aged or older; and more likely to come from professional occupational groups. When compared with those who volunteer, these differences remain, but are less pronounced (Kamerade, 2017). Detailed data on the panel is less comprehensive for other variables (for example, socioeconomic status). The evidence suggests that the MOP panel is not representative of the British population. However, the MOP panel does represent a subset of the population that is actively engaged in voluntary activity, because of their involvement with the MOP. Thus, when sampling for this study we recognised the option for sampling selectively from the panel, to identify subsamples of writers who had been writing for the MOP for some time, and who had specific socioeconomic or other demographic characteristics.

We first identified writers who had been members of the panel since the early 1980s and who had contributed to all 15 directives of interest; we then included those who had responded to declining numbers (14, 13, and so on) of our selected directives. This yielded a cohort of 20 serial responders, 14 women and six men (reflecting a gender imbalance in the MOP overall, which is roughly composed of two-thirds women and one-third men). The majority of these 20 writers began writing for MOP in their mid-30s or later (their average age at start of writing, in the early 1980s, was 46), are now in retirement, and represent voices that offer insights into the volunteering lives of individuals as they move from a midpoint (or further) in their working and family lifecourse into retirement. We then selected a further 18 writers who had written regularly between 1981 and the mid-1990s, or between the mid-1990s and 2012. Our selection criteria included occupation, as a very loose indicator of class and educational background, to provide a mixed sample of writers.[14] We also considered age – we aimed to include some writers at an earlier stage of their working and family lifecourse. An absence of serially responding writers in their 20s meant that the members of the second cohort differed from the first cohort in that they were typically in their 30s or 40s at the time that they started writing (average age at start of writing was 40). The second cohort contributed fewer responses than the first cohort.

We chose the software program, MAXQDA, as a tool for thematic analysis. Pollen (2013) argues that such 'data-mining' tools, with their emphasis on quantifiable results from lexical searches, potentially do violence to the rich individual voice of the MOP writer. In contrast Bulloch and Rivers (2011) contend that, used responsibly, such software is just as flexible, and can be used in the same way, as traditional analytical tools. MAXQDA software performs best when text is in a word-processed format. Since most scripts submitted to the MOP are only available in hard copy (either hand-written, typed or word-processed formats), we digitised and transcribed our selected scripts. We have donated both the PDFs and transcriptions back to the archive, for potential re-use by other researchers. Each writer has been anonymised by the MOA, and is identified by a unique letter and number, for example, B4318. We decided, mainly for ease of reading, to create our own identifiers for the MOP respondents, giving them pseudonyms. These identifiers are used throughout this book. Brief biographical details of our selected writers are presented in an Appendix.[15] We occasionally cite other individual writers, not included in our core group of 38 serial responders, whose responses to The 'Big Society' directive had been drawn upon (Chapter Eight); as we only refer to a small number of these, we have retained the unique letter and number identifier given to them by the MOA staff.

We adopted a *lifecourse approach* to the MOP data, constructing personal, work, volunteering and attitudinal lifecourse histories/ biographies for each writer. This enabled us to look for continuity and change in individual writers' lives, and differences and similarities in their volunteering behaviours and attitudes. In Chapter Seven we present examples of these trajectories.

There were several considerations in analysing the scripts, which we have discussed in more depth elsewhere (Lindsey and Bulloch, 2014). First, when transcribing responses, we reproduced writing and grammatical errors faithfully, and analysed transcripts alongside scanned PDF copies of the scripts, on the grounds that the physical characteristics and format of the scripts offered useful clues about the writers. However, after consultation with the MOA we made the decision not to reproduce spelling mistakes when quoting individual writers.

Second, we noted that the nature of the directives can influence how writers engage with the questions. Consciously or otherwise, writers' responses often mirror the directive in terms of structure or themes covered, and also in relative length (Sheridan, 1993). However, frustratingly, some writers do not answer all of the questions asked. There are many potential reasons why this might be the case, and we need to consider the possibility that omissions reflect the respondent's levels of interest in a question. Failure to answer fully represents one of the drawbacks of using MOP material – in an interview, the interviewer can follow up a non-response. Conversely, however, responses are occasionally accompanied by rich autobiographical reflections that can be off-topic, yet can contain unexpected insights which might not have emerged in a structured interview. Finally, it is worth noting that some writers engage with the reader/researcher consciously and unconsciously. When writing they may, for example, trust the reader with private, personal information, express strong political viewpoints, display unacceptable attitudes (for example, views on race and ethnicity), or seek to impress the reader with knowledge, style of writing, or a particular viewpoint (Sheridan, 1993). This attempt at connecting with the reader can ebb and flow as the writer gets into his or her stride and loses and regains sight of the audience.

The relationship between researcher and the MOP writer is therefore not dissimilar to that between interviewer and interviewee; the relationship can at times be contested, manipulated or controlled by the research subject, thereby challenging the agency of the researcher. However, the nature of the MOA forces the social scientist away from more conventional understandings of the subject of research, into the less familiar territory of the research subject as seen through the lens of other disciplines such as oral history.

How the datasets fit together

Given the disparate origins and purposes of the datasets on which we draw, it is no surprise that the questions on volunteering in our chosen social survey datasets did not always correspond closely with those that were asked through the MO directives. Nevertheless, we perceived our secondary qualitative and quantitative datasets and analyses to be complementary; our mixed-methods approach was to bring these analyses *into dialogue* with each other (we provide a more extensive discussion in Lindsey et al, 2015). Ideally, we wanted to achieve three types of mixed-methods dialogue: a continuous and iterative exchange across the lifetime of the project, described by Tashakkori and Teddlie (2008, 104) as a 'continuous feedback loop'; direct comparisons between qualitative and quantitative analyses where there was a clear fit between the datasets; and combining substantive findings so that the sum of our joint knowledge claims would be greater than the findings from individual elements of the work.

How did we seek to achieve this dialogue? First, we do have an extensive series of qualitative and quantitative sources which can be drawn on for nearly the entire post-1979 period. The degree of temporal correspondence between the survey datasets and MOP

Table 3.1 Survey sources and Mass Observation directives related to voluntary activity, 1981–2012

	Surveys of Volunteering		Cross-sectional surveys of attitudes to voluntary action	Mass Observation directives put to writing panel
	Cross-sectional	Longitudinal		
Early 1980s	NSV, GHS		NSV: place of voluntary action in society	*Unemployment* (1981); *Work* (1983)
Mid-1980s	GHS			*Relatives, Friends and Neighbours* (1984)
Early 1990s	NSV (1991) GHS (1992)		NSV: place of voluntary action in society; BSAS: (1993, 1994, 1996) attitudes to voluntary work	*Social Divisions* (1990); *Membership of Voluntary Organisations* (1990)
Mid-1990s		BHPS (1996, 1998)		*Where You Live* (1995); *Unpaid Work* (1996); *Doing a Job* (1997)
Early 2000s	CS (2001–)	BHPS (2000, 2002)		
Mid-2000s	CS	BHPS (2004, 2006, 2008)	BSAS (attitudes to providers of public services)	*Being Part of Research* (2004); *Core British Values* (2006); *World Financial Crisis* (2008); *Your Life Line* (2008)[1]
Early 2010s	CS (2009–2011), Community Life (2012–)	US (2011)		*Belonging* (2010); *Special Questionnaire on Taking Part in the Mass Observation Project* (2010); *A Working Day* (2010); *The 'Big Society'* (2012)

Note: [1] *Your Life Line* was a directive consulted later in the lifetime of the study, because it offered such strong insights into writers' life-courses.

directives is demonstrated in Table 3.1. There may be no single source covering the entire time period; nevertheless, there are proximate sources of survey data against which our key MOP directives can be compared and, likewise, the MO responses can be used to flesh out the quantitative picture.

We then looked for comparisons between characteristics of the respondents in both our qualitative and quantitative sources of data. The MOP respondents are not the product of a controlled sampling process so it is important to consider differences between them and the rest of the population. As shown in Table 3.2, the MOP respondents are more likely to be female and, on average, are somewhat older than both the general population and those in our core survey datasets, the CS and the BHPS. Although they might be considered unrepresentative of the broader British public, they share similarities to the population that engages in voluntary action (Chapter Five).

We sought to achieve, wherever possible, direct comparisons between qualitative and quantitative analyses where there was a clear fit between the datasets. Thus, for example, some key directives enabled us to estimate the proportions of the MO respondents who were either

Table 3.2: Comparison of data samples: MOP, BHPS/US and Citizenship Survey

	Qualitative		Quantitative		
	Wave 1 MO serial-responders 1981–2012	Wave 2 MO serial responders 1981–96 or 1996–2012	BHPS/US cross-sectional	BHPS/US longitudinal	CS (various waves)
Mean sample size per year	20	18	13337.5	4058	Core sample: 8800–9300
Mean age (year in which measured)	59.8	48.3	44.1	41.8	50
Mean age of volunteers in survey data	N/A		47.3 (in 1996)	45.8 (in 1996)	47–50
Mean % of women per year	65	72	53.8	56	54–56
% female volunteers in survey data	N/A		57	60	55–59

Note: BHPS data refer to 1996, the year in which the question about unpaid voluntary work was first asked. Data in the "BHPS Longitudinal" column refers to the subset of BHPS respondents that answered this question in every wave of the survey.

members of associations or active volunteers. Additionally, the 1996 *Unpaid Work* directive asked writers for accounts of their volunteering behaviour and their views on the role of voluntarism in society, and its questions corresponded well with those about volunteering behaviour in the BHPS and volunteering attitudes in the BSAS in the mid-1990s. Generally, rather than make direct comparisons between qualitative and quantitative analyses, we established an ongoing iterative dialogue, allowing the analytical strengths of both approaches to complement each other.

The ability to build up a portrait of change, over a period of time, in individual behaviour, and to gain a sense of lifetime involvement, is a key reason why the sources we have used have advantages over those deployed in previous work. Cross-sectional surveys ask people to recall actions in relation to a specified reference period – usually the previous month, or the past year. Actions outside those time periods would not be recorded, resulting in an underestimation of lifetime involvement: someone who recalls no volunteering in the past 12 months may have been active at earlier times in their lives. The BHPS/US longitudinal data provided a wealth of representative demographic data for the 1996–2011 period, covering a cohort of individuals, of various ages, who have grown older over time. The data has been used to provide large-scale quantitative analyses of how individual engagement of various kinds has evolved over time (for example, Geyne Rajme and Smith, 2011; McCulloch, 2014). The MOP data brings these trajectories to life, offering in-depth insights that survey data cannot provide, including data on lifetime engagement, or descriptions of changes in people's capacity to engage which are framed in relation to the experience of ageing, working lives, or the changing needs of families (Chapter Seven).

Individually the analyses of survey data offer corroboration of, and comparison with the qualitative material from the MOP. It might be more appropriate, however, to suggest that they offer a different type of descriptive insight into the different demographics of those taking part in volunteering over time.

Conclusion

We have set out the nature of our source materials in some detail here, so that readers can be clear about the claims that can and cannot be made about change or continuity in voluntary action. There is no single source for the study of volunteering over the whole time-period of our study, nor is there agreement about how best to measure it. There is arguably a sharp contrast between the apparent precision offered by survey data, and the very open-ended nature of the MOP material. However, both sources have much to offer, particularly when used in combination. We have also touched on some of the methodological and analytical challenges encountered when reusing and combining longitudinal qualitative and quantitative data to take a lifecourse approach to studying volunteering. Certainly, working through the methodological issues involved could be a messy and difficult process. The temporal and substantive fit between the datasets was not exact and seamless, posing some challenges for direct comparison of qualitative and quantitative data, but we argue that our mixed-methods dialogue enabled us to combine the breadth of an extensive quantitative perspective with the depth of an intensive qualitative approach. In the subsequent chapters we demonstrate the benefits of this approach. Thus Chapter Four juxtaposes analyses of a comprehensive range of statistics from social surveys with discussion of what our MOP writers take to be the meaning of voluntary action. In Chapters Five and Six, we deploy survey data about the content of and motivations for voluntary action as a basis for a much more in-depth assessment of how these issues are perceived in the minds of the MOP writers. Chapter Seven turns to the question of volunteering trajectories, demonstrating how biographical approaches to the study of individuals' engagement complicates and enriches the binary accounts of moves into and out of volunteering offered by social surveys. Finally, Chapter Eight brings together attitudinal material from surveys with individual responses to directives about the terms under which they might – or might not – engage in volunteering or unpaid work. We now explore the extent to which the considerable socioeconomic and political changes over the period we are considering are reflected in volunteering behaviours.

Notes

[1] Of the 38 writers sampled, one writer lives in Northern Ireland, and three writers live in Scotland. None of the writers sampled currently live in Wales, although two of the writers have previously lived in Wales.

[2] The GHS was a continuous annual national study (https://discover.ukdataservice.ac.uk/series/?sn=200019) covering England, Scotland and Wales. Sample size (England and Wales): 17,000–19,000.

[3] The NSV covered England and Wales – sample size: 1,692 respondents.

[4] However, Helping Out only covered England (2,705 respondents)

[5] See UK Data Service archive, http://discover.ukdataservice.ac.uk/series/?sn=200007. The CS covered England and Wales. Sample size (England): 8,700–9,700.

6　The survey has moved from face-to-face interview mode to being delivered largely online. This is known to have had differential effects on the responses to some questions.

7　British Household Panel Survey, www.iser.essex.ac.uk/bhps/

8　See www.iser.essex.ac.uk/bhps. The 1991–98 waves of this survey covered England, Scotland and Wales. Additional samples of 1,500 households in each of Scotland and Wales were added to the main sample in 1999 and in 2001. A sample of 2,000 households from Northern Ireland was added in 2001.

9　Asked every other year from 1996, see, for example, wave 18, 2008: www.iser. essex.ac.uk/bhps/documentation/pdf_versions/survey_docs/wave18/index.html

10　England, Scotland and Wales

11　See www.natcen.ac.uk/our-research/research/british-social-attitudes/

12　To download the full text of any directives used, please see: www.massobs.org.uk/mass-observation-project-directives

13　http://database.massobs.org.uk/

14　Unfortunately the MOA has never recorded the ethnicity of its writers, so we have no data on the ethnic composition of the panel. We are currently in the process of working with the MOA to address this issue. However, for the purposes of this study, our sampling of writers could not take into account writers' ethnic identities.

15　Our decision to use pseudonyms was also influenced by concerns about the level of personal biographical information that we have collected on the 38 writers used, and written about in this book. Researchers seeking to identify the MO number for these writers, for research purposes, should contact the MOA for further information.

FOUR

Trends in volunteering and trends in the voluntary sector

Introduction

In the research which underpinned William Beveridge's (1948) volume, *Voluntary Action*, social investigators found that 'no matter in what sort of area they lived ... less than one-third [of respondents] were found to be giving any sort of regular help to people outside their families' (Beveridge and Wells, 1948, 33). In fact, this was at the higher end of the estimates produced by their local investigators. Seven decades on, regular surveys of volunteering such as the Citizenship Survey (CS), or the subsequent Community Life Survey (CLS), typically find that between 25 and 30 per cent of individuals give unpaid help to organisations outside their households at least once a month. The Beveridge surveyors used a less formalised approach than a modern social survey, but the closeness of the headline figures suggests the intriguing possibility of long-run consistency. What happened, therefore, to volunteering rates during the period in which we are interested? The period has witnessed a combination of an expansion in levels of education (usually thought to be a good predictor of volunteering), a policy environment broadly sympathetic to voluntarism (Chapter Two; Hall, 1999; Kendall, 2003; Alcock, 2010; Hilton et al, 2012), and a steady expansion of the voluntary sector. All of these might be conducive to the growth of volunteering, but what happened in practice?

We begin with a consideration of survey data on volunteering, including statistical evidence from cross-sectional surveys on both formal volunteering for organisations, and on informal neighbourly acts. We consider the broader trends across the period since 1981, as well as evidence of short-term changes within this period. We also utilise longitudinal data from the BHPS, although we rely on that data more fully elsewhere to provide longitudinal profiles for individuals, on the grounds that cross-sectional surveys will underestimate lifetime patterns of involvement.

We flesh this picture out further using Mass Observation Project (MOP) material. This demonstrates how individuals are uncertain about the range of prosocial behaviours that constitute voluntary action; when describing such behaviours (see also Chapter Five), they include a wide range of activities which resist easy characterisation. These rich qualitative descriptions raise questions about whether Mass Observation Project (MOP) respondents would acknowledge the classifications of voluntary action used in social surveys. For example, the distinction often made between formal and informal volunteering is not necessarily visible in individual accounts, and respondents frequently remind us that care of relatives (largely ignored in surveys of engagement, and something which is excluded from definitions of volunteering since the benefits accrue to an individual's family members) accounts for significant proportions of their unpaid contributions to society. One implication, therefore, is whether it is ever possible to capture a 'true' estimate of the level of voluntary action in society, when individuals differ greatly in the actions which they report.

The levels of voluntary action revealed by social surveys demonstrate relative stability, but we also show how the past 35 years has witnessed important changes in the voluntary sector. Allowing for recessionary influences – and acknowledging that the effects of austerity are still working through – we show that there has been growth in the numbers of voluntary organisations, the voluntary sector's workforce, the aggregate level of resources, and public funding for the voluntary sector (at least until recently). We also provide an overview of these developments.

Our work contributes to a wider debate, on levels of social capital in British society, prompted by the work of Hall (1999), building on earlier work (Parry et al, 1992; Almond and Verba, 1963). The emphasis of this literature is on the extent to which individuals, from different social backgrounds, have regular contact with others, in situations of relative equality associated with participation in common endeavours. The core of the argument is that social networks increase trust, and enhance the capacities of societies and communities for collective action. Hall provided a British exploration of the influential claims, made by Robert Putnam (1995; 2000; Putnam et al, 1993), that levels of social capital were in decline. He argued that levels of social capital should be reflected 'both in general levels of trust that people have in others, and in their commitment to voluntary work in the community' (Hall, 1999, 425). His principal substantive focus was on associational membership, social trust and informal sociability, but he also drew upon survey data on voluntary action, covering 1976, 1981 and 1992, though there were important differences between the first of these surveys (conducted for the Wolfenden Committee) and the later General Household Surveys (GHS) (Hall, 1999, 425). With the availability of three decades of survey data we can now speak with much more confidence about levels of voluntary action.

Aggregate trends in voluntary action, 1981–2016

Previous efforts to map trends in voluntary action in post-war Britain have noted the relative absence of consistent social survey data. Hilton et al (2012) provide a very useful tabulation of survey results from 1945 onwards, but variations in the methods used by surveys prior to the 1980s limit the scope for long-term comparisons.[1] However, refinement of survey methods and consistency on the questions to be asked mean that, from 1981 onwards, we can generate reasonably reliable comparisons of trends over time, with a focus on England.

For cross-sectional surveys, we use various waves of the National Surveys of Volunteering (1981, 1991 and 1997; see Humble, 1982; Lynn and Davis-Smith, 1992), their successor, the *Helping Out* survey (Low et al, 2007), the GHS (1981, 1987, 1992) and, most comprehensively, the CS (2001–11) and its successor, the CLS (2012–). As for longitudinal sources, the BHPS began to ask individuals about volunteering activities at two-year intervals from 1996. The MOP material allows tracking of a subset of respondents who replied consistently to specific directives from the 1980s onwards. While the MOP material cannot be considered statistically representative, the levels of voluntary action described in it can be compared with those derived from national surveys. The temporal overlaps between these various studies give us confidence in our judgements about the stability of volunteering rates.

In relation to social survey data, beginning in 1981, with the NSV and GHS, we typically have at least one measure of voluntary action at the beginning and midpoint of each decade, and sometimes more than one. Table 4.1 presents headline figures for both formal and informal volunteering from the four main social surveys conducted over this period. Each survey measures volunteering on at least three occasions, with at least five years between each measure on each survey (although some – BHPS and CS – were conducted more frequently).

Formal volunteering

Our focus initially is on levels of formal volunteering, through organisations. Beginning with changes from the early 1980s onwards, we draw on the NSVs for 1981 and 1991. Though these were based

Table 4.1: Reported rates of formal and informal volunteering, various national household surveys, 1981 to date (% of adult population)

	Sample size	1981	Mid-1980s	1991	Mid-1990s	2001	Mid-2000s	c. 2011	2015–16
Formal volunteering									
NSV (any)	1351–2155	44			47		59		
NSV (at least monthly)		27					39		
GHS	17000	23	24	25					
BHPS/US (at least once a year)	13000				20	19	18	17	
BHPS/US (monthly unpaid help)					11	11	10	13	
CS (any formal)	8000–9000 (core sample)					39	44	41	42
CS (monthly formal)						27	29	25	27
Informal volunteering									
NSV (monthly)	1351–2155	23		35			41		
NSV (at least annually)		'three-quarters'		76			73		
CS (any informal)	8000–9000 (core sample)					67	68	55	60
CS (monthly informal)						34	37	29	34

Sources: Author's calculations for GHS, CS, US; for NSV, tabulations from Humble, 1982; Lynn and Davis-Smith, 1992; see also tabulations in OPCS, 1983, pp 161-180; Matheson, 1987; Goddard, 1992 for GHS.

Notes:

1 BHPS figure in the '2001' column actually refers to 2000 because of minor amendments to questionnaire options for 2002 which influenced the estimate for that year.

2 Geographical units: NSV – Great Britain (1981), England and Wales (1991), England (2006–07 – Helping Out survey): GHS, BHPS, Citizenship Survey – England.

on relatively small samples – the consequence of a deliberate decision to maximise the level of detail obtained – these were arguably the most exhaustive UK-based surveys of voluntary action, in terms of the prompts, options and follow-up questions offered to respondents. Unsurprisingly, therefore, the *lowest* estimates reported in them are well above those produced by general-purpose surveys. The figures for formal volunteering range from 44 per cent (1981) to 59 per cent (2007).

At the same time, the GHS estimated that just under one quarter of the population were engaged in some voluntary work in 1981, a proportion which remained consistent through iterations of the survey in 1987 and 1992, indicating stability over the Thatcher and Major governments. Note that, even within this survey, the definition of voluntary activity varied over time.[2]

The BHPS questions on associational membership have been widely used in important analyses of trends in social capital (for example, Li, 2015; Warde et al, 2003; McCulloch, 2014), but our interest here is in the question about involvement in volunteering. The survey took respondents through a list of 'activities which people carry out in their leisure time', one of which was 'unpaid voluntary work'. No auxiliary information was given to respondents to assist in their deliberations (for example, prompts about types of organisations to which they might (or might not) give assistance). This question was asked of the *same people* at two-year intervals from 1996 to 2008. This provides a consistent estimate of engagement from the end of the Major administration onwards. The proportion of people engaged in unpaid voluntary work at least annually ranges from 17 to 20 per cent; for work carried out *at least monthly*, the figures range between 10–12 per cent. These figures also suggest relative consistency over time. The formulation of this question was not carried forward into the Understanding Society survey (US), the BHPS's much larger successor panel survey. Instead, the US asked about 'unpaid help' to organisations, in a similar way to *Helping Out*, though without the detailed prompts to respondents. The estimate of volunteering produced in this way is roughly on a par with that produced by the BHPS, and is reported here, but while it has been used in the analysis of volunteering (Wheatley et al, 2017, chapter 6) the data may not be strictly comparable.[3]

The CS (2001–11) asked questions about formal volunteering (unpaid help given in an organisational setting) and informal volunteering (help given directly to individuals in the respondent's community) (see Chapter Three, and also Staetsky and Mohan, 2011). The subsequent CLS retained the same questions on volunteering, albeit with a much smaller sample size. Here again we find a consistent picture from 2001 onwards. Estimates of the population involved in formal voluntary action *at least once in the previous year* were 39 per cent for 2001, rising to 44 per cent in 2005, and dropping back to 41 and 42 per cent for 2010–11 and 2015–16 respectively. The rate of formal volunteering *on at least a monthly basis* fluctuated between 25 and 29 per cent in these surveys. Differences in rates between individual years for the proportion of the population volunteering at least annually do not always attain statistical significance, and although the peak figure reported (44 per cent, in 2005) was statistically different from the 2001, 2010–11 and 2014–15 (42 per cent) levels, this would not justify claims that volunteering had either risen or declined over the period.

What of informal volunteering? One criticism, both of discussion of volunteering levels, and of policy designed to increase voluntary activity, has focused on the implicit prioritisation of formal volunteering undertaken through organisations (Rochester et al, 2010; Williams, 2003). However, this view has a longer academic pedigree, going back to David Horton Smith's (1997) arguments about the neglect of the 'dark matter' of the voluntary sector. The key point of these criticisms is that an emphasis solely on formal volunteering risks neglecting other contributions that people make to their communities, and this theme emerges strongly when our MOP respondents describe their own voluntary commitments (Chapter Five).

We use the NSVs (1981 and 1991), the *Helping Out* survey (2006–07), as well as the CS for 2001 and 2011, and the CLS for 2016. The GHS has not investigated informal volunteering (it defined voluntary work as activities which were undertaken through organisations) and neither has the BHPS or US (see Chapter Three).

For the 1980s, the 1981 NSV asked about 'neighbourhood care', offering question options broadly comparable with those used in subsequent surveys of informal volunteering. This found that three-quarters of the population provided neighbourhood care, and that just under a quarter did so at least weekly (Humble, 1982, 13; Lynn and Davis-Smith, 1991, 20, 106). The 1991 NSV found a similar result, and the 2006–07 *Helping Out* survey also estimated that around three-quarters of the adult population were volunteering informally on at least an annual basis.

The survey questions options offered in the NSV and the *Helping Out* survey were broadly comparable with those in the CS and CLS, but the latter generated slightly lower estimates, at around 67 per cent of the population for 2001 and the mid-2000s, dropping to 55–60 per cent in later surveys. More detailed investigations, discussed below, point to the reasons for the latter change but, broadly, we can say that between three-fifths and three-quarters of the population were volunteering informally during the lifetime of the CS and CL. As for monthly rates, there is a suggestion of a dip around 2010 but otherwise engagement has been slightly above one-third of the population.

Interpreting differences between surveys and assessing change over time

Table 4.1 indicates, especially in relation to formal volunteering, that there is considerable variation in the estimates of voluntary action. Before considering change over time, it is important to understand how these variations come about.

The most obvious example is the range of estimates of the proportions engaged in formal volunteering. The BHPS gives a figure for the proportions engaged in unpaid voluntary work of around 20 per cent for any unpaid work and around 10 per cent for monthly engagement; the GHS asks about voluntary work, and generates estimates of around or just under one-quarter for annual involvement. In the CS the reported rates of giving unpaid help to organisations are between 40–45 per cent (at least annually) and 25–29 per cent (at least monthly). In the NSV the proportions involved in formal volunteering were even higher, at between 44–59 per cent for engagement on at least an annual basis and up to 39 per cent for monthly volunteering.

Much of this variation is a function of differences in survey methods. Responses to surveys may be influenced by factors such as mode of data collection (self-completion questionnaire, telephone interview, face-to-face interview), the nature of the social phenomena (for example, attitudes, behaviour) about which information is sought, and the processes whereby people are differentially able to recall or remember aspects of their life (De Vaus, 2002; Groves et al, 2004). Tarling (2000), Rooney et al (2004) and McCulloch (2011) have all shown that reports of volunteering and charitable giving differ depending on the survey instruments used and questions posed to respondents. Staetsky and Mohan (2011, table 2) demonstrate this by considering the questions used in different British surveys of voluntary action. Sometimes involvement in volunteering was measured with a single question; in others a set or a sequence of questions was presented, including extensive prompting, on the basis of which a measure of involvement in volunteering was derived. Thus, volunteering was assessed in the BHPS using a single question within the larger survey framework, and in the GHS the question about voluntary work was not accompanied by prompts to assist the respondent to recall the types of organisation they may (or may not) have helped. In contrast volunteering is a central focus of the CSs and the NSVs. In these surveys, the interviewing process is designed to help the respondents to recall more about volunteering and adopt a more inclusive/broad understanding of it. We would therefore expect a higher level of recall and reporting of volunteering in those surveys than in the BHPS.

We should therefore be cautious about any search for a 'true' estimate of volunteering. But we can say that the *overall* picture is one of stability over time: several surveys apply a consistent methodology for at least a decade and *within each of these surveys* estimates of voluntary activity vary within a narrow range. The GHS and the NSV both illustrate consistency for the Conservative administrations of 1979–97; the measurement baton is then passed, as it were, to the BHPS, which shows little fluctuation in volunteering, from 1996 onwards. The detailed investigations of the CS from 2001 also show little variation over time. It would be hard to conclude that there has been a decisive shift, upwards or downwards, in the proportion of the population engaged in formal voluntary action over the post-1979 period.

Detailed changes in formal and informal volunteering, England, 2001–15

Measurement at approximately five-year intervals across the timeframe of this study allows a broad-brush perspective, but a more detailed investigation of trends is possible using post-2001 data. This allows us to pick up evidence of the effects of recessionary conditions and to provide insights into short-term fluctuations associated with specific events. We use data from the CS and CLS for 2001 onwards to illustrate trends derived from a consistent cross-sectional survey instrument over a 15-year period for England (Figure 4.1). We consider both formal and informal volunteering, by *frequency*.

Between 2001 and 2005 there was an increase in levels of *frequency* of engagement followed by a slight decline in 2008–09, a sharper dip from 2008–09 to 2009–10, followed by an increase between 2010–11 and 2012–13. Later surveys demonstrated a small reduction between 2012–13 and 2014–15. The salient feature of the graph (Figure 4.1), however, is the difference in trends in formal and informal volunteering. Reported rates for formal volunteering remained within much narrower parameters than was the case for informal activity.

The graph of change over time points to the period which accounts for most of this variation. The recessionary conditions from 2008

Figure 4.1: Formal and informal volunteering in England, 2001 to 2015–16

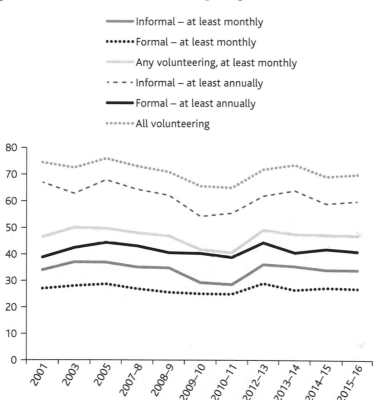

onwards were associated with a significant reduction in the rates of informal volunteering, whether on a monthly or less frequent basis. The proportion engaged *regularly* in informal volunteering dropped from 37 to 29 per cent between 2005 and 2010–11, while the equivalent figures for those engaged *less frequently* fell from 68 to 54 per cent. Recent sophisticated analysis by Lim and Laurence (2015) also indicates that not only did *rates* of engagement in informal volunteering fall, so too did *levels* of engagement, as measured by a reduction in the hours of commitment reported, while the decreases were also the greatest in the most disadvantaged communities. In contrast, levels of formal volunteering remained relatively stable. A further notable feature of their analysis is that because the survey was being conducted continuously, gathering over 2,000 responses in each quarter of the year, it was possible to tie the downward trend very closely to the onset of recessionary conditions from 2008. The scale of the reductions in involvement led Clark and Heath (2014) to conclude that the 'social recession' had been much more substantial than the economic recession.

To what degree is there evidence of a decisive subsequent upwards shift in engagement in the post-recession period and (simultaneously) after the 2010 General Election? If the public had been fired with enthusiasm for the 'Big Society' we would have expected an increase in the rate of engagement. The Coalition government had actually cancelled the CS on account of the need to reduce public spending, but the obvious lack of any instrument with which to measure the success of a flagship policy meant that they reinstated it, on a smaller scale, in the form of the CLS. The first results from this were likely to be a key test and were therefore eagerly awaited. As Figure 4.1 shows, the results from this survey, first conducted in 2012–13, did appear to show a significant increase in volunteering. However, the survey was undertaken from August to October 2012, when the Olympics and the Paralympics gave volunteering a high public profile through the volunteer 'Gamesmakers'. Thus voluntary activity would have been very much in the minds of respondents, possibly prompting them to offer question responses that they believed were likely to elicit approval. Once the full-year results were in, it emerged that the 2012–13 figures were significantly higher than those reported for 2001, but otherwise indistinguishable statistically from most of the CS results for the period from 2001 onwards. Trendless fluctuation might be a more appropriate characterisation. With 15 years of comprehensive survey data there is, as yet, no conclusive evidence that all the initiatives towards volunteering implemented by recent governments have resulted in a decisive upward shift in volunteering rates. Nor has there been a sustained post-Olympic bounce. Subsequent CLSs have shown that volunteering levels have not decisively shifted, one way or another.

Despite this, public pronouncements post-2010 by government ministers and Conservative MPs hailed volunteering rates as a vindication of their policies. Thus David Cameron announced in February 2013 (on the back of the CL results for 2012–13) that 'volunteering is up, charitable giving is up, and the big society is getting bigger'. Later that year the Minister for Civil Society, Nick Hurd, proclaimed that 'volunteering has risen sharply after years of decline'. In June 2015 the Culture Secretary, Maria Miller, suggested that the government had 'successfully reversed a long-term decline started under a Labour government'. In the same debate John Whittingdale pronounced the 'volunteering legacy [to be] one of the most extraordinary achievements' of the Olympic Games.[4] The best that can be said about these statements is that they are somewhat at variance with the facts. 'Bigging up society' might be one way to put it.

In short, bringing together a comprehensive range of survey datasets covering the post-1979 period, there is evidence, broadly, of stability in volunteering rates, as measured in terms of the proportion of the population engaged in volunteering. Surveys may measure volunteering in different ways, but there is consistency within survey datasets and overlap between them. Having said that, there is also strong evidence that adverse economic circumstances had negative effects on informal volunteering during the post-2008 recessionary period. This is consistent with a view that those who are most insulated from economic shocks are best placed to continue the commitments they make to their communities (Clark and Heath, 2014). Unfortunately, the absence of appropriate survey data makes it impossible to comment on the impacts of earlier economic changes (for example, the economic shocks of the early 1980s on voluntary action) (but see Laurence and Lim, 2013).

We have focused on a description of the overall rates of activity here, and are unable to analyse variations in the amounts of effort contributed by individuals, because we lack reliable data from the older studies on time commitments to volunteering. However, recent analysis from ONS, using time use surveys for 2000 and 2015, suggests that there has been a reduction in the amount of time committed to volunteering between the two surveys (ONS, 2017).

The nature of volunteering behaviour 1981–2012: how do MOP writers describe what they do?

Thus far we have emphasised a quantitative, aggregate portrait of voluntary action, but how do individuals characterise their participation when less constrained by the type of prompts found in a social survey? Our qualitative material allows us to explore the consistency between the understandings held by MOP writers of the nature of voluntary action and the evidence from surveys over time. We focus on three principal MOP directives (*Membership of Voluntary Organisations* (1990); *Unpaid Work* (1996); and *The 'Big Society'* (2012)). These all provide some sort of steer on the definition of voluntarism. When responding, some writers have answered these questions using the definitions provided; some have disagreed with these definitions; and some have been unsure as to whether their voluntary contributions count.

1990 Membership of Voluntary Organisations directive

This directive asked respondents to be as inclusive as possible, in reporting everything to which they belong ('If in doubt, list it').

They were also requested to indicate their level of involvement in the organisation, and whether they held office. This directive compares with the 1991 British Household Panel Survey (BHPS) questions on organisational membership, which presented individuals with a list of entities, and asked them to indicate whether they were members of, or active in, them.

Of our chosen 38 MOP writers, 32 writers were registered with the MOP in 1990, of which 29 responded to this directive; all 29 provided lists of their various memberships. Of these 29, 25 provided sufficient information for us to clearly identify 17 writers who were actively involved in the running of, or fundraising for, one or more voluntary organisations. Thus, some three-fifths of the 29 writers for whom we had responses were engaged in formal volunteering – that is, the provision of unpaid help to voluntary organisations. This is higher than the rates identified in the 1991 NSV (with its many prompts) and any subsequent survey. Some of the writers who were actively involved with an organisation also provided retrospective descriptions, indicating where and when they had been actively involved with another organisation but had stopped (Chapter Seven). Several writers who appeared not to be currently engaged in associations provided retrospective descriptions of former levels of activity, including some discussion of their reasons for stopping. Three of the 29 responses were unclear; the writers provided a list of memberships, but did not state how active they were. Given that MOP writers' levels of membership and involvement are at least comparable with social survey data, these responses provide a good basis for the more detailed investigations of the content of volunteering and of the trajectories of respondents (Chapters Five and Seven).

1996 Unpaid Work directive: 'I don't think of this as work, but as a caring friendship'

This directive asked writers to describe any unpaid work that they were undertaking, provided guidance as to what types of activities might count as unpaid work, and offered various prompts about voluntary action. Voluntarism was contextualised as *regular work*, not leisure, and a distinction was made between volunteering taking place through organisational settings and informal acts in the respondent's community. There were 33 (out of a possible maximum of 36) responses to this directive, of whom 20 provided descriptions of regular unpaid activities (of varying levels of intensity from once a year to several times a week) that they were undertaking at the time of writing. This proportion, at approximately three-fifths, is higher than reported in most national surveys of volunteering, which we would expect given the nature of this sample and the fact that writing for the MOP can be considered a form of voluntary action in its own right. Ten writers responded that they were not currently doing unpaid work, but of these, five described regular unpaid work they had undertaken in the past.

Several writers raised concerns as to whether their activities should be defined as unpaid work. Charles Wright, a 74-year-old retired male from London, who had run his own hardware and painting and decorating business, and had undertaken unpaid work in the past, wrote:

> '*I have hesitated more than I normally do...there is not always a clear distinction between unpaid work and activities one might regard as a hobby.*'

He makes what is partly a motivational distinction (see Chapter Six), and echoes the concept of volunteering as 'serious leisure' (Chapter One). He also implicitly questions the definition and conceptualisation of unpaid work: if something is a hobby, that is, a leisure pursuit, can it also be *work*?

Margaret Shaw, a 66-year-old former lecturer from the East of England, describes doing unpaid work for a Citizens Advice Bureau, and involvement in other formal voluntary organisations. However, she wonders whether the '*care and companionship*' that she and her husband provide to elderly people, and her own provision of post-operative care and support to a friend, are unpaid work: '*I don't think of this as "work" but as a caring friendship.*'

Commonly-used definitions of volunteering emphasise the benefits to others. However, there was awareness that there may be direct benefits to the individual volunteer arising from their actions. This was evident in the writing of Caroline Lawson, aged 31, a trained solicitor who described herself as unemployed, disabled and leading a '*restricted lifestyle*' due to her illness, ME (myalgic encephalomyelitis). She questions whether her involvement in a ME support group constitutes voluntary work '*because I'm still operating within a group which directly benefits me*'. This viewpoint resonates with Cnaan et al's (1996) arguments, which suggest that the higher the net cost of the action, and the purer the action (that is, totally voluntary, no reward, formal context and beneficiaries unknown to individual), the more likely someone is to be considered a volunteer.

Denise Rose, a 44-year-old florist from the South East, also did not know whether the range of activities in which she had been involved counted as unpaid work:

> '*I don't really know if I do any unpaid work as such. I look after my mother. I do her shopping, gardening etc. I am driver for my children. I have worked on the school parents' association. I do astrological charts for friends.*'

Formal surveys of volunteering would discount Denise's care for her mother because the beneficiary is a close relative, but the activities reported would identify her as a previous formal volunteer (PTA involvement) and as currently involved in serious leisure (astrological charts). The cognitive difficulties that writers experience when deciding whether an activity is unpaid work, even when examples and definitions have been given, highlight the challenges inherent in capturing evidence on volunteering through large-scale surveys – though we cannot tell whether respondents were over- or under-reporting activity as a result.

Two respondents contested the notion of unpaid work. In 1996, David Gardiner, a 63-year-old male from the South East (who, in other directives, describes himself as a Labour supporter), had been made redundant four years previously from his position as an architect's assistant, and was sourcing small pieces of work as a gardener and a draughtsman. Against this background he stated that doing unpaid work was '*silly ... if you have to earn money in order to live*'; he objected to working without pay, because he was struggling to find work and was running down his savings. He nevertheless described different types of *informal* voluntary activities: '*I have been known to shop for the sick or elderly in foul weather, to take people who haven't a car to the hospital.*' Implicit in this description ('*I have been known to ...*') is that these actions were not taking place regularly; perhaps David discounted them because the directive asked questions about frequency, or he may simply regard these actions as common social courtesies. This has led us to question whether David would have responded negatively or positively to social surveys on volunteering. And might he have answered differently if the 1996 directive had referred to unpaid help, rather than work?

Jack Wilkins, a 70-year-old man, a former construction worker, living in London, who had not worked since losing his job in 1981 (and in responding to other directives describes himself as a Christian socialist) holds similar views to David Gardiner, but expresses these more bluntly: '*I have no time for any voluntary organisations what so ever, as everyone is worth the hire of his or her labour.*' He sounds ideologically opposed to the concept of unpaid work (see also Chapter Eight, on attitudes). His focus on 'voluntary organisations' might suggest that he is opposed to formal voluntarism. Jack goes on to describe the care that he and his wife provided over the years for her dying brother, bedridden following three strokes: '*I suppose this would be termed voluntary work, though my wife was compensated*' – though he does not describe what payments she received. Definitions of volunteering would normally rule this out, on the grounds that this work was remunerated and because it benefited family members. Therefore, the considerable social contributions made by this couple, providing care which would otherwise have had to be provided by statutory services at great expense, would not be picked up by surveys of volunteering. Yet if Jack Wilkins and his wife had provided similar support for a non-relative in a non-domestic environment, that work would most certainly have fitted with a definition of informal volunteering.

2012 The 'Big Society' directive

In this directive (which was commissioned by the authors), we asked writers to consider the voluntary work they do, offering various prompts to aid recall of both formal and informal voluntary action, while also leaving it to the writers to determine what they felt ought to be reported. The intention was to pick up a broad spectrum of voluntary activity, and writers responded accordingly; 11 of the 25 writers who responded (out of a possible 31) provided examples of activities which broadly correspond to survey definitions of formal volunteering. Comparisons with survey instruments indicate that this is slightly below the level shown from the *Helping Out* survey (and its predecessor, the NSV) but comparable with that we would expect from, say, the CSs. A further five described volunteering they had undertaken in the past; three did not state whether they were or had previously been volunteers, but we note that these three writers had described being volunteers in responses to earlier directives; two others reported no volunteering and had not described any volunteering in their responses to other directives.

Some of those responding combined discussions of formal volunteering with accounts of unpaid care: Stephen Johnson, aged 70, was caring for his same-sex partner (see Chapter Five) and two others were providing support and respite care to their children's families (George Tyler and June Foster) (see Chapters Five to Seven). Considering definitions of volunteering, no one could question the unpaid commitment involved, but as we noted with the case of writer Jack Wilkins in 1996, support for close relatives or partners is generally excluded from surveys. Pressures on the social care system mean that it is debatable how much choice individuals have between becoming a carer for a close relative, or taking a chance on what the state can offer.

David Gardiner, quoted earlier, aged 79 in 2012, maintained the position on unpaid/voluntary 'work' that he held in 1996: *'No I don't do voluntary work. I don't enjoy having to do things or working with others'* (see also Chapters Five and Seven). After his redundancy, he had received payments from older people in return for providing assistance with gardening. Once able to draw his state pension, he then declined payment, but continued to offer support to people *'if I'm aware they would accept and like help, shopping, car journeys to hospital, if lonely having a chat.'* Our reading of David's response is that he perceives voluntary work to be a *formal* activity in which he does not engage. Although the 2012 *'Big Society'* directive encouraged respondents to include instances of informal *helping*, he does not concur that his activities might be defined in this way. David's 2012 response also goes some way to consolidate and clarify his 1996 response. He expects to be paid for his labour. While we might regard him as engaged in voluntary acts, he appears opposed ideologically to conceptualising his help as 'voluntary' and/or 'work'. David's political identity – as a left-leaning Labour supporter – might go some way to explain this view; and his sentiments echo those expressed by Christian socialist Jack Wilkins in his response to the 1996 *Unpaid Work* directive (see further discussion in Chapter Eight).

As with survey research instruments, the wording of the MOP directives on voluntarism may have shaped the way in which some respondents have defined and conceptualised volunteering as work, leisure or help. However, we cannot distinguish whether the wording of the directives has led writers consciously to discount particular activities as volunteering or whether they have simply not written about those activities. Therefore, we sampled additional related directives, on the premise that these might prompt insights into activities that researchers would describe as volunteering, even if the writers had not identified them as such.

1984 Relatives, Friends and Neighbours directive

Perhaps unwittingly, Margaret Thatcher's famous speech to the Women's Royal Voluntary Service (WRVS) in 1981 (which we have quoted in the epigraph to Chapter One) contained an allusion to popular understandings of voluntary action and the disjuncture between these and social science terminology. She dismissed, as 'jargon', terminology such as 'informal caring networks' when what people meant was 'family and friends, relatives and neighbours'. In analysing responses to the MOP directives, we certainly find a broad understanding of social action in which support to neighbours in one's immediate community is clearly prominent, if not uppermost, in the minds of respondents.

The 1984 directive asked writers to discuss their relationships with family, friends and neighbours, including the strength of kinship bonds, and expectations of friends and neighbours. Of the 23 writers who were writing for the MOP when this directive was sent out, 20 (three men and 17 women, from a variety of social classes as defined by occupation) responded to the directive, enabling us to identify various types of regular and irregular informal activities that they were performing for, or receiving from, their family, friends and neighbours. This proportion is at least comparable with contemporaneous figures for informal volunteering from social surveys (Table 4.1).

Writers described a variety of different types of relationship with their families, with some providing care for elderly relatives and others discussing the relationship between the state and the family in the provision of care for elderly people (see also Chapter Eight). Some writers discussed providing emotional and practical support to friends, but most were concentrating on relationships with their neighbours. This may be because of the wording of the directive.

Fourteen of our writers described maintaining a reciprocal helping relationship with their neighbours, but commented on the effect of social changes ('*we no longer take in each other's washing if it rains...I think this is mainly because most of us (here at any rate) have tumble driers, so it's not so important*' (Dianne Roberts, aged 41)) and higher levels of participation in the labour market ('*Where I live now, many of the women are out at work all day*' (June Foster, aged 46)). Echoing Pahl's contemporaneous (1985) work on self-provisioning, Frank Driver (aged 50 and a goods vehicle driver) stated that the '*major neighbourly relations are between men who share expertise (car repairs, DIY) plus the loan of major tools*'.

Six of the women writing (some in paid work, some homemakers, of mixed social class), described very strong reciprocal arrangements, where they were – or had recently been – relying on neighbours for particular types of informal help, such as childcare. While two of the women writers, Sylvia Taylor (a 54-year-old shop worker), and Margaret Shaw (a 54-year-old unemployed university lecturer, now homemaker) indicated that they were providing care and help to elderly neighbours at the time of writing. Our interpretation is that these eight different writers were involved in activities that would be characterised as 'informal volunteering'. Six were providing informal help for mutual benefit, and two were providing informal care to close relatives.

Other insights into apparent non-volunteering

Other directives have occasionally provided insights into the activities of individuals who have – in our three key directives – implied that they are non-volunteers. Thus, in responding to the 1995 *Where You Live* directive, which asked writers to describe the locality in which they were living, writer Stephen Johnson describes a time when he had regularly mowed the lawn for an elderly neighbour. This clearly suggests that Stephen had undertaken some regular informal voluntary activity during his working life. Yet only a year later, when considering the *Unpaid Work* directive, Stephen implied that he was too busy in his professional life to do any unpaid work. Similarly, the 2004 *Being Part of Research* directive also prompted recall by Sylvia Taylor of involvement (helping to establish a community centre, and serving on its committee for three decades) that she had not mentioned in her responses to the *Voluntary Organisations* or *Unpaid Work* directives, although having discussed this contribution in 2004, she then described that commitment again in the 2012 directive.

Summary

Such accounts clearly demonstrate the possible measurement errors that may arise in quantifying voluntary action – if someone does not recognise 30 years' involvement in a community centre as unpaid work, then what reliance can be placed on serial responses to the questions in the BHPS on unpaid work? The MOP material also complicates simple narratives about formal or informal engagement; it highlights the contributions these people make to care for relatives, neighbours and friends alongside other volunteering. MOP writers do not always report things that look like the neat and tidy picture of volunteering presented in survey instruments. They talk about caring and family responsibilities almost interchangeably with their commitments to formally structured organisations. Even when a research instrument (in this case a MOP directive) prompts them in relation to volunteering, they don't always recall it. In these contexts, responses to questions from related directives can illustrate previously unmentioned acts that would in fact be recognised as volunteering. We therefore speculate whether these committed and engaged individuals would positively assert that they were engaged in voluntary activity. This suggests that cross-sectional perspectives underestimate the extent of involvement, when considered against the life course of individuals, thereby echoing the comment of the MOP writer Alice Dickens (Chapter One) that the Prime Minister would surely be amazed if it were ever possible to enumerate the scale of voluntary activity in the country.

Trends in the voluntary sector

The discussion so far has emphasised trends in voluntary activity by individuals, but what about trends in the wider voluntary sector? We make reference to charitable giving as well as volunteering, to inform discussion of the extent to which the voluntary sector can be characterised as 'voluntary' in terms of income sources, but the main emphasis is on aggregate growth, expansion in particular funding streams and the growth in numbers of paid personnel. Our purpose is to provide context for the later discussions of the voluntary activities of the MOP respondents.

We have previously demonstrated stability in rates of engagement in voluntary action. Charitable donations by individuals, while substantial, have been static. Studies of individual giving from the mid-1970s show little change in the levels of participation in charitable giving, and the amounts given (Cowley et al, 2011). The proportion of income given by households to charity is broadly comparable with where it was in the mid-1980s, despite increases in the generosity of tax reliefs, and considerable ingenuity and innovation on the part of charities in fundraising techniques. So regardless of hortatory pronouncements by political leaders, such as John Major's aspirational statement, in 1991, that he wanted to 'see charities get a good share of the wealth that is now beginning to cascade down and across the generations' (quoted in Barnett and Saxon-Harrold, 1992, 195), the best that can be said is that charitable giving remains important, generating some £10 billion per annum for English and Welsh charities. It certainly hasn't doubled, however, despite this being the target in at least two reviews (Giving Campaign, 2004; Home Office, 2005a, 4).

There are clear signs of expansion in the voluntary sector, such as a steady increase in the numbers of registered charities in England and Wales, from approximately 125,000 in 1979 to about 160,000 now. Making some allowances for changing regulations and registration criteria (for example, the financial thresholds above which registration is mandatory), and occasional purges of inactive organisations, we can say that the numbers have increased by approximately one third since 1979. Note that in terms of ratios of charities to population, recent years suggest a slowing-down of this expansion.

In terms of resources, aggregate *income* of charities has grown more rapidly than suggested by the growth in the number of charities: it has risen approximately fourfold since 1980. This is based on adjusting the estimates of Lane et al (1994) for inflation and comparing them with the most recent data. How can this be reconciled with the picture of stability in volunteering rates and charitable giving? Two caveats should be entered here: this is not all organic growth, driven by voluntary initiative or public preference; and this is not the result of an increase in charitable donations by individuals.

At the upper end of the size distribution of organisations, the figures are affected by transfers of organisations from public to charitable control (for example, the Canal and River Trust, formerly the British Waterways Board), the registration of new providers of public services as charities (for example, individual academy schools or chains of academies), and by the bringing into the ambit of charity regulation some entities which previously were not required to report to the Commission. Some of these organisations are very large – for example, the Woodard Corporation, a charitable organisation running a number of academy schools, is one of the top 50 charities when measured by income. Therefore, a significant component of apparent growth is the product of deliberate attempts to restructure the state, and not the outcome of voluntary initiative.

Key drivers of financial growth have instead been the growth of statutory funding, and of fees paid by individuals. The work of Unell (1979) and the Wolfenden Committee (1978, 255–8) shows that statutory funding was by no means unknown as far back as the 1970s. Beginning under Thatcher (Brenton, 1985a), however, and accelerating under the Labour administrations (Kendall, 2003), public funding for charities grew to the point where, by 2010/11, it accounted for the largest single component of the sector's income at around 37 per cent in 2010/11. As a source of income of charities, fees from individuals – which includes direct payments for services (school or hospital fees; tickets for artistic events) as well as trading activities (the ubiquitous charity shops) – has also grown rapidly (NCVO, various dates).

Finally, we consider the extent to which the sector is voluntary in relation to the growth of paid employment. Since 1993, the Labour Force Survey has estimated the numbers who work in a 'charity, voluntary organisation or trust'; the figures have risen from a base of

350,000 to a peak of just over 820,000. The addition of around half a million paid personnel at a time of relative stability in volunteering rates clearly represents a substantial change, by any standards, in the nature of the voluntary sector.

Implicit in these aggregate statistics is therefore the effects of a shift in the boundary between the statutory and voluntary sector, and in the funding base of voluntary organisations. In turn these have been associated with growth in paid employment. For some, this signifies a fundamental and regrettable change and in recent times there has been a clear and orchestrated response (for example, Seddon, 2007; Snowden, 2012). Charities have come under fire for payment of high salaries to senior staff, for speaking out publicly against the effects of government policy,[5] and for dependency on public funding. These criticisms have as their subtext an image of voluntary action as something carried out entirely by small entities whose financial base consists entirely of private donations. While there are a number of voluntary organisations that act like businesses, and a small minority that are heavily reliant on public funding, most registered charities have no employees, and (especially in the most prosperous parts of the country) the great majority do not receive statutory funding (Clifford et al, 2013). There are two potential narratives of voluntary sector history here. In one, the voluntary sector has become dominated by large charities delivering services on behalf of the state through paid employees. In the other, a somewhat nostalgic vision of the virtues of small and local, volunteer-led organisations persists, albeit with an underlying concern that these entities are being squeezed out of being able to compete for public service contracts which would sustain their expansion (CSJ, 2014).

There is some evidence of awareness of these trends in surveys of public attitudes to voluntary action (Chapter Eight), although a key feature seems to be ongoing perceptions of proliferation and waste (Mohan and Breeze, 2016, chapter 1). Otherwise, discussion of these changes in the voluntary sector is almost wholly absent from the accounts of MOP writers. This was especially notable in the discussion of The 'Big Society' directive, which was issued at a time when the role of charities was very much in the public eye.

Discussion

Drawing together a substantial body of quantitative evidence, we suggest that volunteering rates have been stable over time. The changes do not justify the claim of an international overview (Salamon et al, 2011) that there have become substantial 'gyrations' in volunteering rates in the

UK. Nor do apparent increases in volunteering merit the unbridled enthusiasm shown, particularly, by Conservative spokespersons in recent times. Our overall conclusion has both optimistic and pessimistic interpretations: despite governments of all persuasions extolling the virtues of voluntarism, we do not find conclusive evidence that rates of engagement have gone up; and despite all the economic shocks which the country has experienced since the 1970s, we do not find conclusive evidence that rates of engagement have gone down.

The second point is that the proportion of the population who are not engaged is small. Based on our survey analyses, between one-quarter and one-third of the adult population have no involvement in volunteering, whether formal or informal. Other work (Brookfield et al, forthcoming) suggests that, in a lifetime context, the proportion of the population who *never* engage in volunteering is even smaller. This is highly relevant for policy: there are no large untapped pools of volunteers out there waiting to be drawn in to voluntary action, and the great majority do report that they already contribute in one or more ways.

This broad consistency in the level of engagement has been taking place against a background of steady expansion in the voluntary sector. Whether measured in terms of employment, resources or numbers of organisations, the trends are generally upwards, though it is also fair to say that evidence is still emerging as to the long-term effects of recession (see Clifford, 2017) and the full effects of public funding reductions still remain to be seen. There are divergent views, from Left and Right, on the merits of these developments, but it is notable that the wider public continue to volunteer in large numbers irrespective of what is going on in voluntary organisations themselves.

What does this voluntary action look like? There is a view that public policy has been excessively focused on formal volunteering through organisations. When we consider responses by individuals to prompts designed to elicit their views on voluntary action, we see a mix of caring, volunteering and participation in associations, the content of which varies from individual to individual, and which is not easily pigeonholed into categories such as formal or informal volunteering. These accounts are often low key, modest and unassuming, seeing volunteering as something that overlaps strongly with neighbourliness and informal care.

To explore this further, we now move from a consideration of levels of engagement to a discussion of the nature of engagement. What does volunteering look like as revealed by national survey data (for example, what sorts of activities are undertaken by volunteers) and, when prompted to write about voluntary action, what immediately attracts the attention of our MOP respondents?

Notes

[1] See www.ngo.bham.ac.uk/appendix/Chapter_6.htm for the data.

[2] See Staestky and Mohan (2011). In 1987, work for a political or trade union organisation was included in the definition but was omitted in 1992.

[3] One illustration of this point can be provided if we compare transitions in volunteering status between different waves of the BHPS, and between the last wave of the BHPS and the first wave of US (see Table 7.1) for respondents who completed the volunteering question on each occasion of the surveys. Between waves of the BHPS, some three-fifths of those who say they volunteer at one wave also report volunteering at the next. Between the last wave of the BHPS and the first wave of US, that proportion is approximately one half. Since these same people are responding each time, this suggests that they are reacting to the question in a different way.

[4] Parliamentary debates: H.C. Deb., v. 558, 13.2.13, c. 858 (Cameron); H.C. Deb., v. 572, 11.12.13 (Hurd), c. 226–8; H.C. Deb., 24.6.15, c. 975 (Miller, Whittingdale).

[5] For example, The Transparency of Lobbying, Non-Party Campaigning and Trade Union Act, 2014.

FIVE

Content and context
of volunteering

Introduction

In the previous chapter, the focus was on levels of voluntary action, as revealed by social surveys, and the extent to which individuals' reports of their engagement do, or do not, conform to the quantitative portrait. Here we go into much more depth as to exactly what it is that individuals do when they volunteer.

We do so, first through analysing social surveys which have asked respondents about the content of their activities – namely, what sorts of organisations they help, the activities they carry out and the roles they play, regardless of whether the activity takes place in organisational settings, or informally in the community. The surveys provide information about the type of groups to which individuals give help (for example, health and social care, sports, religious organisations), the type of help provided (for example, raising money, mentoring, providing transport), and the sorts of informal activities in which individuals engage in their communities (for example, visiting elderly people, home decorating, car repairs). Despite some variation in the approaches taken by various surveys, we provide a broad overview of these activities, and demonstrate whether these have changed over time (for example, have certain forms of activity become more or less prominent?). The measures we use are simply *whether or not* respondents were involved in particular activities; generally the surveys used do not permit quantification of the volume of effort contributed (for example, time spent), nor apportionment by field of activity. However, the information available on hours committed to formal and informal volunteering in the Citizenship Survey (CS) does allow us to make brief reference to arguments concerning a British 'civic core' – a small subset of the population which accounts for the bulk of voluntary effort.

We then provide an extended discussion of material provided by the Mass Observation Project (MOP) writers in relation to the content of their voluntary activities, and where possible, their context – that is, how those activities came about. We emphasise this, because a key point made in the volunteering literature is the importance of *being asked* to engage (Musick and Wilson, 2008, chapter 13). Thus, the social networks in which individuals are embedded, whether through their residential neighbourhood, church, workplace, or other setting, are known to be key to linking people to opportunities for engagement, and to the types of activities which they carry out.

The context of voluntary action is important in understanding the balance between informal and formal voluntary activity. One reading of recent history has suggested that the Labour governments (1997–2010) prioritised formal volunteering, to the neglect of informal activity placing emphasis on specific sorts of activities (essentially, managed volunteering in support of objectives such as delivering public services, taking place in formalised, often bureaucratic settings) at the expense of social and expressive dimensions of engagement (Chapter Two; Rochester et al, 2010; Rochester, 2013). For some academic writers this neglects informal volunteering and renders invisible the people who engage in it and the activities which they carry out (Williams, 2003). If it is true that their Labour predecessors prioritised formal volunteering, the Coalition and Conservative governments since 2010 have instead argued for a generalised increase in voluntary action and expressed no preference as to the type of voluntary activities people carry out (see Chapter Two).

Such arguments raise the question of whether there are variations between individuals in terms of the types of volunteering they do. Egerton and Mullan (2008) investigate this using data from the Time Use Survey for 2000. They show that both informal and formal volunteering are significantly constrained by the time individuals allocate to employment, study, caregiving to relatives, and personal activities. Otherwise, the main difference between formal and informal volunteering is the strong educational gradient in the amount of effort put into formal volunteering. The conclusion that there are socioeconomic and educational gradients in formal voluntary action that are not evident for informal volunteering is echoed by Henriksen et al (2008) for Denmark, and Van Tienen et al (2011) for Holland.

These analyses imply that there is a clear distinction between formal and informal action, but whether this reflects everyday lives would be questioned by our MOP writers. In Chapter Four we have discussed the evidence concerning the proportions of the population which engage in formal and informal volunteering. Here we consider whether formal and informal activities can be easily separated, how one develops into the other, and how they both overlap with caring responsibilities.

Formal volunteering is usually taken to mean activity that takes place through a formal organisational structure. We note, however, that one well-known study differentiates formal and informal volunteering according to the type of organisation being helped. Brodie et al (2011) identify 'social participation' as involvement in 'formal voluntary organisations', 'informal grassroots and community groups', and 'formal and informal mutual aid and self-help' (p 23). Yet, the 'informal grassroots and community groups' to which they refer are often registered charities, and thus actually fall under the definition of formal volunteering, in that they represent voluntary action that takes place through a formal organisational structure. We do not think it is entirely straightforward to classify groups in the way suggested by Brodie et al (2011). Thus, we adhere to the broad categories and terminology of formal and informal volunteering, and when discussing MOP writing we differentiate, as far as is possible, between those activities that take place through an organisational structure, and those that involve direct assistance to individuals in the community.

Quantitative analyses: the balance between formal and informal volunteering, and the nature of the voluntary activities that individuals carry out

Combinations of activity: formal and informal activities and how they vary at the individual level

Arguments for why individuals pursue either formal or informal volunteering revolve around the interaction between socioeconomic status and place of residence. For Egerton and Mullan (2008), professional and managerial groups are more likely to relocate on a number of occasions as they pursue careers. They therefore become detached from the communities in which they grew up; joining formally-constituted voluntary organisations is a way of meeting and forming relationships with people of similar interests and, perhaps, social position. Communities with higher proportions of such people are therefore likely to be characterised by elevated levels of involvement in formal voluntary organisations. Conversely, communities which are undergoing less change, especially those losing rather than gaining more educated members of their population, are likely to be characterised by voluntary action of an informal kind, based on neighbourhood networks established between longstanding residents. These arguments suggest that we should expect differences between individuals in whether or not they are engaged in either formal or informal volunteering, in both of these, or neither. And because of variations in the composition of populations between neighbourhoods, we should also expect variations between communities in the proportion of the population engaged in types of voluntary action. We do not pursue this argument, but see Williams (2003) for the view that there are different 'cultures' of voluntary action which vary according to levels of disadvantage in communities; Morris (1969) had previously made a similar point. There is limited scope in UK survey datasets in the 1980s and 1990s to explore such variations in survey data in great detail, and the number of MOP respondents is too small to permit comparison of whether the activities of our respondents vary depending on the type of place in which they live.

Because of the non-availability of the 1981 National Survey of Volunteering (NSV) data, our ability to investigate combinations of formal and informal volunteering across the full time-frame of our study is constrained to comparisons of the 1991 NSV with data from the CS (in this case, for 2009–10). The discussion relates to England and Wales. Reclassifying the data from these surveys, we create a dependent variable with four categories, namely respondents who: do no formal or informal volunteering; engage only in informal volunteering; engage only in formal volunteering; and engage in both sorts of activity. Our independent variables include: age, sex, tenure, duration of education, length of residence in neighbourhood, and socioeconomic status. A multinomial logistic regression analysis suggests that, in 1991, compared to those who engage in both formal and informal volunteering, the likelihood of being a non-volunteer, or someone who engages in informal volunteering only, was closely related to socioeconomic status and to education. Unskilled manual groups were those who were most likely to be engaged in informal volunteering only, while those who had spent longest in full-time education (the 1991 survey only measures the age at which people ceased to be in education) were least likely to be engaged in informal volunteering only. In addition, predictors of non-engagement also included age, with those in early adulthood and middle age being significantly less likely to report non-engagement. Owner occupation was also a strong predictor of engagement.[1]

We find generally similar patterns 20 years later, with analyses of the CS for 2009–10. Socioeconomic status and educational gradients are strongest in relation to formal volunteering and less evident in relation to informal volunteering, but it is noticeable that the lowest socioeconomic groups are statistically more likely to be engaged in informal volunteering.

In our discussion of trends in Chapter Four, we observed the relatively stable nature of engagement; these results add to this discussion, demonstrating how socioeconomic patterns of engagement have also remained stable over time. Socioeconomic variations exist in the likelihood of individuals doing *any* volunteering at all, and in them doing *particular types* of volunteering. This work extends that of Egerton and Mullan (2008) by showing that these patterns seem to persist. But what of the distribution of *levels* of engagement across the population?

Levels of engagement: debates about the civic core

Voluntary action tends to be heavily concentrated among small subsets of the population. Reed and Selbee (2001) popularised the idea of the 'civic core'; drawing on Canadian survey data they showed that relatively small subsets of the population accounted for disproportionate shares of prosocial behaviours (hours volunteered, money donated to charity, membership of associations). Just under three-tenths of Canadians accounted for around four-fifths, or more, of donations to charity, hours devoted to volunteering, or membership of associations. What does the evidence from the UK suggest and to what extent can we detect change over time?

Again, the content of social survey data imposes some constraints in investigating evidence of a civic core for the earlier years covered by our study. The NSVs in 1981 and 1991 contain very limited information on the hours given to voluntary action by respondents. However, the General Household Surveys (GHS) for 1987 and 1992 asked questions about the number of days on which respondents had volunteered over the course of the year. These were used by Mohan et al (2006) to demonstrate strong socioeconomic gradients in the proportion of the population who were 'committed' volunteers, that is, those who reported volunteering on more than 11 days (thus, at least monthly) over the course of the year. Controlling for other factors, individuals in professional, managerial and technical occupations (social classes I and II) were nearly 2.5 times as likely as their counterparts in partly skilled or unskilled occupations (social classes IV and V) to engage at that level; those aged 55–64 twice as likely as young adults (16–24) to do so; and owner-occupiers 1.6 times as likely as tenants to do so.

In 2012, Mohan and Bulloch were able to identify the British civic core by using the more granular data in the CS (2009–10) on the number of hours volunteered, as well as information on money donated to charity and the numbers of associations of which individuals were members. Following methods initially derived by Reed and Selbee (2001), they found that around 30 per cent of the population was responsible for between 80 and 90 per cent of the total effort.

As an indication of the degree of commitment involved, someone characterised as providing enough effort to qualify for membership of the 'core' would have been volunteering for a minimum of 3.75 hours per week. Mohan and Bulloch (2012) find a degree of social stratification in relation to membership of the core, and there are broad similarities with Mohan et al's (2006) identification of core volunteers in the 1980s and early 1990s. There have been changes in the measurement of social class over time which reduce direct comparability between the two studies. However, what is referred to as the salariat (those in managerial and professional occupations) is broadly comparable to social classes I and II from the socioeconomic classification used in the 1991 survey. Members of the salariat were almost twice as likely to be members of the core than those in routine occupations, or those who had never worked. Likewise, those with degrees, those aged 45–64, and those who were actively practising their religion (note that the latter variable was not available in the dataset used by Mohan et al (2006)) were far more likely to be members of the civic core than the general population.

The comparisons between the two survey datasets do suggest that voluntary effort has been and remains highly concentrated for the two decades between the GHS-based analysis on survey data for 1987 and 1992 by Mohan et al (2006), and Mohan and Bulloch's (2012) work covering 2009–10. Many of our MOP respondents would be classed as members of the core – their voluntary commitments encompass numerous, often sustained, formal and informal activities.

What do people do when they engage? Content of voluntary action as revealed by surveys

The various volunteering surveys have asked questions in a fairly consistent manner since the early 1980s, and so we can provide portraits of the kinds of groups helped and tasks undertaken for formal volunteering, and the activities undertaken in the community for informal volunteering. Variations in the estimates of volunteering provided by the surveys mean that we standardise in the following way. Rather than estimating the proportion of the population who engage in a given activity (for example, 'raising or handling money'), we compare the proportion of the volunteering population who report that they engage in each type of voluntary field, or activity. Thus, for example, for 1991, 30 per cent of respondents said that they were engaged in volunteering for groups concerned with children's education; by 2011 that figure was around 34 per cent of all volunteers. It should be recalled, as was the case with the headline survey figures discussed in Chapter Four, that we are not strictly comparing like with like. Where possible, we focus our attention on England and Wales, partly because the CS/Community Life Survey (CLS) data are comprehensive and available for over a decade, partly because it is not possible to extract data for England alone for 1991. However, the data we used for 1981 are for the UK while those for 2015–16 relate to England only.

Formal volunteering: groups helped

As with the rate of volunteering we find stability in the types of groups helped (Table 5.1). There are some variations in the survey options offered to respondents over time. However, the highest-ranked fields of activity across the timeframe of this study have been sport, groups concerned with children's education, religion, and young people's activities outside school. Groups concerned with welfare and health were near the top of the rankings initially.

There are signs of change over the period with a large increase in the proportion of formal volunteers who say that they are involved in groups such as sports and recreation; there are signs of similar growth for hobbies, recreation and arts from 1991 onwards. Some apparent developments are almost certainly related to changes in the surveys. In 2001 the CS asked respondents to identify types of groups to which they had 'given unpaid help'. However, the question in 2011 and 2016 was less restrictive – it specified groups in which respondents had 'taken part'. This is likely to have influenced, in an upward direction, the proportions indicating involvement in some fields, such as religious, sports and hobby groups. For example, in 2001, when the question referred to 'unpaid help', active volunteers reported involvement in an average of 2.1 types of groups (out of the 13 possibilities) whereas in 2011, when the phrasing changed to 'taking part', they recalled involvement in an average of three types of groups. Engagement in religious groups has experienced a similar proportionate increase, and one might surmise that the shift in emphasis from 'giving help' to 'taking part' has driven at least some of this, notwithstanding the recent prominence of faith-based charities (Spencer, 2016).

Evidence of other changes may also be associated with changes in measurement. Therefore, focusing on the broad rankings of fields of activities may be more informative. A cause for social concern might be that the broad category of groups concerned with welfare and health was close to the top of rankings (second or third) in 1981 in 1991 but slipped to seventh from 2001 onwards. Likewise, despite

Table 5.1: Formal volunteering: percentage of volunteers who report helping, by category of group to which help given, 1981–2011

	1981	Rank	1991	Rank	2001	Rank	2011	Rank	2016	Rank
Education (children)	30	1=	23	2=	29	2	34	3	34	3
Sport	30	1=	26	1	33	1	51	1	53	1
Health/disab/social welfare	25	3	23	2=	15	7	17	7=	17	7=
Religion	23	4	22	4	22	4	32	4	31	4
Youth (outside school)	20	5	19	5	18	6	25	6	24	5=
Community/tenants' groups[1]	18	6	17	6=	21	5	28	5	24	5=
Environmental/animals	4	9=	4	10=	12	8	12	10	16	9
Adult education	N/A	N/A	4	10=	11	10	17	7=	17	7=
Elderly	10	8	13	8	11	9	13	9	14	10
Safety/first aid	0		8	9	9		11		13	
Connected with work[2]	11	7	4	10=	5		0		7	
Justice, rights	0		2		4		6		8	
Politics	4	9=	4		4		6		5	
Hobbies, recreation, arts	N/A	N/A	17	6=	24	3	38	2	38	2

Notes:
[1] Includes 'citizens' groups' from 2001; defined as 'local community and neighbourhood groups' in 2016
[2] For example, professional association, union, works club
Top ten rankings shown for each survey

Source: Humble, 1982; otherwise authors' calculations from survey data

continuing concerns about an ageing population, groups involved with the elderly were some way down the rankings throughout the period. Sport, however, has always been top of the list. Groups focusing on hobbies, recreation and arts were subsumed under other categories prior to 1991, but since this date we can identify steady growth in the proportion of volunteers reporting involvement in them, consistent with an emphasis in the literature on the 'serious leisure' aspects of voluntarism. Children's education, religious groups and youth activities seem to maintain their ranking throughout. Groups concerned with justice and rights, politics, a broad 'citizens' groups' category, trade unions, safety and first aid attract the attention of lower shares of the volunteering population. We note though, that the proportion of the volunteers who are part of environmental groups has quadrupled, which may be a reflection of a more recent tendency for mass membership of these types of organisation. Where there does appear to be substantial change is in the proportions concerned with adult education. However, the definition of the questions on adult education in recent surveys potentially facilitates positive answers from students engaged in university societies and in student volunteering, as well as what is conventionally understood as adult education.

Formal volunteering: types of activities carried out

Fortunately, the questions about the types of activity that people carry out have remained largely stable (with one or two additions) over all surveys of voluntary action. We see general evidence of stability over the period from 1981 to the present date, with around half of the volunteering population engaged in organising or running events, and around one-fifth to one-quarter in visiting people, as part of their volunteering (see Table 5.2).

Perhaps the most striking finding is that while in the 1981 and 1991 surveys two-thirds of volunteers said that they were involved in 'raising or handling money', that proportion is now down to under one half. This may relate to a growth in new ways of raising funds or attracting regular donations such as internet-based platforms (JustGiving being an example), electronic banking, or workplace deductions. Reliance on aggregate estimates of this kind can hide changes in the character of activities being carried out. Automated or routinised forms of donation clearly have limitations if considered as activities that might generate social capital. But as is recognisable from the growth in requests to support people engaged in sponsored walks, fun runs, marathons and the like, as well as simple acts such as the wearing of ribbons or clothing

Table 5.2: Type of tasks undertaken by formal volunteers, 1981–2016

Type of task	1981	1991	2001	2011	2016
Raising/handling money	68	68	56	51	46
Committee member	36	29	34	29	27
Organising/helping run event	54	51	53	48	48
Visiting people		22	23	23	20
Advice/information/counselling	19	15	28	24	25
Secretarial/admin/clerical	22	14	18	15	14
Providing transport/driving	24	28	26	20	20
Other direct service	25	29	36	32	31
Representing	15	22	15	14	15
Other work or help	11	16	36	11	
Befriending or mentoring				17	18
Campaigning			12	8	9
Getting other people involved					42

Sources: 1981: Humble (1982); other dates, authors' analyses of survey data from NSV (1991), Citizenship Survey (2001, 2010–11) and Community Life Survey (2015–16). Note that not all survey options were presented on each occasion.

of particular colours, new forms of fundraising, involving new forms of sociability, have developed. These may generate new social connections or deepen existing ones in a way that standing on the street shaking a collecting tin did not (Moore, 2008).

Some kinds of activity have fluctuated in a trendless manner, and are hard to interpret: examples are the proportions of people who say that they are providing advice, information and counselling, or those who contribute by providing transport. There seems to be no obvious explanation for these variations. Since 2010, surveys have begun to ask questions about activities like befriending or mentoring; one-sixth of respondents declared that this represented part of their voluntary commitments in 2010–11. While we know such work has become more prominent – for example, in the activities of charities concerned with at-risk young people – it is uncertain whether this represents a change. However, it is not obvious from previous surveys where else respondents may have been reporting their involvement in these activities. Finally, the question about 'Getting other people involved' was new to the CLSs (which began in 2012) and has no direct antecedent.

Informal volunteering: types of activities

Generally, again, the picture is one of relative stability across most categories of question and some of the changes are readily explained by changes in survey prompts. Thus, the apparent doubling of those looking after a pet or property arises because of the addition of looking after a property to the question from 2001. Likewise, the apparent decline in visiting an elderly or sick person may be because the 2001 CS question makes a specific reference to 'keeping in touch with or visiting someone who has difficulty getting out', whereas the 1991 equivalent was the broader 'visiting an elderly or sick person' (see Table 5.3).

Table 5.3: Type of activity undertaken by informal volunteers, 1981–2016

Type of activity	1981	1991	2001	2010–11	2015–16
Visiting elderly or sick person	39	33	28	29	32
Shopping for another person	32	28	26	26	25
Giving advice/letters/filling in forms	30	31	46	40	46
Transporting or escorting someone	26	25	31	26	31
Babysitting or caring for children	22	21	29	25	27
Looking after a pet (and property)	17	19	41	34	36
Routine household jobs	17	16	17	18	19
Decorating, home or car repairs	13	11	16	12	14
Improving environment (picking up litter)		38			
Representing someone			6	7	8

Sources: 1981: Humble (1982); other dates, authors' analyses of survey data from NSV (1991), Citizenship Survey (2001, 2010–11) and Community Life Survey (2015–16). Note that not all survey options were presented on each occasion.

Qualitative evidence: the where, to whom and what of voluntary activity

Our analysis of writers' responses to the different MOP directives has enabled us to track and categorise the preferences that individual writers have shown over their lifecourse, both for different types of volunteering, and for where they choose to volunteer. We have identified considerable provision of *informal* help and care to others, some within a reciprocal relationship, and others that involved no reciprocity. We have identified various mostly *formal* activities for organisations, or for people with whom the volunteer was socially or personally connected, such as church or faith, cultural and leisure, or professional/trade organisations. We have identified volunteering for organisations or people with whom writers had no evident strong social connection, such as: acting on behalf of, or for, local communities; formal rights and political work; and providing advice and support.

Some volunteers had focused on specific types of volunteering; others had a broader volunteering 'portfolio'.

As well as enabling us to identify *where* individual writers have volunteered, MOP writing enables us to identify the *beneficiaries* of writers' volunteering. In this chapter we consider how these categories reflect the levels of strong and weak ties that individuals have within their different communities (Granovetter, 1973; 1983); how strongly connected individual writers are to the particular beneficiaries involved; and how these categories are also a measure of volunteers' levels of social capital.

Reciprocal informal help and care for others

Many MOP writers discussed the help and care that they provided to others with whom they were socially connected, writing about this in several directives (*Relatives, Friends and Neighbours* (1984), *Where You Live* (1995), *Unpaid Work* (1996), *A Working Day* (2010), *Belonging* (2010), and *The 'Big Society'* (2012)).

Of the 20 writers (three men and 17 women) who responded to the 1984 *Relatives, Friends and Neighbours* directive, 17 discussed undertaking small reciprocal acts for neighbours. This proportion (85 per cent) is greater than that typically reporting informal volunteering in national surveys. For 16, from varied socioeconomic backgrounds, these activities involved exactly the main categories of informal volunteering investigated in social surveys: feeding pets or watering plants when neighbours went on holiday, taking in parcels, lending tools, helping with tasks such as car repairs, and looking after children. Often, this was described as part of a joint/household activity in cases where the writer was living with a spouse or partner. This is the sort of reciprocal behaviour that Buonfino and Hilder (2006) describe as 'egalitarian neighbouring' (p 15), which contributes to the 'collective efficacy' of communities (Sampson, 2012). However, one writer, Margaret Shaw, felt that there was a class distinction relating to the type of reciprocal acts that she was involved in within her geographical neighbourhood. She mentioned the reciprocal lending of educational toys, giving lifts to neighbours' children, or neighbours' children staying overnight, but insisted that there were class boundaries to her neighbouring relationships and activities:

> 'There is no borrowing of food or other essentials, and no taking in
> of a neighbour's deliveries – all very self-contained in that respect –
> the wrong social set-up for that (middle-class now that previously

rented houses have been sold a year or so ago).' (Relatives, Friends and Neighbours (1984), aged 54)

Other writers mentioned changes to reciprocity as they became more upwardly socially mobile. Looking back on times spent living in less affluent areas, some writers affectionately recalled a greater sense of community, spontaneity and reciprocity (for example, Catherine Neil and Sarah Thomas). Although reciprocal relationships were still evident when they had moved to less deprived/more affluent areas, they felt that there was a greater emotional and social distance between neighbours. This fits with other writing on the relationship between class, place and reciprocal neighbouring, which Buonfino and Hilder (2006) describe as 'detached neighbouring' (p 15); see also Bulmer (1986), and Crow et al (2002).

Two writers, journalist, Alice Dickens, and florist, Denise Rose, both prolific volunteers, talked about the way in which their reciprocal relationships with neighbours had grown into strong friendships. Alice Dickens described how she became friends with her partially-sighted neighbours through their children. Although disabled, Alice's neighbours were able to reciprocate help in many ways, but they also became reliant on Alice for particular types of help:

> '*Inevitably, we have to read, and fill in, forms, write cheques and do various bits of quite confidential business for them…We often say that, if one of us moves, the others will go too so we would have to find two more semis. It probably isn't all that much of a joke. In spite of all our contact, however, at least 80 per cent of our social life is totally independent of each other.' (Relatives, Friends and Neighbours* (1984), aged 42)

In her response to the 2012 '*Big Society*' directive 28 years later, Alice revealed that this strong relationship was still in place, but hinted at changes in the levels of reciprocity, which we discuss below.

Three writers did not report engaging in reciprocal neighbouring relationships in their responses to the 1984 directive. One, Donna Payne (aged 32), living in exceptional circumstances of disadvantage as an unemployed carer for her mother, described receiving some help from neighbours, but not reciprocating such help. Another, farmer Peter Grainger (aged 57), complained that he had nothing in common with his neighbours, who were '*wealthy stock exchange buffs and solicitors*'. A third, Beverley Scott (aged 27) an unemployed teacher experiencing mental health problems, announced that she preferred '*to be on not-too-*

familiar terms with our neighbours' and was relieved, on moving to a more middle-class suburb, to be freed from the pressures for conformity she felt she had experienced while living as a local authority tenant, thus enabling her to engage in 'detached neighbouring', keeping immediate neighbours at a distance.

Non-reciprocal informal help and care to people with whom the volunteer is personally connected

There were some writers who described informal relationships with people in the community, which went beyond reciprocity. Some like Alice Dickens's activity, described above, started with reciprocity and friendship and progressed into help and care. Twenty-eight years later, it sounded as if this relationship had become less reciprocal. Referring to her neighbours, who were registered blind, Alice described how she and her husband (now both retired):

> '*tend to serve as their taxi service to the station, to hospital appointments and the like...[and are] "on call" to do various jobs not easily done by those with minimal sight.*' (*The 'Big Society'* (2012), aged 69)

Alice's neighbouring relationship had evolved over time, and thus it would be hard for her to identify exactly when the transition from reciprocity to dependency took place. This sort of transition is easier to identify in retrospect.

In a similar way, home-maker, Dianne Roberts, described how her *formal* voluntary community work, delivering library books to housebound people in her community, progressed into additional informal activity as her relationships with beneficiaries turned into friendship, despite trying not to '*get too involved*'. Replying to the 1996 *Unpaid Work* directive at the age of 53, she reported having only one regular client, who had '*become a very dear friend*'. Dianne now did '*the odd bit of shopping, reading and filling in forms*' for her, and occasionally accompanied her on shopping trips. This transition (from formal volunteering to informal), illuminates how difficult it can be for quantitative surveys to capture and measure this type of trajectory and activity. It also neatly encapsulates the ways in which volunteering produces wider social benefits and the value of stable relationships between the volunteer and service user.

In all, just over a quarter of MOP writers (n. 10) reported providing un-reciprocated help and care;[2] proportionally more women (30 per cent) than men (18 per cent) contributed. From an occupational class perspective, a range of classes were represented, and the writers were of mixed ages when providing care.[3] The beneficiaries of their help included neighbours and friends. The type of activities provided included help during crises such as hospitalisation and recuperation of the beneficiary or his/her spouse, and bereavement. For Catherine Neil, a mostly informal contributor after having her children, the help she provided to people in crisis formed a large part of her contribution. She describes an elderly neighbour, struggling to balance the demands of visiting her husband in a care home and her own illnesses, who welcomed continued informal support, particularly in terms of the provision of meals:

> *'when she got home, the last thing on her mind was cooking to eat...She can well look after herself. She just doesn't feel like it, sometimes.' (The 'Big Society' (2012), aged 74)*

Other types of informal help and care included regular help with shopping, lawn-cutting, providing company, and cooking of meals, perhaps best summed up by retired shop-manageress, Sylvia Taylor, who describes visiting her elderly neighbour on a weekly basis, doing her neighbour's shopping, while Sylvia's husband did odd jobs. She refers to their involvement as caring, not help:

> *'We have cared for her four years, as she had been our neighbour for over forty years. I don't know how much time we spend with her as it depends on her daily needs.' (Unpaid Work (1996), aged 67)*

Although we have identified this activity as voluntary informal care for someone with whom the writer was personally connected,[4] some writers do not regard such activity as volunteering. David Gardiner (born 1933, an architect's assistant until made redundant in 1992), who, as we describe in Chapter Four, disagrees with the principle of volunteering, does not perceive his activities – the provision of informal *ad hoc* help to various neighbours – to be volunteering.

Although the beneficiaries of most of the help and care provided by these ten writers include friends and neighbours with whom writers are loosely connected, by 1996 Margaret Shaw's beneficiaries appeared to be solely acquaintances and friends, rather than her neighbours and their children (as described in 1984).

'I (with my husband) try to help people I know who live alone and are elderly. We keep in contact with widows and widowers, have them to our house for meals and chat, take them with us for a browse around other parts of Norfolk and finishing with a pub lunch.' (Unpaid Work (1996), aged 66)

The language of most of these ten writers when describing the help and care that they provide suggests that most of their informal voluntary caring is relatively unreciprocated, and that aside from personal gratification and a sense of closeness to the beneficiary, there has been no reward. It also seems that the choice to provide care and help was unasked for, or unprompted by the beneficiary. Relationships can be very practical and business-like, and capable of being terminated, as exemplified by Stephen Johnson's account of why he and his partner curtailed some of the long-term, informal help that they provided to his neighbour, an elderly widow:

'in her latter years we kept an eye on her and doing the occasional shopping or replacing a light bulb etc…Despite being neighbours for 20+ years, we never "Knew" each other…I used to cut her grass but stopped when she wanted to stop and talk for half an hour or so afterwards.' (Where You Live (1995), aged 53)

We note that the provision of help and care to people with whom these ten writers were personally connected, took place across the 30 years in which writers were contributing to the MOP. Some of these activities, such as Catherine Neil's response to crises, would be seen as short-term informal care (see Chapter Seven on trajectories); others, such as Stephen Johnson's regular but low-level and infrequent help given to his neighbour, might be seen as longer-term care.

These neighbourly activities resonate with those which Margaret Thatcher had in mind when thinking about society (Chapter Two), and with the post-2010 Big Society agenda with its emphasis on social action in the immediate locality. As our survey and MOP analyses show, they constitute a stable feature of voluntary action. Individuals seem, in their responses to regard these as a natural part of the order of everyday life, and they are (as far as we can judge) content to continue them over a number of years. There is a limit to what policy might do in this field, but one issue, which we explore in the concluding chapter, is what might be done about facilitating neighbourliness – for example in relation to housing policy or neighbourhood design.

Provision of care to family

Formal survey instruments and academic definitions would not regard help and care to close family members, or beneficiaries who live with their carer, as volunteering (see for example, Musick and Wilson, 2008; Hardill and Baines, 2011), with Taylor (2004) identifying this as informal private domestic labour. This was not necessarily how our writers saw it: several described their provision of help or care to family as volunteering. Writing in 2012, Stephen Johnson (mentioned above, who provided long-term help to his neighbour) described his full-time care for his older male partner as an activity:

> 'which I suppose is called voluntary work, because I don't (and nor do I expect) to be paid for so doing...I can't commit myself to any outside voluntary work because his needs can vary from day to day, even sometimes from hour to hour.' (The 'Big Society' (2012), aged 69)

Stephen does not provide explicit reasons for his perception that being a carer for his partner is both work and volunteering. He suggests that the time used on caring for his partner would otherwise be used on the cultural and leisure-based volunteering that he had begun after his early retirement at the age of 57. Therefore, he may perceive this care as a voluntary alternative. However, Stephen's view may also relate to a tension between his perceptions of his caring activities, and his identity and place within broader British society (and its influence on his accumulation of social and symbolic capital). Having viewed many pieces of Stephen's writing, we found that his first overt reference to his same-sex relationship occurred in 2012 (although we acknowledge the possibility that he may have discussed this previously in responses that we have not seen). Even when responding to the 2010 *Belonging* directive, Stephen describes himself as single:

> 'In what could have been an active social side of my business life, I was at a disadvantage by being a single man. I had few friends outside of work and so no lady partner to take to functions, so quite often I didn't go even if I was invited. Sometimes I minded, but generally I didn't and was sometimes described as "a bit of a loner".' (Belonging (2010), aged 68)

Quite possibly his sexual orientation would have placed him on the margins of business-based social networks which provided routes into conventional forms of voluntary action, and we return (in Chapter Six) to this respondent, where he relates his movement between volunteering roles to a feeling that he doesn't belong. Stephen would have come to adulthood before the 1967 Sexual Offences Act which decriminalised homosexual acts between men aged over 21. Given the lack of recognition accorded to his relationship,[5] it is perhaps not surprising that he does not publicly define his care-work as fitting within the parameters of family and domestic care; his activities come across almost as a covert act of familial care while being defined publicly as an act of civic engagement.

Another writer, Jack Wilkins, who was unemployed from the mid-1980s, also described caring for a co-resident – his terminally ill brother-in-law – as a form of voluntarism, even though he disagreed with volunteering on principle (see Chapter Three). However, unlike Stephen Johnson, Jack constructed this as an acceptance of family responsibilities, saying that he and his wife *'were pleased to be of help, being family'* (*Unpaid Work* (1996), aged 70). Several other writers also discussed caring for family members, such as elderly parents or grandchildren, raising questions about whether their care might be perceived as voluntarism. We note that those writing about providing family care in 2012, such as George Tyler, a man in his 80s providing care to his wife and to a disabled grand-daughter, and June Foster and her husband (both retired and in their 70s), who were providing care for her grandchildren after her son-in-law was brain-damaged in a car-crash, were of relatively advanced years to shoulder the burden of these caring activities.

Personal connections with other volunteers and beneficiaries

Embedded within MOP writers' descriptions of voluntary action are details about their personal connections to the organisations and people for whom they volunteer. They describe being personally connected to the beneficiaries of their volunteering; to other volunteers within the organisation; and being connected as both a volunteer and beneficiary of an organisation.

A typical example of writers being personally connected to the beneficiaries of their voluntary action, is where parents (and in one case a grandparent) described volunteering for organisations and activities where their children (or grandchildren) were the beneficiaries. For example, out of the 29 writers who were parents, half (15) reported having taken active roles in one or more of their children's nurseries or playgroups (6), Parent Teacher Associations (PTAs) (7), school activities (8), youth groups and Scouts (5), and swimming lessons (2). A number of these had engaged in more than one of these activities. All but two of these writers were female; proportionally, over three-fifths of female MOP writer-parents volunteered for organisations attended by their children, and undertook these activities while their children were in receipt of education. This fits with the findings of Brodie et al (2011), and Musick and Wilson (2008, 243). We identified four very active female writers who provided consistent volunteering within an educational context throughout their children's education; and five female writers and one male writer who were involved in one or more educational activity. A further five writers were involved in the provision of extra-curricular activities.

Three writers described intense and frequent involvement in a particular extra-curricular activity: Sylvia Taylor (a retail worker, born 1930) had been involved for many years in a youth club; Sarah Thomas (an agricultural worker, born 1926) described training and volunteering as a swimming instructor for several years; and George Tyler (a transport supervisor, born 1930) was on the youth committee of his local church and had led its Scouting group for 15 years. He had found himself catering for the more specialised needs of senior Scouts to the point where he was:

> 'organising high-level swimming and life-saving courses, adventure training, first aid, and other courses almost every night of the week. As well as supervising more adventurous activity on the downs and in the mountains. Sadly I did not get any younger and in many ways Scouting became more demanding than the job I did to earn a living!' (Unpaid Work (1996), aged 66)

We do not have any measures of just how much time MOP respondents committed to these activities over time, but we can see immediately from the above quote, ('almost every night of the week') that some would fit squarely in the civic core.

A few writers described social connections with others who were volunteers which had triggered their involvement in specific acts, the most common of which were street or neighbourhood collections of money for charities (ten writers). While on the face of it this involved a small-scale and infrequent commitment, of all the types of volunteering described, this face-to-face work seemed the least liked by MOP writers; Dianne Roberts, for example, was not alone in feeling she couldn't say no to a request to support a door-to-door collection of fundraising envelopes (see Chapter Six on motivation), even though she admitted '*I can't say I enjoy it*' (*Unpaid Work* (1996), aged 53).

We also encountered writers who were actively involved in organisations, such as the Rotary Club, which are associated with people with strong economic, cultural, social and symbolic capital (Bourdieu, 1984). Roger King (retired managing-director, born 1920), a prolific formal volunteer, reflected that he had found it '*difficult to refuse*' an invitation to join the Rotary Club from a more senior colleague at work. He had found the Club unsatisfying because its members were local businessmen in the town who were well-networked to begin with, whereas he described his out-of-town workplace as the '*large building up the road*' which reduced his contacts with other Rotarians. He also lived elsewhere, '*so my wife never met any of the other wives and we never "belonged"*'. He was '*relieved*' on being relocated by his employer so that '*I could plead inability to attend the lunches to enable me to explain my resignation*' (*Belonging* (2010), aged 89). What's interesting about this is the pressure on this writer to conform – the normative expectation that someone of a particular occupational position, benefiting from high levels of social capital, *should* engage in particular social networks and, through them, become engaged in forms of voluntary action.

In contrast to Roger King's experience, Margaret Shaw, who was actively involved in the Rotary Club through the Inner Wheel, an organisation for wives of club members, seems to have gained certain benefits from her involvement. Margaret had held office as president of the organisation, and as a committee member. She describes the role of the Rotary Club and the Inner Wheel in fundraising for other local voluntary or charitable organisations:

> '*these change annually, but are currently concerned with fundraising for amenities for the local hospital and for funding the provision of artificial limbs also for a rehabilitation centre in India. An ongoing commitment is helping the Autistics Society locally (through coffee mornings etc) also Oxfam and the Sue Ryder foundation.*' (*Membership of Voluntary Organisations* (1990), aged 60)

Although the overt focus of the organisation was fundraising, Margaret's account suggests there was an equally strong focus on socialising, networking with others, and the accrual of social capital through active engagement in the organisation.

Another writer, retired home-maker, Helen Cook (born 1933), had similar connections through the Women's Institute (WI), of which she had been a lifelong member, holding office as branch president several times. Through this route, she became engaged in cooking and serving for Meals on Wheels, then for lunch clubs for the elderly; being involved in a befriending service; and having active roles in leisure-based clubs and activities. While this local WI looks like the kind of group that Brodie et al (2011) would class as 'informal', it is highly likely to have been a registered charity (in other words, a formal voluntary organisation) and this writer's description certainly suggests that it acted as a springboard for her involvement in more formalised activities. Helen had strong friendships that appeared to cross over between the various organisations in which she was involved. All of her voluntary contributions involved social connections (we examine this in more detail, in Chapter Six).

The nature of the MOP material – the way in which the directives were framed – meant that respondents did not comment at any length on the relationship between their voluntary action and the nature of the communities in which they lived, but from other work (Lindsey, 2013) we suggest that these kinds of connections have a strong rootedness in place. We have observed interconnections between membership of, and involvement, in formal organisations, particularly among individuals who might be perceived as more affluent. This enabled us to explore the concept of 'charitable ecologies', an idea we use to encapsulate the interconnection between different individual charities and organisations, the use of weak social ties for charitable purposes, and the flow of economic resources between organisations within an affluent area. There is an argument to be made about the importance of infrastructure and key institutions in this regard, which can provide a basis for the mobilisation of local community efforts in the voluntary sector.

A number of writers described taking on roles for organisations to which they were personally/socially connected both as a volunteer and a beneficiary. Twelve of our 38 writers described undertaking activities for church/faith organisations, including flower-arranging, committee membership, writing newsletters, being cathedral guides and singing in the church choir. All but two were (or were married to) directors and professionals, the exceptions being George Tyler (transport supervisor, discussed above) and Angela Goode (retail supervisor, born 1953).

Sixteen writers from a range of different occupational classes were active in the running of cultural and leisure organisations. Without wishing to overgeneralise, there was some suggestion that the type of club in which the writers were involved tended to reflect their accumulation of economic and cultural capital, with professionals and directors reporting engagement in music, wine, cricket, golf and art clubs. There was far more cross-over between occupational classes in involvement in literary and creative writing groups. Other clubs mentioned by lower occupational classes included Morris dancing, bowmen, dog clubs, arts clubs and a lorry club.

Activities for organisations or people with whom the volunteer was not personally or socially connected

Seven respondents wrote of involvement in health-related research projects – in some cases because personal or family connections with a specific health condition had led them to become involved – and three had been blood donors (somewhat above the national proportion). Four writers described being involved in teaching basic skills to adults. Derek Prior (born 1929) trained and worked as a voluntary basic skills tutor when he retired as a priest, and was involved in the committee of the local adult education association. Annabel Green (born 1952) retrained as a voluntary basic skills tutor as her children grew older, and after volunteering, subsequently gained employment in this field. Two others – Beverley Scott (see above), and Claire Cooper (retired social worker, born 1925) – had trained as basic skills tutors, volunteered for a short while, then stopped doing so. However, Claire Cooper, who had been a Samaritan in her working life, then went on to provide divorce and bereavement counselling. Two further writers were involved in advice and support work – Margaret Shaw volunteered for her Citizen's Advice Bureau and Angela Goode (see above), a prolific informal and formal volunteer, provided voluntary family support work within a deprived community in the South West, and was also involved in a soup-run (as was prolific formal volunteer, Roger King).

Political activities

Five writers described being actively involved in professional or trade organisations, and four women writers were involved in the National Housewives Register (see Land, 2006, 56). Three writers were involved in work-based trade union activities (see Chapter Seven). Carole Barker, a female teacher (born 1950), had been the local president of the National Association of Schoolmasters and Union of Women Teachers, but when writing in 1990 was no longer involved. However, George Tyler and Frank Driver (born 1934) both involved in transport work, described very active involvement in trade union activities.

Frank Driver was also actively involved in the Labour Party; while Pauline Bennett, a female researcher and counsellor (born 1941) describes being actively involved with local Liberal Democrats, an affiliation she shared with Roger King, who reported distributing newsletters and supporting the party at election time. Annabel Green (see above) and Pamela Clarke (born 1951, d. 2010 – an ex-teacher turned secretary and accounts clerk) stated that they were actively involved with a political party at election time, but did not state which party this was. Even allowing for the small sample size this rate of engagement in politics is well above what would typically be found in the adult population and is an indication that MOP respondents have much to tell us about voluntary action *among the engaged segments of the population* but we should be careful in making inferences about political engagement in the wider population from this source.

Acting on behalf of, or for, local communities

The most popular type of volunteering undertaken was for the local community, where the beneficiary was a local group, organisation, or the community as a whole. Such activities featured in responses to various directives (including *Membership of Voluntary Organisations* (1990), *Where You Live* (1995), *Unpaid Work* (1996), *Belonging* (2010), *A Working Day* (2010) and *The 'Big Society'* (2012)). Almost half (18) of the 38 writers reported this type of activity, several undertook more than one such activity over their lifecourse, and all combined this with another type of volunteering. Contribution to the local community was not the sole type of voluntarism in which writers engaged, alongside their MOP writing.

All but one of these contributions to the local community was formal, and included: activity as a representative of a tenant's association (2); setting up and/or running a community centre or village hall (3); serving as a magistrate (1); monitoring and opposing planning and development (6); running a local environmental trust (1); organising a neighbourhood watch (2); writing and/or delivering local newsletters (4); being involved with a local school or youth group to which the writer had no family connection (3); helping with a community bus initiative (1).

The one informal contribution was reported by David Gardiner, who retrospectively described some of his secret gardening activities prior to being made redundant:

> 'I was the "ghost" gardener at the hospital ... having watched the landscaping carried out around the new buildings which I supervised, I couldn't bear to see weeds swamping the plants so at

weekends ... I went up to garden, so eventually they found out who their ghost was. Similarly I supervised building work at the local Red Cross H.Q. and laid out & took some plants down at the weekends to improve the outlook from office windows, I didn't tell them. I also tidied an overgrown lot behind our garages until the adjacent owner fenced around it and made it part of his garden. But I only did this as I like order and pleasing views.' (Unpaid Work (1996), aged 63)

Although we have categorised David's activity as informal community volunteering, it is important to note that he did not regard this as volunteering and was opposed to the notion of 'unpaid work' (see Chapter Four). Although the beneficiaries of his activities were the communities using the facilities where he gardened, his assertion that he did this because *'I like order and pleasing views'* means that we, the researchers, have to accept that David perceived himself as being the main beneficiary of these activities. He combined his ghost gardening with informal help to neighbours, which again he claimed was not a form of volunteering.

There are obvious limits to what we can say about the demographics of a self-selecting panel of MOP writers. We note, however, that fewer men than women were involved in formal volunteering for community organisations over the lifecourse: only three out of the 11 male writers were engaged in community-based volunteering, compared to 16 of the 27 female writers. In socioeconomic terms, writers from the managerial and professional classes were most actively involved in this type of voluntary activity (15 of the 19 writers came from such backgrounds), even though our sample of MOP writers includes a range of occupational classes. Only four writers involved in these activities were not professionals: Sylvia Taylor and Angela Goode (both were shop-workers – although the latter had a degree), helped to set up and/or run community centres; George Tyler, a male transport mechanic and supervisor, had helped with a community bus initiative; and Maria Dyer, a female hairdresser (born 1947), was a magistrate, served on a committee to monitor the closure of a local psychiatric hospital and rehoming of its patients within the community, and was a governor for a special needs school.

In terms of roles performed, we did find a high proportion of our respondents serving on committees – 17 out of the sample of 38 writers (45 per cent) describe having served on committees, 11 of whom were professionals or had higher education. Note that this is a higher proportion than would typically be suggested by social surveys during the period in question. Even in the most exhaustive studies of volunteering such as the 1991 NSV, where in-depth questioning generates a high estimate of the proportion of the population engaged in volunteering, approximately 30 per cent *of volunteers* say that they have served on committees, though, for professional and managerial groups, the proportion is around 45 per cent (a somewhat lower estimate – around one-third of professionals and managers who are volunteers say that they have served on committees – can be derived from the CSs).

We suggest that this clustering of the professional classes in particular roles within voluntary activities, which is evident within MOP writing and within survey data, will have community-level ramifications. The segregation of individuals with high levels of social, cultural and symbolic capital (Bourdieu, 1984) into particular neighbourhoods substantially accounts for the variations in volunteering rates between communities described by Keohane et al (2011); (see McCulloch et al (2012), and Mohan et al (2006) for discussion of community-level variations in voluntary action). This means that proposals to place greater emphasis on voluntary action to meet the needs of communities are likely to meet with spatially-differentiated responses.

Conclusions

In the previous chapter we have observed what sometimes appears as the tendency of some politicians to fixate on headline figures about volunteering. In this chapter we note that a focus on rates of engagement (proportions of the population who carry out particular activities) overlooks the reality that effort is highly concentrated in small subsets of the population (what we have termed a 'civic core'), and the distribution of volunteers is highly stratified socially. Those who are most likely to engage in *formal*, organisational roles tend to be those with high levels of economic, social and cultural capital. As far as can be shown using survey data, these general patterns have persisted through the time-period of this study.

What of the actual fields of activity in which people are volunteering? In terms of the distribution of the activities which people undertake, again, there has been a picture of stability, one exception to this being the decline in the proportion of volunteers who are involved in raising or handling money. As far as causes are concerned, the main shift seems to be an increase in the proportion of volunteers who say they are involved in sport and leisure, and religion, but this could be partly due to changes in survey methods.

The MOP material adds much depth to the survey data by providing rich insights into the complex mixes of formal and informal engagement being undertaken by individuals, but their descriptions by no means correspond neatly to established typologies of voluntary action. For example, it has been argued that the 'dominant paradigm' for the study of volunteering places undue emphasis on altruistic service to large, formally-structured organisations (Rochester et al, 2010). Survey data can shed little light on this, because (beyond broad categories of activity (education, sport, and so on) there is no detailed investigation of the nature of the organisations which volunteers support. From the accounts the MOP writers give of their voluntary activities, it is also difficult to determine whether the organisations in which they volunteer are the professionalised, large organisations described by the 'dominant paradigm'. Some large organisations are mentioned (Citizens Advice); some of those described are probably smaller, albeit still formal in character (community centre, youth club). Numerous MOP writers also refer to their involvement in committees, again suggesting a degree of formality. Thus, while their volunteering is unquestionably 'formal', the organisations for which this activity is taking place sound like relatively small, albeit organised, entities.

As far as altruism is concerned, we clearly do have descriptions of activities focused on people with whom the volunteer is not directly related, either socially or personally, so one might regard this as altruistic. On the other hand, around one-half of those MOP writers who were parents describe involvement, often extending over a number of years, in activities which directly benefited their immediate family, so whether this would count as genuinely 'altruistic' behaviour is a matter for debate.

We also find ample evidence of involvement in what Rochester et al (2010) would characterise as elements of the 'serious leisure' and 'civil society' paradigms. Close to half of the Mass Observers make reference to engagement in an extensive range of leisure pursuits, going beyond merely taking part in the activities of the organisation to include the acceptance of responsibilities and roles. While it is true that the directives upon which we have drawn did not focus explicitly on questions of campaigning and activism, we find that a significant proportion of our respondents, certainly a higher figure than that revealed by national surveys, are engaged in activism for political parties, unions and tenants' organisations, as well as campaigning around local planning issues.

These respondents are, then, extensively involved in formal volunteering, in a variety of capacities but with significant evidence of engagement in positions of responsibility, to a greater degree than is evident from national survey data. They are also involved in activities which cut across the three paradigms of voluntary action – though the civil society paradigm is less evident in their accounts than the other two.

Formal voluntarism is by no means all they do, however. We have been struck by their extensive involvement in informal volunteering, and also by the ways they prioritise provision of care to both neighbours and relatives in their accounts of voluntary action. Those accounts also point to the very blurred boundary between informal care and informal volunteering. This is acknowledged in theoretical accounts of work, as in the Total Social Organisation of Labour (TSOL) framework of Glucksmann (2005; see also Taylor, 2004; 2005), which refuse any attempts at prioritisation of particular elements of work, regardless of whether it is paid or unpaid, or takes place in the private or public sphere. Most accounts of voluntary activity – especially those based upon survey data – lack information about individual involvement in unpaid care, however. This has also been largely absent from public discussion about volunteering rates. We note that since 2011 there has been an increased focus on familial care within policy debates, with, for example, Jeremy Hunt emphasising the obligation for families to care for elderly relatives (2015);[6] this echoes Thatcher's insistence on familial and neighbourly obligation in the late 1980s.

Those concerned with voluntary action may feel optimistic that, despite considerable socioeconomic change, levels of engagement have remained stable. This chapter, however, demonstrates the great diversity of actions in which individuals engage, and shows that they are often of a small-scale, locally-focused and routine character. Much voluntary action happens in a fairly ad hoc way through routine social practices and connections, is highly valuable for the functioning of communities, but is diverse, unpredictable and probably unmanageable. This raises questions about whether any large-scale shift in favour of private voluntary initiative is feasible. We explore these questions in subsequent chapters, with a focus on individual motivations, individual routes into and out of voluntary action during their lifecourse, and people's attitudes to being asked to do more.

Notes

[1] This is based on unpublished analyses – further details available from John Mohan.

[2] Although ten out of our 38 writers described providing informal help and care to people with whom they were socially connected, we cannot claim that the

remaining 27 writers did not provide this sort of care and help; we can only claim that they did not report this sort of contribution.

3   Half of the ten were born in the 1920s and 1930s, and half were born during or after the Second World War, and thus were young children during the birth of the Welfare State; and might loosely be described as 'baby boomers'.

4   We note that this type of informal activity is omitted from Rochester et al's paradigms of volunteering which relate primarily to formal activity (2010, 10–11), but falls within their description of informal volunteering (p 51) which draws on descriptions of informal activity provided by the CS.

5   This lack of recognition was both cultural and legislative. However there was also a lack of recognition within survey instruments which overlooked the existence of same-sex partnerships (Aspinall, 2009).

6   Speech, 'Personal responsibility', to the Local Government Association annual conference 2015, www.gov.uk/government/speeches/personal-responsibility

SIX

Why people volunteer: contextualising motivation

Introduction: challenges of obtaining accounts of volunteer motivation

Why do people volunteer? Although scholars have advanced a diverse range of accounts of motivation, which we have summarised in Chapter One, significant obstacles stand in the way of gathering data on volunteer motivation which relate to temporality and motive. It is unusual, if not impossible, to be in a position to capture individuals' views on motivation while they are in the process of choosing to volunteer. Consideration of motives will usually be retrospective; however, as Musick and Wilson (2008) have identified, the problem with seeking information about the underlying motives for volunteering is that:

> if they preceded the volunteering act...[the] actual experience of volunteering often leads to such radical changes in attitudes toward the activity that the original goals are forgotten or the volunteer becomes unable to separate her initial reasons for volunteering from the reasons that make sense to her now. (p 71)

Respondents are also likely to conflate their motives for volunteering with more recently acquired views on the actual benefits that their experience of volunteering has brought either to them or to the beneficiaries of their volunteering. Retrospective discussion of motives is also likely to confuse motives with broader attitudinal views. Furthermore, motives overlap with triggers and influences: volunteering may result from the presentation of an opportunity (for example, to someone seeking a move back into employment after a career break). This could be regarded as a trigger, but is then rationalised by the respondent as a motive. Moreover, motive is not just related to the decision as to whether to volunteer or not, it is also related to the decision on *where* to volunteer, and *what role* to take. Given that over the lifecourse an individual may volunteer multiple times, each separate decision to volunteer will involve consideration of whether, where and how to volunteer.

Events that take place after an individual has volunteered may influence or reshape recall of motive, particularly when strong emotions are attached to the memories of these events (Lindsey, 2004; Bal, 1999; Portelli, 1998). Quality of recall can also be affected by over-rehearsal of certain autobiographical memories that are privileged over others (Talarico and Rubin, 2003).

The method of data collection on motivation also influences the answers given. Surveys offer a restricted range of questions that touch on motives for volunteering; qualitative accounts are also influenced by the phrasing of questions asked by an interviewer, or by written questions. Both approaches can be affected by social desirability bias, which may predispose individuals to present the 'right' response (for example, doing something to help someone in need) rather than the instrumental reason (for example, supporting an organisation which directly benefits the respondent or their immediate family). A final point, which really relates to gaps in the literature, is that there has been much less data collected on why people choose *not* to volunteer, than there has been on why people choose to volunteer. Yet it would make sense to consider these two issues together. A consideration of the obverse of motivation, reasons why people do not participate, has the capacity to shed light on our understanding of motive.

Some 35 years ago, Sherrott (1983, 62) argued that research on motives for volunteering paid 'little attention to the circumstances and life histories of which these motives were a product'. Put another way, if a person volunteers out of a desire to help others, where does that desire come from (Leat, 1983; Wilson, 2012)? And what causes that desire to help others to be translated into action? Even those who are highly motivated may not actually volunteer unless they are asked, and people with little motivation to volunteer might do so in face of insistent requests from friends or colleagues. Volunteering is not always entered into through a consciously recognised motivation to fulfil an easily identifiable need, but results, instead, from conjunctures of personal background, social resources and lifecourse events. In this chapter we argue that we may obtain greater insight from investigating the expectations of, and rewards derived from, different types of volunteering against the background of the personal and social circumstances of volunteers (Leat, 1983, 52) – and particularly against the background of how those circumstances change over time.

We do this principally by drawing upon qualitative data from Mass Observation Project (MOP) writers, but we begin, in the next section, with an overview of quantitative and qualitative data, which also serves to demonstrate the challenges and limitations of quantitative work in this field. We follow this in the third section with four vignettes, in which we present accounts of lifecourse trajectories of voluntary actions of selected MOP writers, set against the background of changes in their personal and employment histories. Then in the fourth section we draw out key themes from responses to various MOP directives. These include: parental and cultural influences on volunteering; the influence of being asked to volunteer; peer, family and spousal influences (which we draw together under the theme of triggers and influences); and, in the fifth section, consideration of the motives underpinning volunteering – in other words, whether individuals had volunteered in anticipation of various benefits (personal self-esteem and the building of social capital; therapy; career; and serious leisure).

Data

Survey data

Although various British surveys have asked respondents for information about the reasons why they have become involved in volunteering. However, as Lynn and Davis-Smith (1992, 81) point out, it is difficult to use surveys to distinguish motivations to volunteer from the processes whereby people became involved. These processes include the opportunities or triggers to volunteer that occur over the lifecourse which we discuss in Chapter Seven. To provide an overview of the survey evidence on motivation, and the difficulties in using this evidence, we have used the 1981 and 1991 National Surveys (NSVs), the 2006–07 *Helping Out* survey, the 2010–11 Citizenship Survey (CS) and the 2015–16 Community Life Survey (CLS). Variations in question phrasing, framing and sequencing make it difficult to identify trends in responses. In the 1981 NSV there were questions on the way volunteers became involved; the 1991 NSV featured a module on 'reasons for volunteering'; while in *Helping Out* (2006–07) a module containing similar questions was referred to as 'routes into volunteering'. A crucial question – whether or not someone had begun volunteering because they were *asked* to do so – was put to respondents directly only in the 1981 and 1991 NSVs and (only of those who have recently volunteered through organisations) in the *Helping Out* survey. These different surveys have also sought to elicit opinions about the personal benefits which individuals derive from volunteering – again, not in a consistent manner across surveys.

We consider the reasons why people say they get involved in volunteering by analysing the proportions of *active volunteers* who report a particular reason for their volunteering. If we expressed the figures as percentages of the *population*, variations would reflect differences between surveys in the proportions of the population who say that they volunteer. The 1981 data are not available in electronic format, so we use the tabulations from that survey (Humble, 1982) which appear to give only one response possibility whereas the 1991 and 2006 surveys allow individuals to answer affirmatively to more than one option. We present the results in Table 6.1. This includes those categories of response to which at least 10 per cent of volunteers assented (for 1991 onwards) or which were described by at least 5 per cent of volunteers as the ways in which they had become involved (1981). As can be seen, not all questions were put to respondents in each survey, nor was the wording consistent.

We can see that the most popular reasons given were that the respondent wanted 'to improve things or help people', and that the cause was 'important' to them. The proportion assenting to the former proposition has apparently risen from around two-fifths to three-fifths between the 1991 and 2015–16 surveys. Between two-fifths and one-half of respondents stated that they had been asked to help, though this question was only asked in the specialist NSV and *Helping Out* surveys of 1991 and 2006–07, and only of active volunteers. Note that 'being asked' is by definition the product of social networks of various kinds, but the survey cannot provide access to further detail on what those networks look like. Following these, between one-quarter and one-third of volunteers recorded reasons such as meeting people or making friends, having spare time, connections with needs of one's family, and awareness of need in the community. Then there are two questions which relate to personal values: volunteering because it is part of the respondents 'religious belief' and because it is part of their 'philosophy of life'. Collectively, these are reported by around two-fifths of volunteers. Finally, we note a range of motivations concerned with the acquisition or use of skills and qualifications. The most visible change here is that the proportion who report that they wanted to learn new skills has almost doubled, from 11 to just under 22 per cent. This is likely to be related to the emphasis on voluntary action as a route into employability, which has featured strongly in discussion of the benefits of volunteering in recent years (regardless of the somewhat equivocal evidence for such benefits; see Ellis Paine et al, 2013).

We caution that there are limited possibilities for inferring genuine changes in motivation over time from these surveys, due to changes

Table 6.1: Reasons given for involvement in volunteering

Reasons given for involvement in volunteering	NSV/Helping Out			Citizenship Survey 2010–11	Community Life Survey 2015–16
	1981	1991	2006		
Wanted to improve things/help people		40	53	55	62
The cause was important to me			41	38	40
Someone asked me to help		52	41		
Was asked (no other reason)	14				
Had time to spare	5	29	41	28	31
There was a need in my community		26	29	25	25
Connected with interests or needs of family and friends		43	29	25	26
Altruistic (close personal connections)	14				
No-one else to do it			13	9	7
Part of my philosophy of life			23	22	23
Part of my religious belief	9		17	14	17
Learn new skills		11	19	18	22
Chance to use existing skills			29	23	30
Help me get on in my career/gain a qualification			9	12	12
I am good at it		19			
Connected with paid work		11			
I started the group	5	5			
Enjoyment of work	7				

Notes: With the exception of 1981, figures are percentages of those who stated that they were formal volunteers: 1981 figures are percentages of respondents. 1981 and 1991: survey asked respondents to record various kinds of satisfaction which they receive from volunteering; they could choose as many as were applicable. CS/CL survey question is more directly, why the respondent started volunteering. 2010–11 and 2015–16: respondent could select the five that were most important to them.

Source: Humble, 1982, table 8; elsewhere authors' calculations from survey data.

117

in the menu of questions presented to respondents. The data are interesting as a broad ordering of how respondents rationalise their voluntary activities. There is some suggestion that individuals are more likely to do so in terms of a desire to improve things and help people than was formerly the case, and evidence that instrumental reasons concerned with employability feature more strongly. Given the prominence of voluntary action in public debate the former could reflect social desirability bias as much as a general trend while the latter could be read as a response to an increasingly challenging economic situation. Otherwise, to the extent that it is possible to comment, there has been little change in trends over time in the answers given to questions about motivation.

Mass Observation Project data

The first point to note is that a little less than half (16) of the writers appear to say nothing about their motives for volunteering/not volunteering. Of the remaining 22 writers, responses which address the topic are sometimes confined to a small number of sentences, generally relating to their participation in a particular domain or role. Echoing the wider academic literature, it seems that writers' motivations for volunteering varies, depending on the domain in which it is taking place, and on the role being taken, concurring with Musick and Wilson's observation that 'We cannot separate our thinking about the motivation for volunteering work from our thinking about what that volunteer work entails' (2008, 78).

This dearth of MOP material on motivation is, in part, due to the nature of the questions put to the writers over the last 35 years: only the 1996 directive on *Unpaid Work*, and the 2012 directive on *The 'Big Society'*, have asked specific questions about motives for volunteering. The 1996 directive asked writers about 'getting started': why they began working in a voluntary capacity, why they carried on, and, if they didn't report any unpaid work (or had ceased doing it) why that was the case. Our 2012 *The 'Big Society'* directive simply asked people why they were involved, and how volunteering made them feel. At that point, we had not conceived of the idea of this longitudinal study, so we did not replicate questions from previous directives, nor did we specifically ask about non-volunteering. Most of our information on motivation comes from these directives. A small amount of additional material is found in responses to the 2004 directive, *Being Part of Research*, which asked about being invited to take part in research studies, and experiences and feelings related to such participation.

The 2010 *Special Questionnaire* on *Taking Part in the Mass Observation Project*, and the 2010 *Belonging* directive, both generated responses about belonging to volunteering communities.

Writers tend to sandwich their discussion of motives within descriptions of the type of voluntary activities that they undertake (what they do and for whom), the skills they bring to their volunteering, and the benefits that they receive from taking part. When this material is considered alongside responses to the other directives we have analysed (for example, feelings about their families and communities, their work lives, values and key life events)' we gain insights into their personalities, value systems, and capacity for action. It is this additional *context* about the complexity of these individual lives that informs our understanding of why writers may or may not volunteer over time. For this reason we frame our qualitative evidence about motivation through the context and shape of writers' volunteering lives, examining how motives for volunteering or not can change over the lifecourse.

Vignettes: synopses of writers' volunteering lifecourses

Below we present four non-representative synopses of writers' personal, work and volunteering lifecourses, and then discuss their various reported or implied motives for volunteering, to illustrate the contingent effect of life context on motives; and to reflect on how our findings fit with theories of motivation and UK survey evidence for motive. Choosing which writers to showcase was difficult. Each writer's characteristics, circumstances and volunteering pathway are very different; and the writers we have chosen, Catherine Neil, Roger King, Maria Dyer and Beverley Scott are unique, rather than representative. We interpret and present our interpretations of their writing on volunteering which are based on a close reading of the text of their accounts. We examine the relationship between: motive, influences and values; motive, needs and benefits; motive and personality; motive and sense of belonging; and motive for deciding not to volunteer, or to cease volunteering. We discuss how these compare to the experiences of other writers (providing very short life synopses and context for these writers in parentheses); UK survey data; and international literature on motivation.

Catherine Neil: Brief life, work and volunteering lifecourse

Catherine Neil, a female writer born in 1938 was one of 11 children born to Catholic parents who worked in skilled trades. The family lived in a south coast city, and experienced the Blitz during the Second World War. As a child Catherine undertook various social, educational and charitable voluntary activities. She attended grammar school until 1953 when she and her family moved overseas because of her father's job. While overseas she attended a new school, gained 'O' level qualifications, then left school at 16 to begin a series of retail and banking jobs while learning typing and shorthand at evening classes.

The family returned to the UK in 1955 when she was 17. Catherine continued working in banks, began donating blood and was treasurer for a youth club. At the age of 20, in 1958, she began to travel, spending a year working in France. In 1960, when she was 22 she moved to the South East of the UK, where she joined an amateur drama company. She worked in a variety of jobs. Some of these were unskilled. She writes most fully about working in retail management during this period and the difficulties she experienced with gender inequality. Status within the context of her working identity seems to have been very important to her.

In the mid-1960s, at the age of 26, she got married to a man who worked as a window-cleaner but had trained as a skilled worker in the ship-building industry. She met him when she was working as a barmaid in a hotel where he was captain of the darts team. They lived in rented private accommodation, and their first child was born after they married. She describes having to leave a well-paid job shortly before her first child was born. There was no access to maternity leave, and they had to rely on her husband's income *'We were hard up for years'* (*Social Divisions* (1990), aged 52). She became involved with the running of a voluntary pre-school playgroup. At some point after the birth of her first child she stopped being involved with the drama company.

Catherine and her husband had another child. They moved to a council estate in the late 1960s, where their third child was born. When her children were small Catherine made a conscious decision to no longer get involved in formal voluntary action. However, she joined the MOP in 1984, and was also occasionally involved in short-term formal activities such as collecting donation envelopes. Although she stopped engaging formally, she provided informal help to those she perceived as being in need, and was still providing this help when she responded to the 2012 *'Big Society'* directive.

In the mid-1970s Catherine and her husband secured a mortgage and bought a three-bedroomed house on a new build estate. Catherine seems ambivalent about this move, appreciating the new house, but missing the reciprocity and friendliness of the council estate she had left behind. From the mid-1960s to the mid-1980s Catherine and her husband continued to work in a variety of short-term jobs. Both experienced bouts of unemployment. In the wake of the 1981–82 recession Catherine, her husband, and three children, all experienced three years of unemployment. Their fortunes improved, with all gaining jobs in the mid- to late 1980s. Catherine found a job based in an office in 1986 which she kept until she retired nine years later in 1995. On retirement, she became very involved in the care of her grandchildren.

In her writing Catherine has a self-confessed tendency to *'go off on a tangent'* (2010 MOP Special Questionnaire, aged 72), and her treatment of different subjects within her directive responses can be brief and pithy, or tangentially long and rambling. A close reading of her account is often required in order to identify context, meanings and subtext relating to motivation.

Roger King: Brief life, work and volunteering lifecourse

Roger King, the oldest of our sample of 38 writers, is a male writer born in 1921. He was one of two children born to parents living in a town in the south of England. His father left the army in 1919, and set up and co-owned a small family business. Until 1930, his mother provided bed and breakfast accommodation to tourists. His mother was very religious. In 1928, at the age of 8, he became an Anglican chorister, and later became an altar server after his voice broke.

He gained a scholarship to grammar school. A teacher took him and a small group of other boys for trips where they learnt climbing, walking, camping and sailing skills. Roger matriculated when he was 15, moved to a Commercial School where he learnt office skills, then left still aged 15, for a job as a junior clerk, where he worked from 1936 to 1939, while taking RSA correspondence courses. When the war started he served in a Territorial Army anti-aircraft unit; then joined the army, gained a commission, and was posted overseas. After a chance meeting with a member of the V force, he decided to join this covert intelligence-gathering organisation and parachuted into Burma in 1945, and worked with the Karen hill people.

At the end of the Pacific War he got a job in tropical hardwood logging. During his leave he stayed with his parents, and volunteered to take disabled Barnardo's children out for day trips and was assisted in this by his mother and an aunt. In 1954, aged 34, he contracted TB, left his job and returned to get medical care in England. He met his wife, a nurse, during this time, and they married in 1956, when he was 36.

He retrained as a Chartered Secretary and at the age of 36 started working in the City. He then moved to the north of England with his wife, to work for industry. He gradually worked his way up the company, gaining a series of promotions. He and his wife had four children, who were privately educated, the oldest in a boarding school. His wife worked part-time as an administrator for a medical institute. During this time, he volunteered in a variety of different formal roles: for his church committee for planned giving/Christian Stewardship; for a hospital league of friends; as Chair of the Parent Teacher Association (PTA) for his son's boarding school; as a parent-governor for his son's school; as a governor for a local secondary-modern; as part of the Diocesan training team; and for the Rotary club.

Roger retired from a senior international executive position in 1982 at the age of 61, did some travelling with his wife, and then relocated to a southern cathedral town, where he began to volunteer for a variety of different formal charitable organisations. He worked in various voluntary roles for the cathedral – was on the cathedral council, headed up the cathedral money counting team, was on the Deanery Synod, was a server, sat on the Stewardship Committee, and delivered cathedral newsletters. He was also involved in helping to set up a hospice; helping raise money for the Lib Dems; being a treasurer for a small overseas charity; flag-selling, working in a day-centre for homeless people, and taking part in a longitudinal heart-research project. In 1990 at the age of 69, he joined the MOP. When writing in 2010 aged 89, he described feeling tired and reported that he had osteoarthritis, and was using a mobility scooter. In 2012, when writing for The 'Big Society' directive, he reported that he had downsized many commitments, and was now just working as a door-keeper for the cathedral, but was still treasurer for the overseas charity.

Maria Dyer: Brief life, work and volunteering lifecourse

Maria Dyer is a female writer born in 1947, one of four children born to parents living in a town in the Midlands. Maria's maternal grandfather was a German Jew, her grandmother was Spanish and the two met at an Irish university. Maria's father was an engineer in a car-factory and her mother was a hairdresser. The family moved to a town in the north of England in 1951. Maria was brought up as a Church of England Christian, and both she and her older brother were choristers. She was also a Brownie, and 'lieutenant in Girl Guides/Acting Captain' (The 'Big Society' (2012), aged 65).

She left school when she was 18 with two 'O' levels and was forced to work for her mother as an apprentice hairdresser for five years 'I wasn't allowed to join any groups or clubs', and gained several hair-dressing qualifications. 'My mother was not the easiest person to work for – nothing was right and there was no praise or thanks' (A Working Day (2010), aged 63). She married in 1971, at the age of 24, and moved to another area of the city. 'When we went to visit home after the honeymoon my father said "just because I was married didn't mean I should stop doing the housework for them!!"' (Doing a Job (1997), aged 50). She stopped working for her mother, started work with a new salon, and was promoted to senior stylist. She also worked as a part-time hair-dressing lecturer and gained a teaching qualification. Her husband worked as a financial company director.

In 1978, aged 32, Maria suffered two miscarriages, then became pregnant and gave birth to a child the following year. Complications during pregnancy meant she was unable to work during this time. That same year her brother died suddenly in a road accident. She experienced a post-natal breakdown which she describes as 'post-natal depression' and 'manic depression' (Unpaid Work (1996) aged 49); and she took a two-and-a-half year break from work.

In 1981/2, when she was 34, she began helping out at a local 'spastics (charity) shop' (Relatives, Friends and Neighbours (1984)), and continued volunteering there for eight years, taking on a co-ordinator role. At a similar time, her husband walked out of his job, and did temporary work until finding a more secure job. In 1982 Maria began teaching hair-dressing evening-classes. She joined the MOP in 1984. She took on the role of chair of the PTA at her son's school and continued this role throughout the 1980s. She also cut friends' and neighbours' hair free of charge during this time.

She lost her teaching job in 1985, when she was 38. In 1986, her house had subsidence and she and her family moved to a more rural area. She also got a job as a Welfare Benefits Advisor for a Community Programme Scheme. In 1987, aged 40, she got a job at a museum, then returned to teaching hairdressing. In 1990, when she was 43, her response to the Membership of Voluntary Organisations (1990) directive describes a very full volunteering life: she was helping out at the Spastics Society; an organisation providing care in the community; and the PTA for her son's school; and was deputy leader of the Morris Dancing Group.

She was also a magistrate and sat on the Betting and Gaming Committee and the Juvenile Panel Committee in this capacity.

Maria retired in 1990 aged 43 'as had to look after parents' (Your Life Line (2008), aged 61). In mid-1990, she wrote about a neighbour's comment on her mother's ethnicity and said 'I let the comment go unchallenged but I have decided to move away fairly soon' (Social Divisions (1990), aged 43). In 1991, she and her family moved to a bungalow. She collapsed from pneumonia, experienced chronic back pain and was bedridden with ME for three or four years. In 1996, aged 49, she was active again, and in the Unpaid Work directive describes a very full formal and informal volunteering life: as a magistrate; governor of a special needs school; helping out at her church; cutting friends' hair; teaching Morris dancing and looking after an elderly neighbour.

In 1999, her pension scheme had matured enabling her to use this to contribute to the family income. In 2004, when she was 57, she mentions being the Chair of her local history society. Her husband took early retirement in 2007, when she was 60. In 2010 she mentions being in a choir. In 2012 she says that she doesn't do 'proper volunteering anymore'.

Beverley Scott: Brief life, work and volunteering lifecourse

Beverley Scott is a female writer born overseas in 1957. Her sister was born two years later. The family returned to Scotland in 1962, and lived in a university city. Her father worked away from home in human resources until she was a teenager when he began working close to home; and her mother worked as a school teacher. Beverley stayed at school until she was 18, then spent a year working for a large bookstore, before going to a teacher training college in 1976 when she was 19.

Beverley qualified as a primary school teacher in 1979 when she was 22, and moved to a town not far from her home city. In 1981, aged 24, she got married to another teacher, six years her senior. They lived in a council flat, and disliked their neighbours. They were supposed to take part in a stair- and hall-cleaning rota, but didn't participate fully, and their neighbours reported them to the council.

In 1983, when she was 26, Beverley experienced job stress and depression, and left her job. Over 1983 and 1984, she got a job in a museum through the Manpower Services Commission; began writing for the MOP; moved back to her home city, and made the decision not to have children – she felt her job as a teacher had led her to hate children. In 1984 she became agoraphobic and was unable to work for three years. During her different periods of unemployment, she claimed benefits.

In 1987, aged 30, Beverley's grandmother died, and she and her husband moved into her grandmother's house, returning back to the area where she grew up. She got a job as a part-time library assistant, and signed up for free Adult Basic Education (ABE) training. At the end of the training she volunteered as an ABE trainer for six months. In 1990 she was hospitalised for six weeks 'coming off tranquilisers' (Your Life Line (2008) aged 51). She stayed in her job at the library until 1992. During this time, she spent a year volunteering through Volunteer Development Scotland. She was given a placement providing Occupational Therapy to a patient at a psychiatric hospital for two to three hours once a week. Between 1993 and 1996, she had a series of short-lived jobs. Over this time, Beverley writes about her sister who has moved to England and become a successful artist and lecturer.

In 1996 when she was 39, Beverley began to work as a supply teacher. Her husband retired from work in 2008; and Beverley took retirement in 2009 from supply-teaching when she was 52. Two-and-a-half years into her retirement she decided to volunteer at a local hospital patient library, but the scheme was discontinued the week after she joined. She tried an alternative scheme for a week, and then stopped volunteering.

Influences, triggers or motives – what's the difference?

'Those who set us on our way': parental influence on engagement

Margaret Thatcher argued, in her Women's Royal Voluntary Service (WRVS) speech (see Chapters One and Two) that involvement in voluntary activities owes much to the example of parents and relatives – 'those who set us on our way' – who have stressed the importance of doing something for others.[1] Thatcher's own family background was highly influential on her (to judge from references in her speeches) and indeed David Cameron also referred to the visible voluntary activities of his own adult relatives. What do we discover from MOP writers' accounts?

Catherine Neil became engaged in voluntary action through her parents' involvement in the Catholic church (she joined the Legion of

St Mary, a church-based association providing charitable acts directed towards others) and through her mother's involvement in the Co-operative Society (joining a choir and Pathfinders). Her account of this mixture of organised acts of charity and serious leisure is framed through her parents' involvement.

Catherine also writes about how the religious values absorbed from her parents have influenced her adult civic engagement. She describes herself as a *'cradle Catholic'* (*Belonging* (2010), aged 72) who has maintained lifelong held Christian values that have informed her adult engagement in individual reciprocal informal acts.

> 'I have always relied on friends and neighbours to help me out. It works both ways. I have followed my Christian principles all my life, but it doesn't exclude those of other faiths, or none at all.' (The 'Big Society' (2012), aged 74)

References to her Christianity and religious engagement pervade Catherine's writing, and she makes connections between the tenets of her faith and her decisions as to whether or not to get engaged in voluntary activities. For example, in her response to the 1990 *Membership of Voluntary Organisations* directive, she describes deciding not to get involved in formal group charitable activities when her children were small, although she was engaged in a group which:

> 'cut up tights and old sheets for Mother Theresa...but then the cost of sending it to India became prohibitive. Once again, no one took any notice of Mother's directive not to raise money, but to visit the lonely. I went to one meeting, where plans were being drawn up for a Jumble sale. I didn't join, but like to feel I do my bit privately.' (Membership of Voluntary Organisations (1990), aged 52)

She seems to be implying here that the group's activities were a distraction from more pressing social priorities, such as visiting lonely people. Catherine's writing weaves complex references to her parents' influence on her childhood engagement, their influence on her faith and value systems, and how her faith has influenced her decisions as to whether she should engage as an adult, and how and why she does engage. This makes it difficult to unpick and separate out the motivational relationship between her childhood engagement, her values and the roles of her parents. Although there is an implicit relationship between these issues, we would interpret Catherine's account as relating more to her attitude towards volunteering than her motive for volunteering.

Parental value systems, writer value systems and childhood engagement interact in complex ways to influence whether or how people volunteer. However, we have occasionally noted connections between writers' values and their parents' value systems, and noted how these values can manifest in a writer's volunteering. For example, George Tyler describes his father as a *'staunch trade unionist'* who *'was disappointed that the General Strike [1926] had been so easily defeated'*. In 1974, when George was promoted to *'Transport Superintendent'* at work he urged his workforce to join the union, joined the union himself and became *'quite active at branch meetings'* (*Doing a Job* (1997), aged 67). His account of his engagement in the union makes implicit connections with his father's values.

We have, however, only identified two other MOP writers (from our subset), whose writings have considered the issue of parental influence on their own voluntary action. Margaret Shaw, a prolific female volunteer (born 1930) makes an explicit positive connection between her parents' voluntarism and her own engagement. She had been aware of them *'giving very freely of their time during W.W. II, especially, so I suppose it seemed to me to be normal'* (1996, *Unpaid Work*, aged 66). However, like Catherine Neil's account, this comes across as less about motivation, and more about a disposition towards volunteering – something inherent within the respondent that can be traced back to parental influence.

Roger King also considers this potential connection. He describes his childhood voluntary engagement as a chorister and then altar server at his church as part of his *'upbringing'*. This was arranged by his very religious mother; his recollection is that he could not *'think of any other particular reason for [my] involvement in things'* (*Unpaid Work* (1996), aged 75).

He also considers his knowledge of his parents' engagement, and concludes that they were not involved in voluntary action when he was a child, and thus he had not been directly influenced by their own engagement. We note however, that in his response to the 1996 *Unpaid Work* directive he describes voluntary activities being carried out by his mother when he was an adult. There is, therefore, a strong possibility that she modelled a positive attitude towards engagement to Roger when he was a child. Like Catherine Neil, Roger's accounts show that parental influence on his childhood upbringing and his faith as a Christian, have informed his formal engagement throughout his life. This is seen in some, but not all, of the choices he has made as to where to volunteer; in some of the more charitable/altruistic actions that he performs (see Roger King's text box); and in his views on issues such as charitable giving:

> '*I would far rather be taken for a ride by a plausible rogue than fail to give to someone in desperate need.*' (*Unpaid Work* (1996), aged 75)

This Christian (and in later life what he describes as 'Deist') value system, premised on trust as well as faith, might be viewed more as an inherent attitude rather than a motivation. However, it is important to note that these are not his only motives and attitudes; his accounts of his voluntary activities suggest complex interwoven explanations for his decisions to volunteer, as well as additional value systems that sit alongside his beliefs and faith.

These examples resonate with studies that have demonstrated that children whose parents volunteer are more likely to do so themselves (Musick and Wilson, 2008, 225–32). These studies rely on evidence from surveys that ask specific questions about parental engagement. Whether more specific MOP directive prompts on parental volunteering would have elicited a clearer understanding of parental influences on motivation would depend on how prominent the recall of parental engagement is within the respondent's memory. This represents a potential future avenue of investigation. Nevertheless, we can see how parental behaviours and attitudes – those who, at formative stages of respondents' lives, 'set them on their way' – have shaped the voluntary activities of several of our respondents.

Personal values

If we concentrate on just value systems per se, we can identify more writers for whom value systems represent either a motive for volunteering/not volunteering, decisions on which causes to support, or choices as to the role they should take. Here functional analysis, and in particular the Volunteer Functions Inventory (VFI) 'values' function (Clary et al, 1996; see Chapter One), provides a helpful framework within which to consider values.

Some of the MOP participants write about religious values (the majority of writers who hold religious values are Christians) and discuss formal volunteering activities that are mediated through the church: acts of charity for others through church societies or groups; volunteering acts for the church community (flower-arranging, help in maintaining church premises, or fund-raising), and acts with an arguably evangelical function, such as providing a church-run crèche for shoppers. However, some writers, such as Catherine Neil (described above), discuss how their Christian values underpin their informal volunteering, and the help they extend to others. These descriptions fit with UK survey evidence for underlying values-based motives for volunteering. A significant proportion – between 30 and 40 per cent of regular volunteers – have described volunteering either because it was part of their 'religious belief' or (and somewhat more generally) because it related to their 'philosophy of life' to help people (Table 6.1). This is a wider notion than a purely religious motive. Note, incidentally, that it is 'help' that is being referenced here, not unpaid voluntary 'work'.

These surveys, however, do not have the scope to consider how individual philosophies of life may also play a part in motivating individuals *not* to participate in volunteering. When we consider the case of writer David Gardiner, the male architect's assistant, born in 1933, we note that his socialist conviction that he ought to be paid for his labour was his principal given reason for not volunteering. Yet, despite holding this view, David undertakes various short-term 'episodic' acts for neighbours and strangers that we would consider to be informal volunteering. His given reason for this – '*I believe in being helpful as it costs nothing*' – might have led him (had he regarded this as volunteering) to state that this was part of his philosophy of life. David also mentions he enjoys the appreciation of those he helps '*I enjoy hearing people say "It's nice to know there are still some gentlemen left."*' The short-term nature of his repeated informal acts means that it is possible to see a genuine relationship between motive and benefit. His anticipation of the benefit that he will accrue is an additional motive for his philosophy of being helpful.

Nor do the volunteering surveys we have used identify the political outlook of volunteers, which is a further potential driver for volunteering. Some writers mention volunteering for political causes: Roger King and Pauline Bennett have provided help to the Lib Dems; Frank Driver and George Tyler were both union activists; while Denise Rose and Frank Driver describe having volunteered to assist others with tenancy rights. It seems reasonable to assume that because these writers have been involved in activities with political, human-rights and/or social-justice aims which fall into the civil society paradigm (Rochester et al, 2010), their motives for taking part relate to a politicised outlook, belief or philosophy of life. Some writers, such as Frank Driver who describes himself as a '*left wing, anti-Europe socialist'* (*Unpaid Work* (1996)) wear their political hearts on their sleeves, yet we should not assume that their beliefs are the prime motives for their participation. Our impression from Pauline Bennett's accounts is that the desire to be part of a community – a social function – was her primary motive for her involvement. In contrast, George Tyler's motivation for union activism related to: years of frustration and anger with employers who would not listen to his advice; the pressures of working in local government through years of constant reform and funding pressures; and an implicit link between his union activity and his father's staunch involvement with unionism (described above). We also wonder whether his activism relates to something less tangible: a lack of trust, and a sense of anger with his family background and several events in his life, including his relationship with his mother, whom he describes as controlling and judgemental; the suicide of his disabled brother in 1956; and ongoing continued frustration with working in local government. Our impression is that in George's case, the political and economic context of his working life acted as a key driver in forming his values and leading to his engagement, but strong personal and emotional reasons were also evident.

The most overt relationships between philosophy of life and motive for engagement can be found in the accounts of George Tyler and Sarah Thomas, though they are specifically focused on their reasons for joining the MOP, rather than volunteering more generally. George Tyler saw MOP as:

> '*an opportunity to record alternative views and ideas on issues that the press and media so often distort, according to their political dogma…My opportunity to stir the pot*' (2010 *MOP Special Questionnaire*, aged 80)

Sarah Thomas explained that when she was young, her younger brothers received better education and training and opportunities than her. She married, aged 20, at the end of the Second World war (they lived in straitened circumstances, and her husband was a difficult, controlling man):

> '*Working class life was never easy, however hard we tried…When Mrs Thatcher called working miners 'the enemy within' I felt very hurt. I took part in the MO to tell the truth about working class people.*' (2010 *MOP Special Questionnaire*, aged 84)

Both writers express motives that relate to their philosophy of life. George's desire to '*stir*' resonates with his description of his 'bolshie' (in the non-political sense) attitudes to his employers throughout his work-life. Sarah's account is less antagonistic, but focused on the desire to record the '*truth about working-class people*'. Her preamble on gender also reflects pro-female views that infuse her other accounts, and perhaps may represent an additional implicit motive for writing for MOP. The views of both writers are very much in the spirit of the original Mass Observation, and subsequent ways of thinking about and recording history 'from below'. Other writers' reasons for joining the MOP are more clichéd, on the lines of wanting to leave something of themselves behind for 'posterity'.

Being asked

Musick and Wilson (2008) argue that 'being asked' is one of the most common reasons given for volunteering (pp 7, 269–73, 289–99); it 'influences whether or not we volunteer at all' (p 273), although not necessarily the initial frequency, intensity or level of that commitment. UK survey evidence on 'being asked' is thin. Only the 1991 NSV and the 2006–07 *Helping Out* survey have included a question on this; between 40–50 per cent of regular volunteers said that they had been asked.[2] This tells us that being asked can influence someone to decide to volunteer, but it does not prove that being asked is the reason why they agree to volunteer. This difficulty in interpretation is demonstrated in Catherine Neil's account of one of her first semi-autonomous decisions to take part in voluntary action – blood donation – which took place before she was legally old enough to give her consent (under 21):

> '*I was stopped in the street and asked to give blood. I had to ask Dad's permission for that. Happily he gave it and I eventually became a gold badge holder.*' (2010, *Belonging*, aged 72)

There is an inference that Catherine agreed to give blood because she was asked. However, this is unlikely to have been her sole motivation. Yet, she provides no further information about other recalled motivations. Given how long ago this was, perhaps she can only recall the process of being asked and subsequently negotiating agreement to take part.

Being asked to take part is described by several other MOP writers. It is very clear in Roger King's accounts, as when he was asked by senior executives to get involved:

> *'The Chairman was…President of the local Hospital League
> of Friends. When maladministration got them into financial
> difficulties he stepped in and I was asked if I'd become the Secretary
> to the Friends. Being new to the Company I knew it would do me
> no harm from a career point of view and for about 7 years, until I
> moved house and had a good reason to hand the job over I was very
> involved with an active League.'* (*Unpaid Work* (1996) aged 75)

Although Roger indicates that being asked represented the trigger, he
also saw the opportunities for career progression. He does not reveal
whether he felt he had a real choice, whether saying 'no' would have
been detrimental to his career, or whether he anticipated or received
any other benefits from this decision. But he does sound as if he was
happy to stop when a good enough reason – moving house – provided
by personal lifecourse events, came along. In contrast, Catherine
continued to give blood, which suggests that there was an additional
motive, or benefit, once she started this activity, which motivated her
to continue.

Roger's triggers for volunteering appear to have evolved over time.
Although he gives several examples of being asked to volunteer, he
also recalls, without wishing to sound '*bumptious*', an expectation from
others that he would take a leading role in new initiatives:

> *'people looked to me to take the lead. I was in a job which was of
> some significance compared with the majority of people involved.'*
> (*The 'Big Society'* (2012), aged 91)

He feels such requests were a recognition of his strong social and
professional capital and an expectation from those around that he
would step up to the plate.

Being asked can, however, also provoke negative responses. Catherine
Neil discusses agreeing to participate in an activity after being asked,
but refusing to take part on subsequent occasions. Both she and
David Gardiner describe being asked to collect donation envelopes
in their street and agreeing. They do not comment on any additional
motives, but describe finding the process so unpleasant because of
their neighbours' reluctance to donate, that they refused to repeat the
experience. Here, being asked a second time (and knowledge of what
was involved) represented the trigger for deciding to refuse to take
part. Catherine refers to her replacement collector as '*the other mug*'
(*Unpaid Work* (1996), aged 58). This evocative negative descriptor
suggests that Catherine feels stupid, manipulated or taken advantage of,

for having taken part. Dianne Roberts also found that street collection was unpleasant work.

> '*I got caught for this some years ago...and although I find it a nuisance to do, I haven't the heart to say I won't do it again.*' (*Unpaid Work* (1996), aged 53)

She goes on to describe how she is indeed unable to refuse a face-to-face request from a charity representative, when it is time to do the collection again.

Although Catherine Neil was able to decline repeated requests for assistance with charity collections, she found it impossible to refuse requests for the sustained unpaid work for her extended family during her retirement. She suggests, in effect, that this activity was not voluntary:

> '*My family is very demanding, more so since I retired. Apparently I am 'free' to change library books, hunt for bargains, entertain children, and provide free holidays.*' (2010 *MOP Special Questionnaire*, aged 72)

In several responses, she describes her early unhappy experience of retirement, where she moved from having a working identity to becoming a very reluctant informal carer to her grandchildren. Further on into retirement, she feels unable to say no:

> '*At any time, day or night I might get a call. 'Can you?' NO, I long to say, but never do.*' (*A Working Day* (2010), aged 72)

She sees these family demands as an intrusion on her time, and writes that she would prefer to be writing for MOP, or working on her allotment. She struggles to be heard: '*I can never get a word in with friends, family and can never get through*' (2010 *MOP Special Questionnaire*, aged 72), and feels overridden, not listened to by family members and constantly pressed into taking on caring roles. Although she is able to turn down requests for formal voluntary activity, she is unable to do this with family. The strength of her ties to family, perhaps a sense of obligation or duty, feeling she isn't listened to, and the sustained and established nature of her informal caring, all contribute to her reluctant agreement.

Finally, the accounts of some writers lead us to question how 'voluntary' and uncoerced their actions are. George Tyler describes being *'persuaded'* (*Unpaid Work* (1996)), to become a Scoutmaster for the Church troop, but subsequently uses the word *'coerced'* in 2010 (*Belonging*). Louise Masters describes being put forward for a voluntary role without being asked, when considering the directive question on whether she belongs to friendship groups, and whether she went to other people's houses:

> *'Again when I was secretary to the* [Inland Waterways] *club, I was made secretary without my knowing until we had a meeting, and then was told. I did it for 3 years, then packed up. Then again never* [went] *to anybody's house.'* (*Belonging* (2010), aged 73)

She provides no further details on this episode, nor do we learn whether she was pleased, flattered, appalled, willing or reluctant. The issue is about inability to decline. Like Catherine Neil, George Tyler and Diane Roberts, she could have said 'no', when she was told about being given the role. However, as these other writers indicate, this would have required a certain level of personal confidence, assertiveness and quick thinking.

Peer, family and spousal influences

Discouragement

Although Catherine Neil's writing shows that she was involved in various types of formal voluntary action in her early life, a change in her attitude towards formal volunteering took place at some point during the 1970s, when her children were growing up. Writing in her early 50s, she says: '*I consider joining things a juvenile occupation*' (*Membership of Voluntary Organisations* (1990), aged 52). She echoes this in her response to the 2012 *'Big Society'* directive, when she talks about her youngest child: '*like me she won't join anything*' (aged 74). We note that Catherine does not seem to see her involvement in MOP as 'joining', which might imply that she is referring to formal engagement with others, perhaps within a group/social context, whereas MOP writing constitutes a solitary activity. Catherine's comment sits uneasily with her earlier documented involvement in a youth group, drama group, playgroup and church group. However other references, such as her complaint that she '*can never get a word in with friends, family*' and her reference to the popularity of her younger sister (mentioned below) might indicate that Catherine's anti-social attitude relates to shyness/

introverted personality, and she has become more withdrawn at some point between her 30s and early 50s.

Catherine also hints at the negative influence of her husband:

> '*I haven't been physically prevented from joining anything, but my spouse has such a downer on good works, that it has rubbed off*' (Membership of Voluntary Organisations (1990), aged 52)

Here, Catherine conflates voluntary organisations (the theme of the directive) with good works (the 'dominant paradigm'). We know from her writing that she is not against the idea of doing good works. It would seem that Catherine and her husband have come to share an attitude of 'not joining in' with formal volunteering, and she describes how his negative attitude is shared by her (now adult) children: '*My husband would not give you his toe nail clippings. The children sadly take after him*' (Social Divisions (1990), aged 52).

Negative influences from spouses, family and peers are a recognised barrier to take-up of volunteering (Rotolo and Wilson, 2006). In this case, it seems that attrition is responsible for Catherine's change in attitude, after years of living with her husband and children. However, we have wondered whether Catherine is conflating charity and altruism with other types of voluntarism. In a later account Catherine questions her family's attitudes:

> '*My family insist they don't do anything for nothing. This is simply not true. They have done baby sitting and Red Cross duty and my husband has run the dart league for thirty years. He used to get an honorarium, but not now. Not even the phone.*' (Unpaid Work (1996), aged 58)

This suggests that Catherine's immediate family members' attitudes are complex and cannot be reduced to an outright refusal to take part in voluntary activity. There are some domains, such as informal help and serious leisure, and some roles, in which they will and do engage. As we know from survey data, there are actually very small numbers of adults who are not engaged in any way at all with voluntary activity.

Family needs

Spouses and family members can also have the effect of encouraging or influencing each other to volunteer. Survey questions that frame volunteering in terms of the influence of friends and family have revealed that at least 25–30 per cent of respondents said that their volunteering was 'connected with the needs of family or friends' (Table 6.1). Around one-fifth of respondents said that the reason they began volunteering was because 'family or friends did it'.

These questions are not synonymous. One references activities that meet needs in some way, while the other relates to how family connections or friendship groups draw people into volunteering. The former is referenced by MOP writers in several ways. A number of (primarily female) MOP writers with children describe *formally* volunteering: for their children's pre-schools in various roles; for their children's schools as parent-governors; or for the school PTA. In these contexts, the 'needs' of family could not be described as particularly pressing or demanding, but the parent is clearly supporting their child, indirectly. While these writers occasionally refer to the benefits of taking part, very few discuss their motives. An exception is Angela Goode who writes about motive and her involvement in all three of these roles. She became a Parent Governor:

> 'to ensure that my own children's education was of a high standard. I wanted a say in policy making, staff appointments & the state of the surroundings, but I'd known so many of the other children for so many years that I had an interest in their welfare too.' (Unpaid Work (1996), aged 43)

Here, the key motive seems to be the need to influence the quality of her children's education, so there is a degree of self-interest.

None of the MOP writers discuss formal volunteering because of a need created by a family member's disability or illness, but several discuss being involved in fundraising for charities, such as hospices, that became meaningful to them after the death of a friend or family member. This type of engagement may be picked up by questions in the 2006–07 *Helping Out* survey, and the later CS and CLS, where around two-fifths of volunteers said that they volunteered because 'the cause was really important to me'. However, the wording of the question is rather ambiguous, and we cannot infer the reason why a cause is important. Respondents may be referring to a vast range of causes, whether connected to their life experience or not, and individuals might contribute to them in very diverse ways.

MOP writers provide a clearer description of responding to the pressing need of friends and family through the provision of *informal care and help* (see Chapter Five) to ageing or ill parents, siblings, spouses, and to young grandchildren; some describe providing informal care to friends or neighbours. They say little about their motives except to hint at feelings of duty, obligation and love, and also having little choice as to whether to provide this care (Catherine Neil). Several MOP writers describe providing care in intense circumstances, to dying relatives, or to relatives who are profoundly dependent on care. Donna Payne (born 1952) attended very little school, and from the age of nine provided fulltime care to her mother and other family members, until her mother died in 1996. She writes about an extreme and abusive situation where she had no choice about providing care '*I really really felt very ill, & trapped. Life as a carer is not easy*' (*Unpaid Work* (1996), aged 44). Less extreme, but nevertheless demanding is the situation of June Foster who, with her retired husband, cared for seven grandchildren, including twin babies, after her daughter's husband was institutionalised following a car crash, so that her daughter could continue to work (*The 'Big Society'* (2012), aged 74). George Tyler, writing in his 80s, describes regularly supporting his wife and divorced son to care for his son's teenage twins, one of whom has a profound disability. Besides providing physical help, he and his wife support their son by being witnesses to the care that their son provides to his children, after unfounded allegations of abuse made by his son's ex-wife during an extremely acrimonious divorce and custody battle. The motive here combines family obligation, desire to help and protectiveness.

The 2011 Census found that in England and Wales there are more than 6 million unpaid carers providing care to '*an ill, frail or disabled family member or friend*' (ONS, 2017). There are continuing national debates about the duties and obligations of family carers and the increase in an ageing population. This type of informal care is usually not investigated by social surveys of voluntarism (Chapter Five), although it is often referred to by the MOP writers. They might feel that from the perspective of motive, they have no choice and thus care is not voluntary. Yet as male writer Stephen Johnson points out, his provision of full-time care for his partner could be interpreted as '*voluntary work, because I don't (and nor do I expect) to be paid for so doing*' (*The 'Big Society'* (2010), aged 70; see also Chapter Five).

Volunteering with family or friends

Several writers describe formal volunteering with their spouses; the majority describe joint involvement in church/religious organisation activities. These co-volunteers do not say anything about their motives for volunteering or explain why they do this with their spouses. Angela

Goode writes about her 'delight' when her husband asked to join her on a weekly Hare Krishna soup-run:

> '*He has always supported me in my ventures...but by going out onto the streets he has finally come to understand that immense satisfaction can be gained by putting a little effort in to a project.*' (*Unpaid Work* (1996), aged 43)

She emphasises the benefits they have received from this joint activity, rather than the reasons why her husband became involved. Conversely, Roger King, who has been a lifelong and prolific volunteer, states that his wife '*had no time to give to voluntary work*' before their retirement, but attributes this to '*Bringing up 4 children and having a part-time job as Administrator of the local Medical Institute.*' We note that Roger himself was able to undertake a succession of voluntary roles despite being in an executive position, since, in their domestic division of labour, his wife was entirely responsible for the children. However, on his retirement and their associated relocation to the south coast, '*we made the deliberate decision that we would have different activities so that we would meet different people and make life generally more interesting*' (*Unpaid Work* (1996), aged 75). Although this couple do not volunteer for the same activities, they have influenced each other by deciding that they should both volunteer, in part for social reasons ('*meeting different people*').

One can thus see a range of potential family influences, both positive and negative, which come together at key points in the lifecourse to provide triggers for voluntary action, such as retirement, or the needs of one's children. But this evidence also points to how individuals can in effect become trapped in domestic circumstances which either prevent or seriously inhibit engagement.

Motive and recall of anticipation of benefits

One of the barriers to identifying people's motives for volunteering (or not doing so) is inaccurate recall, which can result in respondents confusing retrospective views of the benefits accrued from volunteering with their original motives for taking part. Below we examine what MOP writers and survey respondents say about the benefits that volunteers have anticipated receiving when deciding whether to volunteer. We base our interpretations of MOP writing on a close reading of writers' accounts, and an understanding of their life context, to identify whether stated motives are founded on *anticipated* benefits prior to volunteering, or whether there has been muddling of anticipated and received benefits. We divide the actual or potential benefits into several categories: personal validation and self-esteem; therapy; career; and leisure.

The 1981 and 1991 NSVs, and the 2006–07 *Helping Out* survey, asked respondents to describe the benefits they receive from volunteering in relation to a number of pre-given categories. In most cases, the reasons given relate to the personal satisfaction which they derive from it: pure enjoyment, satisfaction from seeing the results, or a sense of personal achievement. Table 6.2 shows that at least four-fifths of respondents referred to one or more of these benefits.

Table 6.2: Main benefits reported by volunteers, 1981–2006 (%[1])

	1981[2]	1991	2006	2010–11
The satisfaction of seeing the results	50	93	97	63
I do it because I really enjoy it	51	93	96	60
I meet people and make friends through it	38	85	86	47
It gives me a sense of personal achievement	30	78	88	30
It's because I feel that so many people are less fortunate than I am	30			
It gets me 'out of myself'	26	65	69	12
I like to feel needed	25			11
It broadens my experience of life	25	75	82	27
It gives me a chance to do things I'm good at	23	69	83	25
It makes me feel less selfish as a person	22	62	72	21
It gives me a position in the community	8	29	37	

Notes:

[1] Figures are percentages of those who are active volunteers

[2] 1981 figures are lower because of restrictions on the number of boxes respondents could tick; in 1991, 2006 and 2010, respondents were able to list as many as seemed relevant to them.

Sources: 1981: NSV (Humble, 1982); 1991, 2006, 2010–11: authors' tabulations from NSV/Helping Out/ CS. 2015–16 CL data does not include data on satisfactions/benefits reported by volunteers.

Many of the MOP writers also talk about the benefits they receive from volunteering in these terms. However, it is rarer for MOP writers to anticipate such types of benefit and identify them as one of their motives for volunteering. One of the few that have done this is Derek Prior. He describes undertaking various types of rewarding voluntary work after retiring, but his given motives for teaching Adult Basic Education are the most redolent with anticipation of satisfaction:

*'I have always felt a very strong emotional thing about the freedom – indeed liberation that education can bring (*Educating Rita *brings me to tears every time I watch it) and wanted to do something in this area now that I have the time.' (Unpaid Work (1996), aged 67)*

His life-story is of coming from humble origins, qualifying as a librarian, becoming a mature student, then becoming a priest, but always slightly regretting not being a teacher. He appears to have strong personal experience and empathy for the power of education; and his motives for his volunteering in this domain are not simply satisfaction, but also because the cause is clearly important to him.

Personal validation, self-esteem and building social capital

Conscious ego-building

Respondents to the 1991 NSV and 2006–07 *Helping Out* surveys were shown a list of potential personal benefits associated with volunteering and asked to say how important these were to them (Low et al, 2007, 61–2). The list included a question on the social status associated with volunteering ('it gives me a position in the community'). Responses to these questions from regular volunteers suggest that some 30–40 per cent thought that this was important or very important. As such these benefits rank lower in the list than other response categories. What we cannot judge from this survey data is whether individuals avoid giving positive responses to these questions because they believe it to be inappropriate to reveal particular reasons for volunteering/continued volunteering – such as recognising the instrumental benefits for one's position in the community of being engaged in volunteering. There may be similar bias in MOP writing; we do not find many writers who discuss choosing to volunteer in order to improve their social status. Writers are guaranteed anonymity, but some still seem aware of how they might be perceived by their 'imagined audience' (Shaw, 1994), leading us to question whether some self-censoring takes place. However, Charles Wright does not seem to self-censor, and discusses volunteering and social status overtly, while acknowledging the retrospective nature of his recall:

'I have in the past served on various committees, mostly of trade organisations, and although I would not call that work exactly, attendance at some meetings meant my paying less attention to

more remunerative tasks Why I should have given up so much time to these is hard to explain in retrospect. Prestige, I suppose. To be proposed and elected to such committees, as well as serving two terms as President, was an honour at that time and was not deflating to my ego.' (Unpaid Work (1996), aged 74)

Here the motive suggested by the writer is his anticipation of increased self-esteem, prestige, and presumably an increase in social capital. Roger King discusses a complex mix of motives for his prolific volunteering. Although self-esteem and ego do not seem to be his primary motives, he demonstrates awareness of the social recognition he received from people because of his high-powered job. As discussed earlier in this chapter, he remarks that *'people looked to me to take the lead'* (*The 'Big Society'* (2012), aged 91), and there is an implicit sense that this recognition was not unwelcome. However, he does not discuss volunteering and social status as overtly as Charles Wright.

Subconscious ego-building

The issue of ego-building and self-esteem are difficult to identify unless a respondent discusses them openly and overtly. However, longitudinal qualitative data offers the opportunity to look for implicit or inferred ego-building motives, particularly where the respondent describes taking on a role requiring some form of responsibility, leadership, power or control. There appear to be two different potential implicit motives, the first being where the respondent may have relatively low social capital, or self-esteem, and is volunteering in order to increase this. For example, Catherine Neil began attending a youth club with her *'very pretty and popular little sister'* when she was 19, and subsequently became the treasurer of the club. She struggles to recall her motivation and suggests that this was more accident than choice:

'I don't quite know how it happened, but I soon found myself collecting the subs.' (Belonging (2010), aged 72)

Subsequently she reconsiders her involvement in the club:

'Looking back it was so informal. I don't recall a committee as such, but most of the members were 16 – my sister's age. I was 19 as were a couple of others. What were we doing playing with them?' (Belonging (2010))

The comparisons she makes between herself and her sister, who is the right age for the club and a popular attendee, might suggest that she took on this role to justify her presence/belonging, at the youth club, both to herself and other attendees.

Maria Dyer describes a difficult passage to adulthood, gaining just two 'O' Levels by the age of 18, and then being apprenticed as a hairdresser to a salon run by her domineering and controlling mother who would not allow her daughter to '*join any groups or clubs*' during her apprenticeship (*Doing a Job* (1997), aged 50). Maria lists her prolific volunteering history in her responses to the 1990, 1996 and 2012 directives. These read almost like lists of rebellion against her mother. If so, we might read her motive/trigger for volunteering as related to the acquisition of increased personal self-esteem and new personal values. However, there are other readings available. She describes experiencing '*post-natal depression (manic depression)*' after the birth of her son; recovering; returning to work; and in 1982 '*feeling I could do more*', leading to her taking up a volunteering role. This represents her recalled primary trigger or motive for her first experience of adult volunteering. She then discovered the therapeutic benefits of volunteering (see below) which provided a motive for her sustained involvement. After this she '*became a coordinator for three/four two week periods per year for about 7 years*' (*Unpaid Work* (1996), aged 49), and took on additional formal and informal voluntary work throughout her lifecourse. She has held several responsible, leadership roles, such as being a magistrate, a governor at a special needs school, chair of her son's school's PTA, deputy leader of a Morris Dancing group, and chair of her local history society. She does not discuss why she takes on such roles, but her other writings demonstrate a need to be in control of her life (while lacking such control in her relationship with her parents, her mental and physical health, and events such as the loss of her brother in a road accident). Control may represent a motive for this type of voluntary role. We also note that the formal titles for her volunteering roles seem important to her. When responding to the '*Your Life Line*' directive, which asked writers to '*mark up the key events of your life*', she records that at the age of 18 she gained a leadership role as '*acting captain for local girl guides*' (2008, aged 60). How many would recall a temporary role such as that over four decades later? As well as anticipating other benefits, our reading of Maria's accounts is that she chose and sustained voluntary leadership roles that would increase her pride, self-esteem and social capital. There are other MOP writers who, like Maria, seem to want or need leadership roles in their volunteering to increase and sustain their social status and self-esteem.

Strong self-esteem

Other MOP writers seem to have strong self-esteem, established strong social networks, and enjoy taking on voluntary leadership roles for different reasons. Roger King hints at this with his description of others looking to him to take the lead. Other writers, such as Angela Goode, describe enjoying building networks and taking the lead in different voluntary activities. Angela's first volunteering role, setting up and running a mother and toddler group, came about because:

> 'When I found myself at home with my new baby, I felt it would be an advantage to have contact with other mums, to swap anecdotes & problems & generally have some fun. There was no local Mother & Toddler Group running, so I approached the local community centre & started my own!' (Unpaid work (1996), aged 43)

The motive was social, but the benefits of this action seem to have been the development of her skills, personal growth and understanding of leadership. After this Angela took on other voluntary leadership roles:

> 'many local families supported my application to become a Parent Governor. I was more confident & articulate than many of them & they know I would represent their views. I was a very active governor, & once I'd learned the ropes played a prominent role in meetings & the life of the primary school – organising fund raising events, listening to reading groups, helping with outings etc.' (Unpaid work (1996), aged 43)

She moved on to roles at other schools and a further education college. This demonstrates a volunteering trajectory, where the first volunteering activity undertaken provided benefits that had not initially been anticipated, leading to enhanced self-confidence, new motives and additional volunteering. In Chapter Seven we examine this type of trajectory from a different perspective, identifying this writer and Roger King as serial volunteers.

Therapy

Shaw (1994, 1396) observes that 'There are clearly some disturbed people writing for the Archive (Mass Observation) as well as some very unhappy ones.' The relationship between writer and the archive/reader can resemble that of patient and analyst, with writers providing 'painful and intimate' details of their lives. Some MOP writers used in this study have described traumatic events, such as: bullying at school; failure in exams; the deaths of siblings, friends and parents; emotional and physical neglect or abuse by parents; sexual assaults; and abusive marriages. Some also describe experiences of anxiety and depression as adults. Not many of these writers discuss the role that MOP has had in helping them to deal with their experience of trauma; and the potential therapeutic benefits of writing for MOP have been considered by a very small proportion (this would be the protective function within the functional analysis of volunteering discussed in Chapter One). Catherine Neil acknowledges a therapeutic motive in her response to the 2010 *MOP Special Questionnaire*; she and her mother had regularly exchanged letters and, after her mother died, she heard about the MOP on the radio:

> '*I missed writing long letters, and so just changed the recipient. I am also a "people watcher".*' (2010 *MOP Special Questionnaire*, aged 72)

Being an observer of others and a desire to write are important, but the key motive seems to have been grief, and the desire to transfer her writing relationship with her mother to the MOP.

Two other writers, Alice Dickens and Beverley Scott, both of whom have had problems with mental health at some point in their lives, describe joining the MOP for therapeutic reasons. Alice began writing for the MOP:

> '*in the throes of post-natal depression, to prove to myself that I could still write a coherent sentence…It was the trigger that set me on the freelance path which developed into a staff post…I realised it could be a safety valve on occasions. Directives on families & the NHS were particular examples.*' (2010 *MOP Special Questionnaire*, aged 68)

Her primary motive for joining the MOP was therapeutic. She continued her involvement in the project because she recognised the therapeutic benefits that writing afforded her mental health and recovery from post-natal depression. She also found that writing for the MOP enabled her to resume her career in journalism.

Beverley's motives for joining the MOP were similar to those of Alice Dickens. She resigned from her job as a teacher after experiencing a mental health breakdown. She joined the MOP in 1983, three months after leaving work. She describes her experience of claiming benefits at a time of high unemployment, applying for jobs through the Manpower Services Commission, and seeing the MOP as a route back into employment:

> '*I needed something to challenge me mentally. This whole scheme which I am writing for, for the first time has helped me enormously to formulate my thoughts, organize myself, to see if I can write logically and still be interesting as well. This was my first real "test" and I am so pleased to have been chosen to write for the scheme.*' (*Work* (1983), aged 26)

Like Alice Dickens, Beverley used MOP as a route out of her mental health crisis. Her subsequent volunteering behaviour has been less prolific than many other writers. She describes three episodes of volunteering: one was a very brief experience (two attendances) after she retired; the other two took place during her working life when she was trying to decide whether she wanted to change career. However, Beverley has continued to contribute to the MOP for the last 34 years (at the time of writing) and is a frequent and prolific writer.

Maria Dyer (see above) also experienced post-natal depression after the birth of her son (and death of her brother). She first decided to volunteer after she had recovered from her depression, when her son was aged about three:

> '*I felt settled and fully recovered from a break down post-natal. I'd gone back to lecturing (part-time) and felt I could do more.*' (*Unpaid Work* (1996), aged 49)

The motive of feeling she '*could do more*' is rather vague and might relate to values/altruism, but may also relate to the notion of 'having time'. She then discovered the therapeutic benefits of volunteering:

> '*I've found I like to help others…when I went to help others I forget about my problems and the more I helped others the better I felt.*' (*Unpaid Work* (1996), aged 49)

The anticipation of these benefits of volunteering then became a key reason for her volunteering, and like Alice Dickens, Maria went on to become a prolific volunteer. However, as we have suggested above, her motivation for choice of specific volunteering roles seems to have been driven by different needs, related to social status and control.

Caroline Lawson, who is disabled by ME, describes volunteering for a Women's Centre for a few months when she first became ill, but stopping because she found the work too stressful and tiring. She had been attending an ME support group, felt she gained a lot from it, and proceeded to volunteer as a committee member and editor of the group newsletter for several years, before reducing her commitment. She provides multiple motives for this volunteering: altruism, using skills, having time, feeling useful, meeting others.

> '*I wanted to help other sufferers in the ways I'd been helped when I first joined the group, and I wanted to eradicate the feelings of "worthlessness" which I've experienced since becoming ill. I also wanted a little project with which to occupy my time when I wasn't asleep or resting in bed...*
>
> *While doing this "work", I used many of the skills I'd acquired + which would have been put to use were I able to practise as a solicitor. That was a very important motivation for me. I felt (still feel) that I have a great deal to offer despite the limitations of my illness.*
>
> *The flexibility of voluntarily work appealed to me when I was thinking of ways to occupy my "well" hours. Also, the prospect of meeting people and getting out of the house.'* (Unpaid Work (1996), aged 31)

The chosen domain, the ME support group, and particularly the strong emotional language used ('*I wanted to eradicate the feelings of "worthlessness"*') suggest, however, that therapeutic motives were the most prominent drivers. Caroline's query as to whether she can call this volunteering because '*I'm still operating within a group which directly benefits me*' shows a consideration of the boundaries between therapy and voluntarism, and the relationship between volunteering and mutual benefit.

Career

The conceptualisation of volunteer motives as being centred on personal benefit sits uneasily with the 'dominant paradigm' (Rochester et al, 2010) which constructs altruism as the primary motive for volunteering. However, both MOP and survey respondents have identified motives which are not altruistic, but provide mutual benefit to the volunteer and beneficiary. As we have already noted, Roger King realised that agreeing, when asked by his firm, to volunteer for the Hospital League of Friends, *'would not harm his career'*, and Alice Dickens recognised that her MOP writing enabled her to regain confidence in her capacity to do journalism. In these examples, there were additional motives for taking part. Beverley Scott, however, described career as being her primary motive for her two experiences of consistent volunteering:

> '*In the past I have done voluntary work more – usually when I was thinking about changing jobs and wanted experience…to see if I liked it. To that end I did Adult Basic Education…I went to an evening training course (6–8 weeks) and subsequently did ABE for about 6 months, then gave up. It was fine but wasn't what I was wanting, and I didn't see any suitable job opportunities arising from it, so I felt I'd given them back their time training me by doing ABE for the 6 months, and gave it up with no guilt, no regrets.*' (*Unpaid Work* (1996), aged 39)

She also considered a career in occupational therapy, and found a volunteer placement at a long stay psychiatric hospital, working with a patient for a couple of hours, once a week. Beverley's description of motive, relationship with the voluntary organisation with whom she was volunteering, and the mutual benefits of the relationship sound contractual; there is no evidence of altruism or the dominant paradigm in this account.

Beverley's forays into testing out other potential careers took place in the late 1980s and early 1990s. Although her account shows a personal lack of altruism in motive, these types of contractual volunteering agreements – exchanging training for tuition – do have altruism at the heart of the agreements, in that they provide clear benefits to others. The situation in the late 2010s is somewhat different. Individuals have had little choice but to accept unpaid work, including internships, on whatever terms are offered, sometimes on pain of loss of welfare benefits, with no expectation or guarantee that such work will lead anywhere. Such 'volunteering' comes with a range of ethical and moral concerns about exploitation of those doing the 'volunteering' (see Leonard et al, 2016).

Leisure

Various MOP writers also report volunteering for 'serious leisure' (Stebbins, 1996) activities. Arguably, the primary beneficiaries, for some of these activities, are solely those taking part in them (and fellow club members). For example, Jim Banks describes becoming the secretary for his cricket team and golf club. Some of the other activities mentioned by our writers, such as local history societies, museums, choirs, or dog-training organisations have cultural and/or educational value, so that benefit extends beyond direct participants. The primary motive for those undertaking 'serious leisure' volunteering seems to be a strong interest in the sport or cultural activity for which they are volunteering. Additional motives are also evident: for example, Jim Banks indicates a desire for control and management:

> '*I have always felt the urge, if that is the term, to get involved in the management of any organisation I have joined or have taken an interest in, and strangely enough I have found others on various committees have the same outlook.*' (*Unpaid Work* (1996), aged 70)

Perhaps he is recreating elements of his role in his professional life, seeking out like-minded individuals sharing attitudinal and behavioural dispositions. Few writers mention additional social motives, but it is our feeling that these may also represent motives for those taking part in 'serious leisure' volunteering. Equally, if there is a perception that serious leisure and social motivations go hand in hand, we note that this does not work for everyone. An example is Stephen Johnson, who volunteered for the committee of a local art group, once he felt that he was '*accepted as part of the group*'. But he also realized that once engaged at a certain level, '*you have to open up and let people into your life, which I've discovered over the years is something that I want to do with only carefully selected people*' (*Belonging* (2010), aged 68). As a result, he reduced his involvement with the group. He describes his reticence with others as partly learnt as a child, when his mother's illness meant that he was unable to bring friends back to the family home. But his reticence may also relate to his feeling, as an older man in a publicly-undisclosed same-sex relationship, of not fitting or belonging within a very heterosexual world.

Social need, personality and belonging

Between 25 and 30 per cent of volunteers responding to a range of social surveys (see Table 6.1), stated that they volunteered because they wanted to meet people and make friends. Over recent years there has been growing public concern about greater social isolation and fragmentation, but the proportion of people citing social motives for volunteering has remained consistent. Given the survey results, we were surprised that very few of the MOP writers describe volunteering because they wanted to meet others. Having said that, the directives did not specifically ask the respondents whether their volunteering had a social context, so we cannot rule out the possibility that their motives encompassed social reasons. We might speculate whether MOP writers are less sociable than the representative UK population, and whether there is something specific about the act of writing that attracts more solitary people to the MOP, but we are not able to form subjective impressions of writers' personalities from their writing. We are reliant on them telling us, very specifically, about their personalities, and their levels of sociability – such as the older Catherine Neil saying she is not a joiner of things – through their own accounts.

Helen Cook is the only writer who describes herself as gregarious, she also says that she is quick to make friends, has a strong personality, and is frank and outspoken. Social motives are important for her; she has sought volunteering domains and roles that bring her into contact with other people: '*I like being part of the community, I need to be with others, this suits me well*' (*Unpaid Work* (1996), aged 73). In contrast Pauline Bennett (see above) describes herself as:

> '*someone always on the outside looking in. I'm a behind-the-scenes sort of person and took naturally to journalism – on the features rather than news side.*' (*Belonging* (2010), aged 69)

She welcomes, however, the sense of being involved in the community that she derives from volunteering. Pauline describes moving house and area several times, and engaging in a series of serious leisure activities with her husband, such as editing local free newsletters and newspapers, that fit her skills and social needs, and welcoming the feeling of being part of the community (*Unpaid Work* (1996), aged 55). Likewise, Roger King describes he and his wife jointly deciding to do separate volunteering so that '*we would meet different people and make life generally more interesting*' (*Unpaid Work* (1996), aged 75). But he also describes avoiding roles that involve selling and persuading, and admits that he is '*not a gregarious person*' (*A Working Day* (2010), aged 88).

> '*I have always thought of myself as a "loner". I am sure I am. I have never felt lonely – if I ever did it is something that I have grown out of. Even in a group I have often felt people looked upon me as someone separate.*' (*Belonging* (2010), aged 89)

Around one half of our writers, when responding to the *Belonging* directive, described themselves as 'outsiders', with some attributing this to their personalities, but others, such as Stephen Johnson, referenced their personal life context or circumstances. The differences between Helen Cook, Pauline Bennett and Roger King are interesting. Social motives for volunteering are important to all three: their personalities do not have an impact on why they decide to volunteer, but they do seem to have an impact on the reasons why those individuals choose certain domains and roles. Moreover, although Pauline Bennett and Roger King are less gregarious and outgoing than Helen Cook, feelings of belonging are important to all three. Perceiving social motives for volunteering as 'wanting to meet or make friends with people', is therefore too simplistic. The broader, functional analysis description of social motives – wanting to integrate with social groups and communities – is more informative (Clary et al, 1996).

Conclusion: volunteering motives and the lifecourse

We have discussed some of the influences, triggers, desires and needs that result in people's volunteering, such as: parental role-modelling and guidance; childhood volunteering; value systems; being asked; the need for therapeutic activities, leisure, and career advancement; and the need to belong. We have also discussed some of the negative influences and triggers that can result in what is perceived as coerced volunteering, people refusing to take part or becoming disillusioned in their volunteering. These influences, triggers, desires and anticipated needs occur throughout the lifecourse, and are contingent on life events. They do not exist in isolation, but converge to provide multiple and complex explanations as to why an individual decides to volunteer, and why they choose a particular type of volunteering and role. The accounts on which we draw illustrate how complex volunteering motives can be.

This chapter has also identified, however, that often volunteers are not consciously aware of some of their motives, and were we to classify them, they may or may not agree with our interpretation. Some seem clear enough – such as the psychological benefits identified by Hustinx et al (2010) and which are stressed by one writer who welcomed the social status conferred by volunteer roles (*'not deflating to my ego'*). Considering accounts of possible motivations summarised in the introduction (such as the VFI) we find elements of several of these – personal growth and understanding; career enhancement; social motives; protective influences (the therapeutic benefits of volunteering); and personal values. While there are strong resonances here, we have not sought to assign the MOP responses to one category or another.

Given the longitudinal nature of the evidence, when we began our study of volunteering, we had intended to place motivation into specific synchronic, political and social and economic policy eras. We were surprised as to how infrequently MOP writers referenced contemporaneous political policies and events in relation to their volunteering. This may be because of the nature of the available MOP material on motive. Only two directives provided strong evidence of motive at two time-points. However, our view is that MOP writing on reasons for volunteering demonstrates that for most people, motives are personal and relate to their individual life-events and lifecourses.

One of the key things we note about motive from this evidence is that motivation encompasses triggers, attitudes, influences and more instrumental events. One can easily sympathise with Leat's (1983, 52) observation, that discussions of motive become bogged down in 'esoteric speculation about "real" and "underlying" motives, and sooner or later end up in the lap of the psychoanalysts'. Although it is useful to interrogate the issue of motive, we also agree with Leat in suggesting that it may be more helpful to reframe the question. This chapter has argued that an individual's choice of domain, role, and form of volunteering is contingent on personal circumstances, skills, values, identity and personality. Focusing on *when* in their lifecourse people volunteer, and *how* the roles and domains in which they choose to volunteer fit their life circumstances, skills and personality may offer more insight for both academic and practitioner purposes. We continue this argument in the following chapter on trajectories of volunteering.

Notes

[a] Margaret Thatcher, speech to the Women's Royal Voluntary Service National Conference ('Facing the new challenge'), 19 January 1981, www.margaretthatcher. org/document/104551

[b] Some surveys also ask respondents what they would do if they were asked to volunteer, but this is a more hypothetical question and one obviously prone to individuals giving socially-desirable responses.

SEVEN

Volunteering trajectories: individual patterns of volunteering over the lifecourse

Introduction

When recent British governments have attempted to promote volunteering, there has been a tendency to issue general exhortations, focus on specific groups believed to be underrepresented, or target attention on disadvantaged areas, rather than focusing on *how* and *when* people volunteer (Chapter Two). In this chapter, which considers volunteering behaviour *over time*, we argue for a deeper understanding of the volunteering trajectories taken by individuals across their lifecourse, relating these to individual and household characteristics, and key trigger points in the lives of the respondents. The insights from this may be of value to those who seek to increase levels of voluntary action.

Using longitudinal approaches may also provide a different perspective on underlying rates of engagement in voluntary action. Analyses of volunteering often use cross-sectional surveys – snapshots of evidence at specific points in time. Survey participants are identified as having volunteered if they answer affirmatively to a question usually framed within a reference period (4 weeks, 12 months). However, someone who has volunteered extensively outside of the given timeframe might not be identified as a volunteer. This has led analysts of some cross-sectional surveys, such as Low et al (2007), to identify those who have taken part in volunteering in the past, but not in the previous 12 months and to describe these participants as 'ex-volunteers' (pp 11–12). Are they truly 'ex'-volunteers – people who no longer volunteer? Or are they simply people who happen not to have done any voluntary activity in the 12-month reference period? If these people were surveyed repeatedly over a long timeframe then we would identify many people who, while not volunteering every year, do so from time to time. The 'true' rate of volunteering may thus be higher than is suggested by cross-sectional surveys. To answer these questions we need longitudinal understandings of patterns of volunteering across individual lifecourses (Musick and Wilson, 2008, 221–3).

There has been no single longitudinal quantitative study of patterns of volunteering that is representative of the UK population across the whole of 1981 to 2012 timeframe. The British Household Panel Survey (BHPS) began in 1991 and first asked about 'unpaid voluntary work' in 1996; the survey questions were carried forward into the significantly-expanded Understanding Society (US) survey from 2011. Quantitative work using these sources has highlighted the stability in volunteering rates in the BHPS/US panel, with typically between 18 and 22 per cent of adult respondents indicating that they do unpaid voluntary work as part of their leisure activities (Chapter Four). The study has been used in significant analyses which have explored connections between volunteering and various aspects of health, wellbeing, employability and return to volunteering. These have operationalised regression models which explore the independent effects of changes in volunteering status (for example, a transition from being a non-volunteer at one wave of the study to being a volunteer at the next wave) on a social outcome, such as mental health (Binder and Freytag, 2013; Ellis Paine et al., 2013; Sauer, 2015; Tabassum et al, 2016). We use the data in a more descriptive way here, focusing simply on measurement of volunteering in a lifecourse perspective, and assessing the degree of transitions in volunteering within individuals over the time-period in question. The questions being analysed are straightforward: did individuals carry out unpaid voluntary work? And if so, how many times did they report it, and what was the pattern of their moves into and out of voluntarism over time?

Our longitudinal qualitative approach also provides useful insights into the potential fluidity of volunteering patterns across time (hinted at in Low et al's (2007) conceptualisation of 'ex-volunteers'). Qualitative studies of individual volunteering patterns over the lifecourse (Sherrott, 1983; Davis-Smith and Gay, 2005; Brodie et al, 2011; Hogg, 2016) all provide some detail on trajectories. However, these are heavily dependent on individual recall at the time of interview. While analysing MOP writers' accounts we have found that recall of past voluntarism is dependent on the questions being asked and the mindset of the writer at that time. Writers do not always give comprehensive accounts of their engagement at one sitting. Unlike interviews undertaken at one timepoint, MOP writing also offers accounts of contemporaneous engagement over several time-points, enabling us to identify change and continuity in the volunteering being undertaken by individual writers, and providing insights on how they felt at the time they were volunteering.

In this chapter, we present our mixed-methods findings relating to *individual* volunteering patterns across the lifecourse. We first explore the length, frequency and intensity of voluntary engagement, investigate when in their lifecourses people volunteer, and then move on to examine how their volunteering behaviour changes or continues over time, using panel data for the period 1996–2011. In the next section we use the Mass Observation Project (MOP) data to explore the shape of people's volunteering trajectories, describing the various patterns of stopping and starting engagement among our writers. The remainder of the chapter contains a discussion of the importance of life-events as triggers for routes into and out of volunteering, looking specifically at the conceptualisation of volunteering as work or leisure when considering triggers for stopping and starting, the influence of free time and capacity, and examples of routes in and out of volunteering.

Quantitative evidence

We have described our data sources more fully in Chapters One and Three, but to recap, the BHPS has questions on volunteering behaviour on alternate years from 1996, offering 'doing unpaid voluntary work' as one of over a dozen possible responses to a question about what people do in their *leisure* time. Our analysis considers responses to eight sets of volunteering questions (8 time-points) within the timeframe 1996–2011 (2011 being the first year of US).

We constructed a sample of respondents from the BHPS/US comprising individuals who had responded in each wave of the survey to questions on volunteering behaviour, and who had reported volunteering at least once between 1996 and 2008. The first finding to emerge is that while in any *one* wave of the BHPS we identify around 20 per cent of respondents who say that they have done some volunteering, some 40 per cent of respondents have volunteered at least once in this 15-year period (Geyne Rajme and Smith, 2011). This suggests that, if measured in a lifetime context, a much higher proportion of the population has been a volunteer at some stage than is revealed by cross-sectional studies. An obvious conclusion is that the 'true' proportion of volunteers in the population is somewhat higher than previously acknowledged. A practical implication is to learn from volunteers about what would facilitate more continuous involvement, and about the circumstances which have led to them ceasing to engage.

We can unpack this quantitative picture a little by considering transitions in volunteering status between waves of the survey, and individual trajectories through it. First, there is a very small group (some 3 per cent of those who provide a clear answer to the question about unpaid work at every wave of the survey) of individuals who continuously volunteer through the 1996–2011 timeframe. We then look at transitions between pairs of waves of the study (for example, between 1996 and 1998). There is underlying stability in non-engagement: over 90 per cent of those individuals who do not report unpaid voluntary work at one wave of the survey also do so at the next (Table 7.1). Turning to volunteers, we first find that only a small proportion (less than 10 per cent) of those who are not volunteering at one wave will report that they are doing so at the next wave. For those who say that they are engaged in volunteering at one point in time, between 58 and 66 per cent will report that they are volunteering at the next wave of the survey. Thus, if 20 per cent of respondents say that they are volunteering at one wave, then between 11.6 and 13.2 per cent will volunteer at the next wave (Table 7.1). It also follows that around two-fifths of volunteers report that they *stop* volunteering over each of the two-year intervals at which this question is asked. The exception to this is the transition between the BHPS and US, where the pattern of responses may suggest a need for further work, but does not, we argue, undermine the inclusion of this cell in the table.[1]

Table 7.1: Transition matrices for volunteers, 1996–2011

		1998				2000				2002	
		Yes	No			Yes	No			Yes	No
1996	Yes	58	42	1998	Yes	65	35	2000	Yes	65	35
	No	8	92		No	8	92		No	9	91
		2004				2006				2008	
		Yes	No			Yes	No			Yes	No
2002	Yes	64	36	2004	Yes	66	34	2006	Yes	64	36
	No	8	92		No	8	92		No	14	86
		2011	
		Yes	No
2008	Yes	52	48
	No	10	90

Note: based on 3203 BHPS panel members in England who responded to the volunteering question in every one of the seven waves in which it was asked, as well as in wave 2 of *Understanding Society*. The cells show the percentages answering that they did (or did not) volunteer at time period t, crosstabulated against those for time period t + 1. Thus, of those who said they volunteered in 1996, 58% also said they volunteering in 1998, but 42% did not.

Source: Authors' calculations from BHPS/US.

The proportion (up to two-fifths of respondents) who volunteer at one time-point moving to a 'non-volunteering' status when they are next surveyed may seem high. It is possible, though we have not tested it in the context of this work, that the very general question used about unpaid voluntary work, and its placement in a suite of questions about leisure, means that people are less easily able to recall instances of volunteering. Second, these findings may suggest that once an individual is on a particular trajectory, they are more likely to remain on it. We also found that few individuals transition from non-volunteering to volunteering between one wave of the survey and the next. Does this suggest that there is a division between a long-term volunteering 'core' and a broader population which has intermittent engagement with volunteering? The final point to make is that, as with other studies of volunteering, the groups who are most likely to stick with volunteering are those members of society with the greatest resources. Other related work on individual volunteering trajectories, and on the frequencies with which individuals reported volunteering in the BHPS (Geyne Rajme and Smith, 2011) provides clear evidence of socioeconomic gradients in the likelihood that individuals report volunteering two or more times over the same period of the BHPS.

We sought further insight using sequence analysis (optimal matching) to understand the evolution of individuals' volunteering behaviour over time. For these purposes, we selected responses to the question on 'doing unpaid voluntary work' as a *leisure* activity. We defined a volunteer as someone who responded as doing unpaid work several times a year, or more regularly. This does not include people who stated they volunteered once a year, or less frequently, so is a more restrictive definition than used in Table 7.1, covering a smaller number of respondents. Sensitivity analysis of dissimilarity matrices was undertaken to check the consistency of the optimal matching process, and repeated with groups of individuals of different age ranges to explore whether the findings were consistent over different age ranges (this is similar to the approach taken by the Pensions Policy Institute, 2017). This was followed by hierarchical clustering to extract general patterns of individual movement in and out of volunteering over time.

The optimal partitioning of the sample identified two broad patterns of behaviour: those who volunteered occasionally, whom we have described as short-term volunteers; and those who volunteered continuously over several years within this timeframe, whom we have described as long-term volunteers. The former group includes those BHPS/US participants who reported volunteering four times or fewer between 1996 and 2011, and who usually did so discontinuously

(1,525 respondents). The mean (sd) number of times that an individual in this group reported volunteering was 2 (1.2) out of a potential 8 time-points (see Figure 7.1). This figure is a graphical representation of individual trajectories, grouped together. Thus, in the top left-hand corner of the diagram, there is a grouping of respondents who do not volunteer at all initially, but then (proceeding from top to bottom) do so in the last wave, or in the penultimate wave, both of the last two waves, and so on. Conversely, and reading up from the bottom of the diagram, there are individuals who volunteer consecutively in several waves, but cease to do so thereafter.

Of the 2,151 BHPS/US participants in this analysis who reported volunteering at least several times a year on at least one wave of the survey between 1996 and 2011, we consider 71 per cent (n=1525) to be short-term volunteers. Short-term volunteering thus makes up the largest proportion of BHPS/US volunteering activity – though note that the largest single group, not represented in these diagrams, is those who never volunteered on any occasion (which accounted for around three-fifths of BHPS panel members). However, in terms of frequency and intensity of volunteering, this high proportion of short-term volunteers contributed less than half of the episodes of volunteering activity (46 per cent) undertaken by BHPS/US participants in this timeframe. The greater contribution came from a smaller proportion

Figure 7.1: Sample of short-term volunteers' trajectories of volunteering, 1996–2011

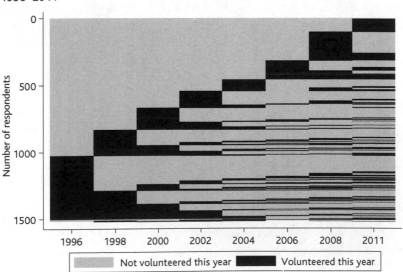

of long-term volunteers. The short-term volunteers whom we have identified have strong similarities with the general British population, and little in common with the demographic characteristics of long-term volunteers (see Chapter Three), who are more likely to be women, and over the age of 50.

Figure 7.2 Sample of long-term volunteers' trajectories of volunteering

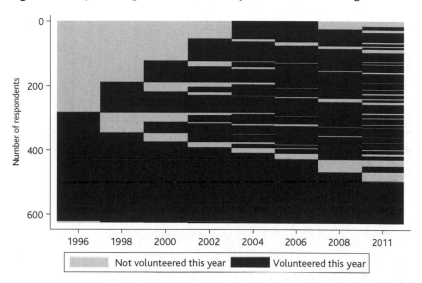

Hierarchical clustering identified a group of BHPS/US respondents who had taken part in formal volunteering *several times a year or more*, for a large proportion of the 15-year timeframe (1996–2011).These 626 individuals accounted for 29 per cent of the 2,151 individuals who were included in this analysis. They reported volunteering on average 5.9 (sd = 1.6) out of a potential 8 time-points. As can be seen the majority of trajectories suggest a strong and consistent engagement over time. At the bottom of the diagram, around 100 respondents volunteered at every single wave of the survey. The 626 long-term volunteers included in this group contributed 54 per cent of the episodes of volunteering activity (defined as the proportion of people who reported undertaking voluntary activity) across this timeframe. This implies that *slightly less than one-third* of the longitudinal BHPS/US sample of volunteers contributed *over half* of the total episodes of voluntary activity (we cannot quantify the amount of time contributed since that was not investigated) reported by survey respondents. This resonates with the notion of a civic core, flagged by Mohan and Bulloch (2012; see also Chapter Five above, pp 87-90), not least in terms of the socioeconomic makeup of the long-term volunteers, which is skewed towards the better-off, middle-class sections of society.

Although only available for a relatively limited number of years, this data has considerable advantages. First of all, it suggests strongly that 'true' levels of engagement are underestimated. Second, it illuminates not just cross-sectional (synchronic) variation, but also variation over time for individuals. Third, it points to socioeconomic gradients in the depth of involvement over time. We turn now to the qualitative picture on volunteering trajectories over the lifecourse.

The shape of writers' trajectories

Survey data, whether longitudinal or cross-sectional, cannot provide depth insights into volunteering behaviour, or examine the dynamic relationship between volunteering and the lifecourse, such as, for example, explaining the transitions noted in the longitudinal BHPS data. Our 38 MOP writers, whose demographic characteristics broadly reflect those of long-term volunteers within the BHPS sample (see Chapter Three and the Appendix), and whom we see as long-term volunteers or 'stayers' because of their long-term commitment to the MOP, do provide these kinds of insights through their contemporary and retrospective accounts of their different volunteering behaviours. In Chapters Five and Six we have described the different types of volunteering they undertake and the motivations and barriers associated with their volunteering. In this chapter, we focus on their volunteering trajectories, not just across the timeframe during which these individuals were writing (1981–2012), but across the whole of their lifecourses. To enable this, we drew on key MOP directives that deal specifically with volunteering: *Membership of Voluntary Organisations* (1990), *Unpaid Work* (1996), *Being Part of Research* (2004), and *The 'Big Society'* (2012). We also, however, utilised the other MOP directives outlined in Chapters One and Three, drawing on writers' contemporary and retrospective discussion of personal events and life-experiences to construct personal, volunteering and employment biographies for each writer in our sample. This enabled us to map each writer's movement in and out of paid work and volunteering across time, alongside personal life events, observing how changes and continuities in patterns of engagement were situated alongside different lifecourse events.

First, we discuss the distinctive longitudinal shapes of individual writers' volunteering trajectories, which have led us to postulate a typology for volunteering patterns across the lifecourse. Second, we discuss how writers have entered and exited volunteering at specific points in their lives. The identification of key times, or life-events, at which people transition in and out of volunteering, represents an insight that is not available from other sources and throws novel light on the commencement, continuation and cessation of voluntary action.

Our sample of volunteer MOP writers are all serial-responders to MOP directives. However, not all writers would perceive their contribution to the MOP, and other activities that they carry out without pay, as volunteering. Although some of our writers might disagree with our interpretation, from a research perspective we view these writers as having engaged in voluntary action. With two exceptions, all of our selected MOP writers have been involved in other volunteering acts throughout their adult lifecourses.[2] The distinctive shape of their trajectories in, out, and through their volunteering is described below. With such a small number of respondents, claims to authoritative taxonomy are limited, but the trajectory shapes suggested, seem, to us, to make intuitive sense.

Stickers: continuous committed volunteers

We identified eight writers (representing just over one-fifth of the sample) who provided *continuous* voluntary commitment to one or more organisations or individuals (in addition to their commitment to the MOP), in formal and/or informal caring capacities. These writers fit Davis-Smith and Gay's (2005) taxonomy of 'constant volunteers'. For some writers, this additional long-term activity involved a complex and evolving relationship between the volunteer and the beneficiary. Female writer, Dianne Roberts (born 1943), a home-maker who had formerly been a book-keeper, provided informal help and care to neighbours throughout her adult lifecourse. From 1976, when her son was small, she volunteered as a library home-visitor delivering books to housebound beneficiaries until her husband, a manager in an engineering business, took early retirement in 2000. Writing about her unpaid work in 1996, she states:

> 'There have been times when I've found it very difficult to fit it in to my week and have wished I could get out of it, but once committed to something I will always see it through.' (*Unpaid Work* (1996), aged 53)

Over the 24 years in which she volunteered, her relationship with her clients, all elderly widows, grew beyond the supply of library books to friendship, and the provision of informal support, such as companionship, phone-calls and shopping. Dianne describes herself as a solitary person, who does not like the company of others, is conservative in her lifestyle and attitudes, and is someone who does not embrace change. This type of personality may be likely to stick with a cause once they have committed to it initially.

Natural switchers: long-term volunteers who move between causes or organisations

Social surveys can measure some longitudinal aspects of voluntary action, but cannot measure movement between volunteering opportunities. Thus, they cannot identify what Musick and Wilson (2008) describe as individuals who 'pursue a "career" in volunteering, moving from one volunteer opportunity to another' (p 224). Having identified people who volunteer continuously for one organisation or beneficiary, we also looked for other types of long-term volunteering behaviours. We did not find evidence of short-term hopping from one volunteering opportunity to another, but we did identify individuals who committed several years to volunteering for an organisation or beneficiary, then moved on. An example is Roger King (see biographical synopsis in Chapter Six) who, in his response to the *Unpaid Work* directive in 1996, aged 75 and still an active *formal* volunteer, stated:

> '*As with most of my activities I have moved on after a time. Looking back I can see that even my working life has been like that. Not that I get bored; it just seems that something else might be more interesting and I dislike routine.*'

In his working-life he had held professional senior managerial positions and was still volunteering when writing for the MOP as a 91-year-old in 2012. His voluntarism included a mix of one-off actions (for example, irregular street-collections), and longer-term commitments, such as being the treasurer of a charity assisting a poor, overseas community. He described his routes into different volunteering activities as 'being asked' by individuals with whom he had both weak social ties (line-managers at work and church members) and strong social ties (members of his extended family) (Granovetter, 1973; 1983). Later, when retired, he also self-selected various voluntary activities. While some of his one-off and long-term volunteering activities were of a consecutive nature, others were undertaken simultaneously. All could be characterised as formal volunteering.

Female writer, Pauline Bennett (born 1941) worked full-time and part-time throughout her life, married three times, and described regularly changing employment, place of residence and *formal* volunteering activities. Her volunteering began when she started writing for the MOP, as a mature student in her late 30s. Subsequently she also started, stopped, and/or continued, a variety of other types of volunteering, mostly in committee and administration roles. Her routes into and out of these activities were self-selected and linked to other lifecourse events and changes. For example, in the mid-1990s she described volunteering, with her husband, to work on a local free newspaper after a house move, stating '*It has helped us to get known in a new area and there's a great feeling of being involved on the community*' (*Unpaid Work* (1996), aged 55). Like Roger King, some of her long-term volunteering activities were of a consecutive nature, and others were undertaken concurrently.

We have identified ten MOP writers (just over a quarter of our sample), who were long-term volunteers who describe wanting or needing to vary and swap their volunteering activities throughout their lifecourse. Their contribution was primarily formal, with only one writer contributing a mix of informal and formal engagement.

Pragmatic switchers: people whose volunteering evolves to fit their life needs

We also identified MOP writers who like the writers discussed above moved across different volunteering activities, but whose routes into volunteering seem to have been determined by lifecourse events and family needs. For example, several mothers (some home-makers, and some undertaking paid work) describe first volunteering when they identified a need for help at their children's pre-school.

> '*I wanted her* [daughter] *to join the local playgroup, but I wasn't much impressed with what was on offer…I decided I could do better myself and having joined the group took it over.*' (1996, *Unpaid Work*, Carole Barker, aged 46)

Such respondents describe moving onto involvement in their children's primary school, and then their children's secondary school. We interpreted the behaviours of 11 MOP writers (just over a quarter of our sample) as encompassing this kind of pragmatic switching. Three of these reported contributing informal voluntary acts alongside their formal volunteering. We make distinctions between these subgroups of 'switchers' because in one case the volunteering trajectory seems to follow from *family* circumstances whereas the other seems more closely related to *personality* and *motivation*. Combined, these subgroups represent more than half of our sample of 38 writers.

Stop-starters: people whose additional volunteering is of a short-term or interim nature

We identified seven writers whose other volunteering activities, beyond their contribution to the MOP, did not meet our definition of long-term volunteering. Without our knowledge of their involvement in the MOP, we might have classified them as short-term formal or informal – possibly even episodic (Macduff, 2005) – volunteers. Trying to categorise these writers is quite complicated; each had unique routes into their short-term voluntary engagement. Female writer Beverley Scott (see biographical synopsis in Chapter Six) has consistently written for the MOP since 1983, when she was 26. She joined the project shortly after leaving her job as a primary-school teacher due to stress-related depression. The process of writing for MOP seems to have been therapeutic. Beverley's routes into other types of formal volunteering were triggered by her search for an alternative career, while balancing her mental health needs. This additional volunteering was of an interim nature (fitting MacDuff's (2005) category of episodic volunteering). She took up an opportunity to learn to teach basic skills to adults in return for committing to volunteer-teaching for six months; after which she stopped. She also volunteered for a half-day a week for a year at the occupational therapy unit of a psychiatric hospital. After securing a job as a supply teacher in 1996, aged 39, she did not volunteer again until her early retirement in 2009 (aged 52), where she undertook a trial afternoon working for a hospital charity, which was curtailed when this avenue of work was shut down shortly after she joined. Beverley's voluntary experiences are *formal*, and she does not mention engaging in any informal volunteering activities. In her early accounts when depressed, she describes a tension in her relationship with her neighbours, and her choice not to undertake informal activities with or for them.

Catherine Neil (see biographical synopsis in Chapter Six) began writing for the MOP in 1984 when she was 46. She, and her husband and children, have had varied working lives, including several years of unemployment during the 1980s' recession. She describes herself as someone who does not volunteer, yet her writing suggests that she appears to have engaged in several stints of formal volunteering over her lifecourse. Both she and her partner are very actively engaged in their community, providing different types of *informal* support for friends and neighbours. We have placed Catherine in the 'stop-starter' category because she describes these as a series of one-off activities. However, if it were possible to map out all Catherine's informal engagement – the nature of the MOP responses means that we do not have exact timelines for when particular activities began or ceased – we might find that it is actually long-term and continuous.

Another stop-starter is female writer, Emily Major (born 1974, see Chapter Six), a former hedge-fund manager who began writing for MOP in 2003 aged 29. In 2008, aged 34 she left her job to get married, and volunteered for a fistula charity while living briefly in Sierra Leone with her husband in order 'to do something'. This was her first experience of volunteering. By 2012, she had a 2-year-old child and was living in England. Categorising this writer is difficult; she may be at the beginning of her volunteering journey, and may go on to do other formal voluntary work later in life as a parent. However, at the cross-sectional moment in time when our analysis of MOP writing finishes – 2012 – the shape of her volunteering behaviour/trajectory makes her appear to be a 'stop-starter'.

Interpreting MOP writing on the shape of volunteering trajectories

Our descriptions and examples of different long-term volunteering behaviours among our sample of MOP writers, particularly those of the stop-starters, illustrate that it is difficult to define and categorise volunteering behaviour. Taxonomies can be affected by the quality of the evidence provided, the lifecourse context and age of the respondent, and the timeframes being examined. Fortunately, the MOP writing that we have drawn on offered diverse accounts of volunteering at different time-points, enabling us to identify and address gaps and inconsistencies in these accounts. During this process we have noted that there is also a mismatch between the definitions of volunteering used in national surveys and individual awareness and perceptions of what volunteering entails that can affect respondent recall and reporting, and researcher interpretation. This is substantively important given the emphasis placed by political and policy discourses on generating robust estimates of voluntary activity.

Routes into and out of volunteering

As well as providing information that enables us to identify the shape of their volunteering lives, MOP writers often provide accounts of how they commenced or ceased volunteering, sometimes accompanied by brief discussions of the reasons for those events. Routes into volunteering are, therefore, strongly connected with motivations and barriers (Low et al, 2007; Musick and Wilson, 2008; Brodie et al 2011), and 'triggers' and 'critical moments' in volunteers' lives (Brodie et al, 2011). The central focus here is on a key finding from our analysis of MOP writers: when describing stopping and starting volunteering at key points in their lifecourse, an exit point for one writer may represent an entry point for another (Figure 7.3). This signposts how important individual life context is to understanding how and when people volunteer. We therefore look again at motivations, barriers and routes, this time focusing on how individual conceptualisations of formal and informal voluntarism affect people's decisions to stop or start providing voluntary action at certain key points in their lives. We frame this within a discussion on writers' notions of spare time and capacity.

Figure 7.3: Routes into and out of volunteering

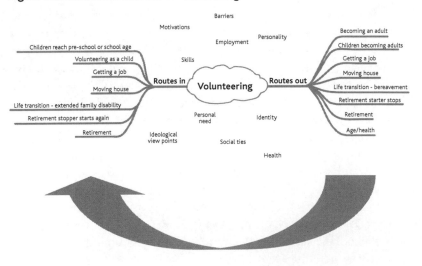

Spare time, capacity and conceptualisation of volunteering as work or leisure

In Chapter Six we did not discuss the availability (or otherwise) of 'spare time' as a motivation or trigger for engagement or non-engagement. Although the availability of time constitutes a resource which individuals can deploy in whatever way they choose, merely having spare time cannot constitute an adequate explanation as to why individuals choose to commit that time to volunteering rather than any other activity. Yet having spare time was identified as a motive to begin volunteering by significant proportions of survey respondents: around 30 per cent in the Citizenship/Community Life Surveys, with some fluctuation (29–41 per cent) between the 1991 and 2006 National Surveys of Voluntary Activity (NSVs) (see Table 6.1). Respondents may report that 'spare time' was a reason for volunteering because it is a familiar trope (along the lines of wanting to 'give something back', 'doing something for others', or 'wanting to be of use to others') that fits alongside the 'dominant paradigm' (Rochester et al, 2010), while making the volunteer look less narrowly altruistic (see Wuthnow, 1991). However, 'spare time' is also related to other broad volunteering motives, the conceptualisation of volunteering as work or leisure, and perceptions of capacity. MOP writing on volunteering and spare time helps to shed some insights on these relationships.

Volunteering conceptualised as work

We have discussed male writer, David Gardiner, at several junctures in this book, in the main because of contradictions in his attitudes towards volunteering. He describes providing unpaid help to others on numerous occasions, but holds staunch anti-volunteering attitudes, conceptualising voluntary action as work, while believing that he should be paid for his labour. Thus, he also provided *paid* help for old people who needed it, principally with gardening (when made redundant after 35 years as an architect's assistant). He admits to increasing the intensity and frequency of his informal helping once he received his state pension and was not in need of an income, extending his repertoire to include assistance with shopping and journeys to hospital (*The 'Big Society'* (2012)). This shift in identity from being '*redundant*' to formally retired, allowed him to conceptualise his time as being free for helping others, which he is then able to donate to those in need. Qualifying for his pension, achieving a measure of financial stability, and a change in his working-identity, were the triggers for this increase in his voluntary activity.

Long-term volunteer, Dianne Roberts, states that having *'free time'* and *'wanting to be of use to others'* are the reasons why she began volunteering:

> *'I started doing this little job just after my youngest had started school. I felt that I had some free time available, and wanted to use it to be of some use to others. I saw a notice appealing for volunteers in the library, so I applied.'* (*Unpaid Work* (1996), aged 53)

Her reference to *'this little job'* shows that she conceptualises her voluntarism as a form of work, undertaken during the day when she has time off from her home-making and mothering duties: labour that is performed within the 'dominant paradigm' of voluntary action. It thus seems unsurprising that she decided to give up voluntary work when her husband retired. In several accounts written after her husband's retirement, Dianne clearly states that retirement is associated with leisure:

> *'Since we are retired now, life is very little to do with work, even around the home, and much more to do with leisure time and enjoying ourselves.'* (*A Working Day* (2010), aged 67)

In this writer's case, retirement represents a withdrawal from the world of work, and instead she sees it as an opportunity for leisure and enjoyment, primarily undertaken through expensive holidays and time spent together. Dianne makes little reference to her involvement in associational membership, taking part in group leisure activities, or 'serious leisure' in her responses to directives used in this study. In 2010, she remarks:

> *'my husband and I tend to act as a unit of our own and neither of us feels the need to interact with others. We have always preferred our own company, so we don't belong to groups, clubs etc. I can't say that I have ever felt a sense of belonging particularly when I've been in the company of others.'* (*Belonging* (2010), aged 67)

Spousal influence on volunteering within this relationship seems very strong. Retirement, and the desire to give up work and share leisure time with her husband seem to have triggered Dianne's decision to cease her voluntary action: volunteering was associated with work, a phase of life that had passed.

For some of the MOP respondents, spare time has been created by their transition into retirement, providing a trigger to stop or start, increase or decrease, their voluntary commitments. Others, such as Emily Major, find that they have spare time on their hands through family circumstances: in her case, newly married, she left her job as a hedge-fund manager in 2008 to join her husband who was working in Sierra Leone. She describes volunteering for the Mercy Ships charity who were working with women with fistulas:

> '*I did it to do something. To be honest it made me depressed and sad hearing these terrible stories and also frustrated that I couldn't do anything more useful than data entry.*' (*The 'Big Society'* (2012), aged 38)

Emily's transition from working to having free time could be compared to that of Dianne Roberts, who came into time when her son started school. However, Emily's transition seems to have been more sudden and less planned for. Looking at the phrase '*I did it to do something*', this could come across as the use of a traditional trope associated with how people explain their volunteering; it might also be interpreted as the frustration or despair of someone wanting and needing to fill their time. She evinces sympathy with the charity's beneficiaries, but does not convey passion for the cause, and says little about how and why she chose this specific charity. This is not a novel situation, as Leonard's (2010) work makes clear: many partners of overseas workers – sometimes referred to as 'trailing wives' – have found themselves in a situation in which volunteering offers a sense of identity, provides contacts and relieves boredom (and in a British context, see Land (2006)).

Volunteering conceptualised as leisure

Male newspaper executive, Stephen Johnson, describes a volunteering trajectory which is the opposite of Dianne Roberts' route into and out of volunteering, where Dianne conceptualised volunteering as a form of work. In previous chapters we have seen that Stephen had provided informal help to a neighbour for some years, but had not been involved in formal volunteering during his working life. In his response to the 1996 *Unpaid Work* directive (aged 54) he says:

> *'This is going to be a very short reply – because I don't do any! Not that I don't want to, but I really don't have enough spare time. My job is fairly demanding and by the time I get home in the evening and we've had a meal, I'm usually only fit for falling asleep in front of the television or over the crossword.'*

He follows this up, however, with a declaration of intent to volunteer when he retires.

> *'I'm hoping to retire in the year 2000 – like big business and all the political parties, I've developed a slogan "A new millennium, a new life" and then I expect to spend some of my time helping others (and thus helping myself at the same time!).*
>
> *Send me this directive again in the first few years of the next century and hopefully I'll be able to write several pages.'*

There is an anticipation of helping others in retirement, but this is tempered by the suggestion that his voluntary action will be of mutual benefit. As we discovered by reading his response to the *The 'Big Society'* directive in 2012, Stephen made good on his plan, taking early retirement in 1999, at the age of 57, and undertaking *'voluntary work from the word "go"'* (*The 'Big Society'* (2012)). His transition from work to retirement volunteer neatly fits Davis-Smith and Gay's (2005) and Hogg's (2016) descriptions of a 'trigger volunteer'. Stephen took up several consecutive and simultaneous volunteering opportunities, which included cultural activities such as working for the Mass Observation Archive (MOA), a transport museum, and being on the committee of an art group. He also passed the driving test for the Institute of Advanced Motorists, which he:

> *'had wanted to do for years but had never had the time and, at their suggestion, became an Observer, that is, taking people out for an hour on a Sunday morning and advise on ways they could improve their motoring skills. I enjoyed this very much but I was having back problems at the time and found that getting in and out of other people's cars on damp winter mornings and (sometimes if they weren't very proficient) living on one's nerves for an hour not conducive to my health, so I reluctantly had to give it up after a couple of years.'*

The roles and domains in which Stephen chose to volunteer all relate to his own interests, and could be described as leisure activities. He curtails these activities for a variety of different reasons: health, boredom, anti-social feelings. However, 13 years into his retirement he withdrew from formal volunteering when he became a full-time carer for his partner. His obligation to care meant that he had no capacity to volunteer.

Conceptualising volunteering as both work and leisure

Female writer Louise Masters holds the view that voluntary work '*is giving your time free – to help when and as much as you can*' (*Unpaid Work* (1996), aged 59). She describes working in a charity shop for three mornings a week, when she was in her 50s, but stopping in 1994 because of a knee injury, which restricted her ability to spend any length of time on her feet, so that she couldn't '*do any voluntary work, like door-to-door collecting, or helping in the shop*' (*Unpaid Work* (1996), aged 59). Louise clearly characterises her voluntary actions prior to her injury as voluntary work. She also describes her habit of knitting squares for Oxfam, and how in the year of her injury, she began sewing up blankets for Oxfam:

> '*One day I took a bag of knitted squares to the Oxfam Shop and the manageress asked if I'd sew the squares up to make the… blanket, the lady who did the sewing was unable to do it any more, as her sight was going. I said "Yes I'll do a couple and see if they would be okay." So since 1994 I've sewed 265 blankets, I've had 3 letters from Head Office thanking me for my work.*' (*The 'Big Society'* (2012), aged 75)

Her narrative suggests that although she was already knitting, the task of sewing blankets replaced her charity shop work. We note that she uses the word '*work*' when describing the letters from Oxfam's Head Office. She does not say directly that this activity fills her time, but there is an inference that she treats her knitting as a hobby. When she mentions it in different directives over the course of 16 years, she provides a different count on the number of blankets she has sewn, and this is a source of some pride. After her husband died in the mid-2000s, she moved to be nearer to her son and grandchildren, but describes a subsequent, disappointing lack of contact with her son's family:

> '*I did think I'd see more of them, the move was also to be near my two grandsons but that has not happened.*' (*Belonging* (2010), aged 73)

171

She attends an 'OAP' (Old Age Pensioner) social group, and regularly has her lunches at pubs frequented by other OAPs, but there is a strong sense of loneliness in her accounts. Knitting and sewing continues to fill her time, gives her a sense of purpose, pride, belonging and identity, and we interpret Louise's view of this activity as something she became involved in which comprises both work and leisure, and which she was able to do despite increasing problems with mobility.

Lack of free time and capacity

Several MOP writers describe feeling that they do not have the free time or capacity to volunteer, citing pressures of work, family commitments, personal and/or family events such as birth, death, illness, disability and ageing. Conversely, other writers describe continuing to volunteer despite these events or commitments, or even cite family or personal events as the triggers for beginning volunteering (see Figure 7.3). A lack of spare time does not seem to be an adequate explanation as to why individuals choose not to volunteer, or why they stop volunteering. Constraints on spare time or capacity should therefore be considered alongside other individual lifecourse events and circumstances.

Family commitments

Stephen Johnson (see above) appears to have stopped volunteering because of his need to look after his partner. Catherine Neil's (see above) involvement in formal volunteering appears to have waned when her children were small. She does not explain why, but she hints that her husband's membership of a darts team took priority over childcare responsibilities, which made it difficult for her to engage in local societies such as a drama group (*The 'Big Society'* (2012), aged 72).

We have gained the impression from some of her writing that the pressures of family life, and competition for her time, have influenced her decisions on whether to volunteer or not. We do not know when, how and why she stopped her engagement with the drama group, but references to it in her directive responses suggest that pressure from family commitments had some influence on her decision to stop.

Family events, such as death, birth, illness and disability, can draw intensively on individual emotional and physical spare time, and represent a barrier to the continuation of people's volunteering, particularly when there is an obligation for care. However, we also note that prolific volunteer, Roger King (see above), describes continuing to volunteer throughout his working life, while his children were growing up, and family commitments appear not to have affected his volunteering career. He states: '*I do not enjoy standing aside if I think something needs to be done, or I can contribute in any way.*' But he notes that his volunteering:

> '*took quite a bit of my free time, and I was in a demanding job at the time. I sometimes wonder if my family suffered as a result – I often look back and think how little time I seemed to have spent with my children when they were young.*' (*Unpaid Work* (1996), aged 75)

He acknowledges that there was a cost to this type of volunteering trajectory, though elsewhere rationalises it (Chapter Six) on the basis that there was a normative expectation that someone in his position would be expected to play their part in leading voluntary activities.

Disadvantaged lives

Gillian Reddy describes herself as someone with neither the time or capacity for volunteering, and apart from her MOP writing appears to have never volunteered. Her mother left home when she was 11, her father died when she was 20. From the age of 24, until her retirement in 2005, she worked in a frozen food factory. The work became increasingly hard. In 1997, Gillian complained that for the last year or so she had been required to do 12-hour shifts: '*It is terrible and I don't know how long I can carry on as I feel so tired*' (*Doing a Job* (1997), aged 52). She began writing for MOP in 1991, and her responses are usually very brief, often comprising just a few lines of writing. In response to the 1996 directive on *Unpaid Work*, she states:

> '*I don't do any unpaid work. But I do admire people who do. If I was financially better off I would devote my life to helping other people. That might sound awful. But at the moment I have people in my own family who I need to help, a brother who has M.S., a sister who has cancer, and the only help I can give is financial. So I need to have a job. When I retire, God willing, I will still be fit & well, I will devote my spare time to helping others.*
>
> *I do so admire people who help others, and you have made me feel so guilty that I don't.*'[3] (aged 51)

Gillian's conceptualisation of voluntarism falls into the 'dominant paradigm' of good works, in which volunteering is conceived of as an act of altruism. She suggests – possibly in acknowledgement that the MOP directive has made her feel 'guilty' – that she wants to be involved in volunteering when she retires. However, her response to the 2010 *A Working Day* directive, which details how she spends a typical week as a retired person, shows that, in contrast to Stephen Johnson (discussed above), and despite previous good intentions, she is doing no voluntary work.

Gillian's sole close support seems to have been her husband (none of the responses we have analysed mention children). Her life post-retirement sounds more comfortable, providing respite from the drudgery of the factory. In her response to the 2010 *Working Day* directive, she describes a weekly routine of cooking, gardening, housework, shopping, having coffee with her sister-in-law once a week '*otherwise my time is spent at home with my husband*' (aged 65). She also mentions that the factory work that she had done all her working life, no longer exists '*I assume I would be one of the unemployed* (had she been of working age).' Our impression is that from an emotional perspective, after retirement, Gillian still does not have spare time, and that she is finally enjoying a life without either the pressures of an unpleasant and physically-demanding job, or financial worries.

Donna Payne (see Chapter Six) is a disabled adult who began writing for MOP in 1981, aged 29. As a child, then adult, she acted as a full-time carer for her disabled mother, until her mother died in 1996, when Donna was 44:

> '*Being a carer for relations is a lonely depressing job, you don't get much sleep & [are] on the go all the time.*' (*Unpaid Work* (1996), aged 45)

She recounts some extremely difficult life-experiences that affected her mental, physical and emotional wellbeing, leaving her unable to work or volunteer. After her mother's death, she describes feeling extremely lonely and wanting to volunteer for social reasons, but was worried about incurring benefit sanctions:

> '*I would dearly love to do unpaid work, but at the moment I don't know if I'm allowed to do it as* [the job centre] *keep stopping my money even now 7 months since mum died they [are] still stopping it & only last week took my book away again from me.*'

In other subsequent responses Donna described experiencing problems with her eyes, and not being able to access the right care. In 2007 she stopped contributing to the MOP because of these difficulties.[4] The impression gained is not that she is unwilling, but lacks the skills, social contacts and knowledge required to move into volunteering. Both Gillian and Donna appear to lack education, social capital and both weak and strong social ties, which as various studies show (see Musick and Wilson, 2008, 119–47) are linked to a lack of civic engagement. Their writing suggests that they feel exhausted by their individual life situations.

Sarah Thomas (born 1926, see Chapter Six) also describes a difficult life, with the traumatic death of a much-loved sibling when she was a child, emotional and physical abuse from a mentally ill mother, the death of her much-loved father when she was in her early 20s, a difficult marriage, and the subsequent illness and death of her husband when she was in her late 50s. She describes a close, loving relationship with her six children, however, and a 'soldiering on' attitude when describing her working life. Unlike Gillian Reddy and Donna Payne, Sarah has been a volunteer. She joined a local swimming club and taught her children to swim after one of her daughters almost drowned in a duckpond. This led to her volunteering as a swimming instructor, which she conceptualises as:

> 'unpaid work …[at] the local swimming club. I enjoyed teaching children to swim. I passed an exam to be a teacher and I paid for the examination. Every week I used to spend approx 6 hours helping children to swim at our open air swimming pool.' (Unpaid Work (1996), aged 70)

However, after becoming pregnant with her sixth child at a late age, she gave up this role.

> 'My work at the swimming pool ended when a new baby turned up when I was 46 years old. I would have gone back but the Council sold our park and swimming pool…and they built a Superstore on top of it.' (Unpaid Work (1996), aged 70)

We are not sure why Sarah seems to have fared better than Donna or Gillian, and found the capacity, time, resilience and tenacity to volunteer.

Physical and mental health

Several of the MOP writers discuss how their health has affected their capacity to volunteer, altered the type of work they do, or influenced the amount of time they can spend on volunteering activities. We note for example, Louise Master's discussion of her knee injury, above, which forced her to change her volunteering role. We also note that Caroline Lawson's (see Chapter Six) volunteering life began with her diagnosis of ME. However, the greatest challenge to writers' volunteering trajectories seems to be the onset of later old age, and the ailments and tiredness these bring. Even prolific volunteer, Roger King, describes having to reduce his numerous commitments, and says that he is now only able to continue with one or two activities (*The 'Big Society'* (2012), aged 91). Bennett et al (2012) have noted how the hours contributed by volunteers fluctuate much more widely in later life – it is not so much that the proportion of the population who are volunteering declines, but that the hours which they contribute are more variable.

Several writers who have been long-term volunteers, however, describe transitioning into contributing and engaging in other ways as they age. Roger King states *'Now my support – as with lots of things I was actively involved with – is purely financial'* (*The 'Big Society'* (2012), aged 91). Union man, Frank Driver, who experienced a loss of political and volunteering efficacy in his late 50s, while looking after his ill wife (see Chapter Six) describes returning to political engagement in later years, and taking part in online campaigning:

> *'I re-joined the Labour Party. I am not sure if it was a good idea but it is the nearest thing to an organisation that's views are similar to mine. Although some of its aims these days would have been thought 'right wing' in the days* [of] *Clem, Harold and by Tony Benn. I also 'belong' to Avaaz, 38 Degrees, Unlock Democracy and the Campaign for an English Parliament. All of which have the aim of banding together to make something happen.'* (*The 'Big Society'* (2012), aged 78)

From a personal perspective, these writers still seem to view and define their contribution as voluntary action, even though the nature of this contribution has shifted to membership of organisations, financial support and online engagement.

As regards mental health, Beverley Scott (see above) who experienced poor mental health in her 20s and 30s, undertook two short-term stints of volunteering during this time. When she got a job as a supply teacher in 1996, she stated that she was unable to volunteer because of lack of time and energy and the ability for forward planning because:

> 'I don't know from one day to the next what I'm doing, let alone week to week, so fitting in anything, other than at weekends, is virtually impossible. And at weekends I usually have hoovering, cooking, tidying etc to do, so I really have no time then either to do voluntary work – I'm usually exhausted as well, and have no inclination to do it, even if I did have time, and energy.' (Unpaid Work (1996), aged 39)

We do not have anyone in our sample on zero-hours contracts, but one can easily imagine similar responses from people in that position. Like Gillian Reddy, Beverley anticipates that she would 'do more voluntary work again if my hours of work were regular. Certainly in the future I would eg if I retired' (Unpaid Work (1996), aged 39). After retiring at 52, she did indeed make a brief foray into volunteering, but the project was shut down at the point at which she joined. She did not find any alternative opportunities that appealed to her. She was reluctant to visit her local volunteer office, stating that 'I'm scared I would get talked into doing something I didn't want to do' (The 'Big Society' (2012), aged 55). The impression we have gained from reading Beverley's account is one of lack of confidence; although she has considered volunteering, she does not really want to volunteer, and has a fear of committing to something that she is not sure that she wants to do. Although Beverley writes comprehensively about her husband and her family over 30 years, these accounts suggest some tensions with her weak social ties – family and neighbours (see Chapter Five for one example). Her history of mental health problems and lack of long-term work security, also suggest that she may have less social capital than some of the other MOP writers in our sample.

Although Beverley's mental health problems, lack of confidence and work insecurity seem to have prevented her from resuming volunteering, other writers, such as Maria Dyer (see biographical synopsis in Chapter Six) describe continuous volunteering despite, or because of, their mental health problems. However, this may be an unfair comparison. We do not know the diagnoses given to these different writers, except that some (not Beverley Scott, who has no children) have experienced post-natal depression; nor do we know the severity of their conditions. However, a key question is why do some people fail to engage, and others gain immense therapeutic gain from their engagement? We wonder whether personality also affects levels of engagement. Although there has been considerable discussion of the relationship between personality and volunteering, the relationship is difficult to evidence. Musick and Wilson (2008), for example, devote a chapter to a discussion of the literature on engagement and personality, and argue that the field would benefit from studies of the quantitative correlation between personality and sociological variables in volunteers and non-volunteers. There is room for further work on the relationship between personality, mental health and levels of engagement.

Routes out: negative experiences of volunteering

MOP writers provide a range of different reasons for stopping volunteering. We find references to lifecourse events, such as a health transition or the birth of a child, or to an attitudinal issue, such as getting bored, or wanting to move onto something else. However, some writers discuss other, more negative, reasons for becoming demotivated in their volunteering. We have been struck by the three examples below, where writers have talked about their disillusionment with the causes or organisations with which they are involved.

Caroline Lawson, the ME sufferer, left a committee role because of frustration and disillusionment with in-fighting and power struggles.

> '*The bureaucracy, the pettiness, the political in-fighting, the bitchiness and the ineptitude soured most attempts to improve the quality of life for group members…it particularly angered me that one or two difficult personalities were able to influence the direction of the group so dramatically.*' (*Unpaid Work* (1996), aged 31)

Concerns about power-struggles were also the reasons noted by several other writers for not wanting to undertake certain roles.

George Tyler, who worked for his church council, and also worked for many years as a Scoutmaster for his church-based Scout troop, left these roles, and then the church, in the late 1970s, when one of his sons died in a motorbike accident. He made these decisions because he felt unsupported in his grief by a changing church community '*I felt my wife and myself were not really wanted. It was time to move on*' (*Belonging* (2010), aged 80). After a lifetime of involvement in unionism and the Labour Party, transport worker, Frank Driver, ended his involvement with both. This was partly because of the need to look after his increasingly disabled wife. His decision was, however, also driven by his dislike of the way that unions and the Labour Party had evolved from the late

1980s onwards. In his view, the unions had been '*emasculated*', and '*the snare of "buy your cheap council house" had been firmly set*' (*Unpaid Work* (1996), aged 63). The rightward drift of the Labour Party under Tony Blair led him to resign. Frank lambasts the way in which the individual and the private sphere have eroded collective political values, and was disillusioned with individuals who had sold out. However, he notes the irony that he has purchased a 'bargain' ex-council house and owns shares in the privatised National Freight Corporation. '*I believe in Marx's dictum that there is no harm in benefiting from capitalism even if you don't believe in it*' (*Being Part of Research* (2004), aged 71). Interestingly, after his wife's death, in 2000, he rejoined the Labour Party, and since then has been involved in online political lobbying.

All three MOP writers stopped volunteering because of disillusionment with the organisations and communities for which they were volunteering, or in the causes they were supporting, leading to a growing lack of trust and reduction in self-efficacy in all three writers. This did not lead to the three writers becoming anti-volunteering; they have continued or resumed prosocial activities since their withdrawal from particular roles and domains. However, we wonder what role disillusionment might play in reducing the self-efficacy, and interest in volunteering, of less prosocial and established volunteers.

Conclusion

In this chapter we have focused on individual volunteering behaviour over time, tracking the trajectories into and out of volunteering of BHPS/US participants and MOP writers. When individuals are followed up regularly over a number of years we find evidence that a much larger proportion of them are involved in voluntary action, compared to the picture that one would obtain from a cross-sectional survey at one point in time. This raises questions about the 'true' level of engagement in society: people who are apparently disengaged at one wave of the survey may well re-engage at the next one. In other words, volunteering is fluid. When we consider transitions from one wave of the BHPS/US to the next, we find that people move in and out, or dip in and out, of volunteering, but just as is the case with cross-sectional analyses, a small core of individuals contribute the greatest effort.

While such longitudinal survey data offers novel insights, it needs to be complemented with qualitative accounts of voluntary action by individuals. Looking at the activities of the MOP writers, we find various patterns of long-term voluntary activity over the course of writers' volunteering lives. More than a fifth were individuals who had stayed committed to an individual organisation or cause. More than half regularly swapped the roles or domains in which they volunteered, either for pragmatic reasons, such as the changing needs of their children, or because they liked change. And less than a fifth of writers stopped and started their volunteering, for a variety of different reasons. Apart from the writers who were continuous volunteers, it would not be possible to pick up the level of churn demonstrated by writers in their volunteering lifecourses, through survey data. This brings us back to Low et al's (2007) conceptualisation of 'ex-volunteers', briefly mentioned at the start of this chapter, and to our MOP writers who were stoppers and starters. If we consider volunteering from a lifecourse perspective can we really describe anyone as an ex-volunteer, or a non-volunteer, unless they are deceased? Until we can describe the whole of a person's volunteering lifecourse, any categories imposed might be inaccurate. There is always a possibility that behaviour may evolve, change or continue.

A key observation is that writers discussed triggers and transitions in their volunteering behaviour in some detail, providing rich qualitative data which allowed us to relate those transitions to their lifecourses. Certain types of life events, such as starting or stopping work, a child starting school, illness and disability, house-moves, retirement, can influence people to start and stop, or increase and decrease their volunteering. One writer's stopping point may represent another's starting point. The insights we have gained into the lifelong volunteering patterns of these writer-volunteers, their different volunteering exit and entry points, and the amount of volunteering they contribute, provides a perspective of volunteering that might enable policy-makers and practitioners to anticipate and predict volunteering behaviour, and inform volunteer retention and recruitment strategies based on life-events, rather than on demographic predictors such as age. At the same time, the examples given in this chapter show how routes into voluntary action are heavily contingent on conjunctures of circumstances that are often unique to the individual.

It is also possible, however, that we have been exploring the volunteering trajectories of people who grew up in fortunate circumstances and fortunate times (our youngest writer was aged 37 in 2012), and that the conditions for engagement are no longer what they were. Wilensky (1961) emphasised the role of 'orderly careers' in underpinning social participation, drawing a contrast between those in the more 'chaotic' sectors of the Labour market and those in secure career niches. Some 50 years later, Laurence and Lim (2013) have shown how the engagement trajectories of those expelled forcibly from the labour market during the collapse in employment in the early 1980s had been set on a very different, downward, path, compared to those in more secure positions. The past decade has seen similar economic turbulence, particularly affecting young people, whose prospects are further hampered by significant student debt. Many of our MOP writers grew up in propitious circumstances, but this will not be the experience of rising generations. What will be the engagement 'penalty' of the economic circumstances of the first 15 years of the twenty-first century?

Notes

[1] This table includes data from both the BHPS and the first wave of US, notwithstanding our previous comment that the nature of the question about voluntary action has changed. There are in fact several issues which arise in use of the BHPS / US data which are worth pointing out. A priori, consider the transition between 2008 (BHPS) and 2011 (US) in Table 7.1. This suggests that around half of respondents who previously have declared that they were undertaking 'unpaid voluntary work' in the BHPS are now saying that they are providing unpaid help to a voluntary organisation in the closely related question in US. In previous transitions in the BHPS the equivalent was approximately 60–65 per cent. This might be held to invalidate the incorporation of the 2008–11 cell in this transition matrix. On the other hand, this still means that there is a substantial degree of consistency in individuals' responses between the two surveys.

Does this also mean that we should not use the data in the graphs of individual volunteering trajectories (Figures 7.2 and 7.3)? The principal aim of these is to illustrate the diversity of those trajectories and so, even if volunteering status is mis-measured in 2011 compared to 2008, the number of observations affected is very small relative to the size of the datasets (some 2,100 individuals observed 8 eight times feature in those graphs).

[2] In their cross-sectional survey, Low et al (2007) found that 'Seventy one percent of volunteers undertook more than one volunteering activity' (p 23). When we compare this to the proportion of MOP volunteer writers undertaking more than one volunteering activity, the MOP sample is substantially larger, 36 out of 38 writers. However, the additional volunteering acts considered took place across multiple time-points.

[3] Gillian Reddy writes her responses in upper case. However, for ease of reading we have reproduced these in lower case.

[4] Staff at the Mass Observation Archive have stated that Donna Payne has subsequently returned to writing for the MOP.

EIGHT

Attitudes to voluntary action

Introduction

We have previously shown that rates of engagement in volunteering have been stable over the time period covered by this book. However, knowing that members of the public engage in voluntary action at a relatively high and stable level does not tell us about their attitudes to voluntary action. Do they regard volunteering as a duty? What is their view of the position of volunteering in British society? What do they think about the importance of volunteering and of the balance between statutory and voluntary provision of public services?

An inquiry into attitudes to voluntary action could encompass consideration of the public's understanding of the social and individual benefits of volunteering, their perception of the roles and efficiency of voluntary organisations, and the contribution of voluntary organisations to the delivery of public services. It might also investigate public attitudes to specific issues, such as the recently topical issue of fundraising tactics by UK charities. Few of these topics have been the subject of robust national surveys. The major surveys of volunteering in 1981 and 1991 incorporated various questions on individuals' understanding of volunteering and attitudes regarding its wider social benefits. The long-running British Social Attitudes Survey (BSAS) has intermittently included some relevant questions, such as: whether individuals were 'currently a member of voluntary groups to help the sick/elderly/children/other vulnerable group' (1997, 1998, 2000, 2012); whether people had done 'volunteer work' (note, not 'unpaid help') in any of the following areas – charitable, political, religious and church-related; whether they had undertaken any other kind of voluntary activities (asked in two waves, in 1998 and 2000); and whether they were members of a broader range of local community or voluntary groups (1994, 1997, 1998, 2000, 2012). Frustratingly, these hardly ever coincided with other BSAS questions on whether society relied too much on volunteers (1993, 1996); on whether 'everyone has a duty to do voluntary work at some time in our lives' (1993, 1996); and on whether doing voluntary work was a good thing for volunteers because it makes them feel that they are contributing to society (1994, 1996).

As for voluntary organisations, public perceptions of and trust in charities received some attention from the BSAS during the Major governments (Barnett and Saxon-Harrold, 1992), while awareness of the growing role of the third sector in welfare delivery led to questions being asked in 2007 and 2012 about public attitudes to a diversity of providers in public services (Curtice and Heath, 2009). Relating this to our discussion of the changing character of the voluntary sector (Chapter Four), however, we do not have enough survey evidence to determine whether or not public attitudes have changed over time in response to the changing character of the voluntary sector, or indeed whether the public is aware of the changes that have taken place.

This overview suggests that there is little systematic evidence on public attitudes to voluntary action; nevertheless, in the next section we present some salient findings from the evidence that is available. We do, however, have a considerable body of attitudinal material from our Mass Observation Project (MOP) writers, which we focus on in the third section. We examine responses to the 1996 *Unpaid Work* and the 2012 *'Big Society'* directives, looking for changes in attitudes. In the fourth section we then focus on the 2012 directive to investigate individual responses to a clear appeal from the Coalition government (2010–15) for greater engagement in voluntary action, and to explore perceptions of the capacities of communities and individuals to do more.

Survey data from the British Social Attitudes Survey and from the National Survey of Voluntary Activity

The 1981 and 1991 National Survey of Voluntary Activity (NSV) respondents were offered statements about the place of voluntary action in society and its contribution (Table 8.1). The survey asked about responses to propositions that 'a society with voluntary workers shows that it is a caring society' and that voluntary workers 'offer something different that can never be provided by the state'. Note that this wording was also used by the 1996 *Unpaid Work* directive, and it is quite possible that this was deliberate on the part of the postgraduate student who commissioned the directive. We would expect few people to answer negatively to the first of these survey statements, and nearly nine-tenths of respondents agreed with it; over three-quarters agreed with the second, in both 1981 and 1991. Conversely there was very strong disagreement with the argument that 'voluntary workers are less efficient than paid professional workers'. Consider responses to the final

Table 8.1: Attitudes to voluntary work within the NSV, 1981 and 1991 (%)

	1981	1991
A society with voluntary workers shows that it is a caring society	87	92
Voluntary workers offer something different that could never be provided by the state system	77	75
If the government fulfilled all its responsibilities, there should be no need for voluntary workers	23	49
On the whole, voluntary workers are less efficient than paid professional workers	13	14

Source: Humble, 1982, 5; Lynn and Davis-Smith, 1992, 127–8

statement, however: 'if government fulfilled all its responsibilities there should be no need for voluntary workers'. The proportion agreeing with this statement rose from 23 per cent to 49 per cent in ten years. Thus, while there was positive support for volunteering, this was not unqualified, and the statement may reflect awareness of the rolling back of the state during the Thatcher and Major years. At around the same time, the proportion of BSAS respondents agreeing that 'government should spend more money on welfare' was steadily decreasing, while the proportion agreeing that 'if welfare was not as generous people would learn to stand on their own two feet' was gradually rising.

More specific questions on volunteering were asked by the BSAS in 1993, 1994 and 1996, a time when the Major government was seeking, through its 'Active Citizenship' policy rhetoric, to encourage greater voluntary action by individuals. The surveys asked individuals to indicate their assent, or otherwise, to statements that:

- Everyone has a duty to do voluntary work at some time in their lives. (1993 and 1996)
- As a society, we rely too much on volunteers. (1993 and 1996)
- Doing voluntary work is a good thing for volunteers because it makes them feel they are contributing to society (1994 and 1996)

Table 8.2 shows the proportion of respondents who agreed, disagreed or did not feel strongly either way towards these statements. The majority felt that volunteering benefits the people who volunteer, making volunteers feel as if they are contributing to society (86 per cent in 1994 and 81 per cent in 1996); fewer than 4 per cent disagreed in either wave. This echoes the positive views of volunteering from the 1981 and 1991 NSVs. However, three-fifths of the population also felt that British society was too reliant on volunteers (59 per cent in 1993 and 61 per cent in 1996). The question of whether volunteering

Table 8.2: Attitudes towards volunteerism within the BSAS

	Good for volunteers		Too reliant		Duty to volunteer	
	1994	1996	1993	1996	1993	1996
Disagree n (%)	28 (3)	33 (3)	223 (18)	154 (16)	488 (38)	369 (37)
Neither n (%)	109 (11)	157 (16)	296 (23)	236 (24)	338 (27)	304 (31)
Agree n (%)	811 (86)	808 (81)	745 (59)	598 (61)	449 (35)	314 (331)

Note: Percentages are rounded down or up; may not sum to 100. The BSAS has a sample size of around 3000 but the questions on this topic were put only to approximately one-third of the sample, hence the numbers given above.

Source: British Social Attitudes Survey.

was seen as a duty generated a mixed response with around one-third agreeing, and a slightly larger proportion disagreeing. As we will see from the responses of Mass Observers to the 1996 directive on unpaid work, there was some degree of scepticism about the place of voluntary action in society, mainly related to the relationship between statutory and private initiative. These survey findings are, therefore, interesting particularly in relation to society's reliance on volunteers and the question of duty to volunteer, and they perhaps provide context for the views expressed by our Mass Observers when they describe their own attitudes to and experience of voluntary action.

We can also explore trends in relation to attitudes to statements regarding statutory versus private responsibility for welfare. In contrast to evidence of stability of the underlying level of involvement in volunteering since the early 1980s (Chapter Four), the BSASs, covering the same time period, have revealed a cyclical pattern of attitudes either for or against greater government intervention, self-reliance and higher welfare payments (Taylor and Taylor-Gooby, 2015). Support for government intervention (for example, spending more money on welfare, or raising levels of taxation to support public service provision) rose during the 1980s and through the mid-1990s before declining. Conversely, support for the proposition that 'if welfare benefits weren't so generous, people would learn to cope' has increased steadily from the late 1990s to the present day. Neither of these trends bears any relationship to levels of voluntary action. Thus, although attitudes were swinging away from support for state intervention, behaviour was not switching in favour of greater voluntarism by individuals. Unfortunately, we do not have survey data on which we might base further discussion – for example, more comprehensive data on attitudes to voluntarism – which would enable us to explore the relationships between attitudes and pro-social behaviours in more depth.

Attitudinal material from the Mass Observation Project, 1996 and 2012

Only two Mass Observation Project (MOP) directives – the 1996 *Unpaid Work* and 2012 *The 'Big Society'* directives – have asked writers about their attitudes towards voluntary action. The first directive was sent out to MOP writers after 17 years of Conservative governments, the year before Labour's landslide victory at the 1997 General Election. The second directive (commissioned by the authors) was sent out two years into the Conservative–Lib-Dem Coalition administration (2010–15), when that administration was implementing austerity cuts following the 2008 financial crisis. (A small number of writers also provided attitudinal views in their responses to the 1990 *Membership of Voluntary Organisations* directive.) Given the time-points at which these directives were issued, we are, therefore, unable to identify any change in the attitudes of individuals during the Thatcher/Major or New Labour administrations.

As well as probing the extent and character of voluntary action undertaken by writers (as described in Chapter Three), the 1996 and 2012 directives also investigated attitudes towards voluntary action. The 1996 *Unpaid Work* directive asked the following questions:

- *The meanings of words*: how you would define the words '*voluntary organisation*' and '*charity*'?
- *Voluntary work in our society*: do you feel the work *should* be left to voluntary effort or that it should be taken over by the State or some other body? Does a society with voluntary workers show it is a caring society?
- *Voluntary workers*: what do you think about them? Do you think voluntary workers are less efficient than paid professional workers, on the whole? Do you think voluntary workers are taking away opportunities for paid employment for others?
- Traditionally voluntary workers have tended to come from the better-off sections of society. Would you say this still remains true, or have you observed changes?

The 2012 *'Big Society'* directive asked:

- Do you feel you could do more voluntary work? Or do you think that you are doing the maximum that you can?

- What about our society? Do we do enough/too much voluntary work?
- Are there certain jobs that should only be carried out by the State or some other body? If so, what jobs are these? If these are not carried out by the State, who should carry them out? Who should fund these jobs?

Although there are differences between the questions asked (for example, the 2012 directive did not ask writers to define 'voluntary organisations' and 'charity'), there are enough areas of common ground, such as questions on the relationship between voluntarism and the state, to enable us to examine whether individual writers have changed their views on voluntarism (the sample being too small and unrepresentative to investigate collective views). We also note that the wording of the 1996 directive question 'Does a society with voluntary workers show it is a caring society?' is the same as that asked by the 1981 and 1991 NSVs. Although this question was asked some five years after the later of those two surveys, writers' responses offer some insights into the complex discussion this question can prompt, when not simply required to answer 'yes' or 'no'. Of our sample of 38 writers, 33 writers responded to the 1996 directive, 25 to the 2012 directive, and 22 writers responded to both directives. Not all of those 22 discussed attitudes to voluntarism: four expressed no views, and two answered the attitudinal questions in only one of the directives, thus reducing the potential to measure change in views to 16 writers.

Change and continuity in attitudes to voluntary action

Although there is evidence that writers' volunteering behaviours have changed over time – with writers either reducing or increasing their voluntary input, or changing where they volunteer (see Chapter Seven on trajectories) – there seems to have been little change to their views on voluntary action *per se*. We observed only three examples of change in writers' viewpoints among the 22 writers for whom we have longitudinal data on attitudes. Catherine Neil had been involved in formal volunteering for some years, but in 1990 declared '*I consider joining things a juvenile occupation*' (*Membership of Voluntary Organisations* (1990); in Chapter Six we discussed the influence of spouse, family and capacity in changing her views).

The second attitudinal change came from writer, Dianne Roberts, a lifelong fan of Margaret Thatcher, who opined, nearly two decades after Thatcher had been ejected from office, that the country would have been a much better place if Thatcher were still in charge (2008 *World Financial Crisis* directive). Dianne had volunteered continuously for the same organisation for 24 years, commencing in the 1970s because she had '*some free time available*' when her youngest child started school (*Unpaid Work* (1996); in Chapters Five and Seven we discussed her conceptualisation of volunteering as work that you do when you have free/spare time). She maintains this attitude in her responses to different directives written after 2000, but appears to change her views on the relationship between the state, and public and voluntary services. When answering the 1996 *Unpaid Work* directive question on whether or not voluntary work '*should* be left to voluntary effort' she argues:

> '*Yes I think we should have more volunteers to carry out many tasks that do not require intervention from the State. Why should we rely on the State for everything? Ultimately anything the State does we have to pay for anyway, so let's cut out the middle man and do it ourselves.*' (*Unpaid Work* (1996), aged 52)

This type of liberal non-interventionist response might be expected from a supporter of Margaret Thatcher. However, when asked in 2012 whether there were 'certain jobs that should only be carried out by the State or some other body', she was much less certain. While she did not expect the state to provide '*things like charity shops, the WVS, volunteer gardeners and guides in National Trust houses*' she stated:

> '*I do feel that a lot of services that are already supplied by volunteers should perhaps be provided by the state in one way or another. I'm always confused by Special Constables, as I gather they are purely volunteers and receive no pay and that just doesn't seem right, although they obviously enjoy doing it. I'm sure there are loads of other positions similar to that but I'm afraid I can't think of any at the moment.*' (*The 'Big Society'* (2012), aged 69)

The context of this potential shift in view is worth consideration. Dianne's framing of her views within a discussion of Special Constables, might suggest that concerns with law and order services are uppermost in her mind (this had been a key element of Thatcherism's electoral appeal) compared to the provision of voluntary or statutory social care services; thus this statement is in line with her political attitudes. But she appears out of her 'comfort zone' in this directive, stating that she knows more about charity shops and the National Trust than about services that could be made statutory, and exclaiming:

'I have not enjoyed this section at all, as I find the whole subject such utter rubbish and therefore very difficult to know what to say about it.' (The 'Big Society' (2012), aged 69)

When we unpick Dianne's writing, and the context of her response to the 2012 *'Big Society'* directive, it may be more accurate to characterise her views not as indicating a change in her attitude but rather a lack of confidence in her ability to comment on voluntarism and the state.

The third example of a change in view on voluntary action comes from George Tyler. Almost the antithesis of Dianne Roberts, George is a virulently anti-Thatcher writer who holds left-wing viewpoints. In his response to the 1996 *Unpaid Work* directive, he describes his extensive voluntary experience: on his church council, as a Scoutmaster, undertaking union activity, and with a community transport initiative. During his somewhat discursive, retrospective account he discusses how he was made redundant from a local government post at the age of 59:

'I became involved in the Community bus project as much as anything through my anger and resentment at being prematurely retired...I had been in the transport industry all my working life.' (Unpaid Work (1996), aged 66).

He also announces:

'I have to say myself that Thatcherism has made me hostile to the notion of voluntary work.' (Unpaid Work (1996), aged 66)

This seems like quite a radical change in attitude from a man who has contributed so much of his time and energy to formal voluntary endeavours. However, here we note that George's formal volunteering seems to have stopped at some point in the early 1990s, and we do not think that he ceased to volunteer solely because of this change in attitude. Instead, George describes how his caring duties for his wife limited the intensity and frequency of his contribution to the community bus project, while in later writing he describes his involvement in the care of a profoundly disabled grandchild born in 1995, and the informal help he provides to friends and neighbours. These changes in his behaviours may relate to his caring responsibilities as much as to his change in attitude to formal voluntary action. In terms of the consistency of his views over time, George's response to the 2012 *'Big Society'* directive, where he seems to present himself as a *former* supporter of voluntarism, might indicate that between 1996 and 2012 he maintained his hostility to voluntary action:

> 'There have always been people wanting to produce a better society. Going back to Victorian times and beyond. I was such a person myself once. Then along came Maggie Thatcher who, having made so many municipal services a shambles, began talking about the voluntary sector sorting out all the things she had cocked up! Cameron would still have been a Bullingdon Club drunk then.'
> (*The 'Big Society'* (2012), aged 82)

Our conclusion is that a small number of our writers, two (possibly three, if we count Dianne Roberts), have discussed changes to their views and attitudes, over time. Catherine Neil's change in attitude is private, related to family and the private sphere, and manifests itself as a change in behaviour. George Tyler's is political and rhetorical, but we are uncertain whether this is evidenced in his behaviour. In such an account, voluntary action cannot be reduced to a simple expression of political attitudes, but instead needs to be primarily understood in relation to an individual's particular circumstances.

In terms of continuity of attitude, some of the writers who have responded to both the 1996 and 2012 directives highlight very similar issues on both occasions. This may be as much about the continuity of writers' views across time as it is about responses to the similarities between the social and economic policies implemented by the 1979–97 Conservative administration and the post-2010 Coalition government (see Abrams et al, 1989; Glennerster, 2007; Bochel, 2011; Glasby, 2011). Key subjects causing interest and concern among writers were social care, cuts to public services, and the relationship between voluntarism and the welfare state. As well as diachronic similarities (across time) in individual accounts, we also note certain synchronic 'reading formations' (Bennett, 1983) within the responses to the 2012 *'Big Society'* directive, with many writers making references to the financial crisis and austerity measures by drawing on specific tropes, such as quoting Thatcher's 'No such thing as society' assertion, and discussing individualism, greed and selfishness.

Influence of individual beliefs on attitudes

We begin our discussion of writers' views by considering the influence of individual writers' beliefs, world views and personal ideologies on their attitudes towards voluntarism and on their writing on and interest in British political and economic policies. Several writers make *no* reference to such beliefs or ideologies, have little to say on British policies and politics, and appear to lack political efficacy. Beverley Scott provides an explanation of her distrust of, and disengagement with, political discourses. In 2012, she writes that she has never heard of the 'Big Society', but after discussing this with her husband while writing her response to that directive, states:

> *My husband had just said that David Cameron talks about the*
> *Big Society. Well, I wouldn't believe a word any politician says…*
> *programmes like Question Time just make me want to scream at*
> *the idiot politicians on them, they drive me mad, so I generally*
> *avoid them. (The 'Big Society' (2012), aged 54)*

Then there is a group of writers whose writing includes a mix of views and attitudes on social and economic issues, alongside personal anecdotes, for whom we cannot identify a political affiliation. We might hazard that they are a mix of Lib-Dem and Labour supporters, but we cannot exclude the possibility that some may be Conservative voters (even when writers describe their political affiliations, their views are sometimes inconsistent with the policies of the parties they support). These writers are all females (in 1996, their ages ranged from 72 to 44), most of whom have had experience of higher education. Some draw on the tropes of individualism, greed and Thatcherism; for example, Susan Leonard, writes:

> *But the society created by Thatcher, and continued by Blair, seems*
> *to demand* everything they want *too, irrespective of how they*
> *get it. (The 'Big Society' (2012), aged 60)*

Others in this group, however, comment more specifically on particular issues such as social care.

Some writers consistently mention specific themes or issues in their responses. For example, writers Catherine Neil and Linda Pope often discuss the influence of their religious faith on their lives, and on their attitudes to formal and informal voluntarism. However, they say little about political affiliation or politics, although they will occasionally comment on policy. Some are explicit about their political views in their responses to directives. For example, Charles Wright holds strong anti-immigration views, and is the most explicitly right-wing writer in the sample. His response to the 1996 *Unpaid Work* directive includes his thoughts on the pointlessness of charities providing overseas aid:

> *For all the years these unpaid workers have been operating and money spent, these evils persist. Would they know when they have won their battle? Would they then quietly go away?* (*Unpaid Work* (1996), aged 74)

Dianne Roberts, mentioned above, is less consistently explicit about her political views, but is very clear about her support of Thatcherism in some of her responses. Roger King and Pauline Bennett both mention actively supporting the Lib-Dem party. Roger King makes some minor comments on policy, but surprisingly, Pauline Bennett does not discuss policies or politics in any of the writing used for this study. At the opposite end of the political spectrum, David Gardiner, Jack Wilkins and Frank Driver describe themselves as left-wing; others, such as Gordon Page, George Tyler and Sarah Thomas, use left-leaning language and discuss political issues from a left-wing perspective, but do not identify their political orientation in the responses used in this study. These six left-leaning writers often comment on policies and politics in their responses, drawing on specific tropes, for example, quoting Thatcher's comment 'There is no such thing as society'. David Gardiner writes in 2006:

> '*Since Margaret Thatcher in the 1980s and her "There's no such thing as society" materialism, selfishness and greed have sadly come to the fore. The "I must have" mentality. All things in moderation has been swept aside and forgotten.*' (*Core British Values* (2006), aged 72)

We discuss the responses of left-aligning writers below, grouping their responses together because of their clear expression of their political affiliations, and we provide evidence of the relationship between their attitudes and their behaviours.

Left-leaning writers: voluntarism and the labour market

In his response to the 1996 *Unpaid Work* directive, David Gardiner states that having been made redundant six years before he was officially due to retire he does not believe in unpaid work, and argues that he should be paid for any labour he undertakes. In 2012, he states that he maintained this view until he was in receipt of a state pension and officially retired, after which he felt he could donate his time and help to individuals in need (see Chapters Five to Seven). Jack Wilkins writing in 1996 believes that volunteers are cutting the floor from underneath the labour market:

> '*I, who only had my labour to sell and keep me solvent, I would ask the volunteers to not uphold such systems and allow a decent set of standards of pay to apply throughout, especially concerning today's chaotic climate.*' (Unpaid Work (1996), aged 70)

Similar views are also expressed by Sarah Thomas and George Tyler (see above) in their responses to the 1996 *Unpaid Work* directive:

> '*Voluntary work within a club is ok but if it takes away the work opportunities for paid employment that's not fair.*' (Unpaid Work (1996), Sarah Thomas, aged 70)

> '*I have heard more than one Tory politician suggest that volunteers might like to take on some of the functions that once provided employment opportunities. Suggestions that I find more than a little offensive.*' (Unpaid Work (1996), George Tyler, aged 66)

George continues this discussion in 2012:

> '*Politicians and chief executives cannot have enough mugs to work for nothing. On the other hand, if you are desperate for paid employment or on the receiving end of efforts to put you out of work volunteers can be a pain.*' (The 'Big Society' (2012), aged 82)

Although these writers demonstrate left-wing attitudes in these responses, their perspectives are also informed by personal or family experiences of unemployment, and their empathy for people whose job situations are precarious. David Gardiner, George Tyler and Jack Wilkins were made redundant while in their 50s, and never regained full and sustained employment. Sarah Thomas held on to her job as an agricultural worker, but her husband and other family members were all unemployed for several years during the 1980s' recessions; she discusses how poor the family were during these periods.

We note that various non-politicised writers, writing in 1996, did not support this view that volunteers deprive unemployed people of opportunities for paid work. However, responses in 2012 were somewhat different, because writers were making connections between the government's cutting of public expenditure and the Big Society call for more volunteers. Had there been no change in the policy environment, we wonder whether these writers would have maintained the attitudes which they held in 1996.

Left-wing writer, Frank Driver, also comments on the relationship between voluntarism and the labour market in relation to statutory services, focusing (as did Dianne Roberts, a strong supporter of Margaret Thatcher), on the issue of Special Constables:

'We need more constables, so we get someone to do it for nothing in their spare time. If they are really capable of and want to be PCs let them enrol properly. Just think how you would feel if you were a lecturer short[1] and the University said "we are not going to employ another one, we've lined up a couple of policemen to come in and do the job on their rest days. Best of all they will do it for free".' (Unpaid Work (1996), aged 63)

Ironically, although Frank Driver is more articulate and clear about his views on this issue, we see a convergence of views between him and Thatcherite Dianne Roberts, who had been puzzled by the position of Special Constables.

Voluntarism and the state

George Tyler, who describes having feelings of hostility to voluntarism, contemplates the relationship between reductions in public funding and voluntary action:

'I have seen at first hand the effect of [the government's] policies upon the public services. How a public service has been undermined, even withdrawn, because there was no money in it. Having seen so many good people lose their jobs [under this government] it annoys me intensely when I hear [Conservative supporters] suggest that voluntary workers might like to step in and restore a service that has been undermined even terminated by their political creed. Muggins working for nothing to overcome the disasters of [this government].'

George actually wrote this in 1996, making specific retrospective references to Margaret Thatcher and Thatcherism. We were struck by how easily it could have formed part of a response in 2012 if, as we have done, references to Margaret Thatcher were removed. George's concerns anticipate views held by less–politicised MOP writers, in their responses to the 2012 'Big Society' directive, 16 years later. June Foster, who does not identify her political affiliations, regards the possibility of placing greater responsibility for public services on volunteers as:

> '*very unfair, as most people need to earn a living. I suppose that part of the thinking behind this idea is that now so many people are unemployed, due to huge Govt cutbacks etc, they need to be kept busy!*' (*The 'Big Society'* (2012), aged 73)

A sense of distrust with politicians' attitudes towards voluntarism and public services is evident in responses to both the 1996 and 2012 directives.

Gordon Page, another left-wing writer, echoes these views on public services in 2012, and argues for certain public services such as health and social care to be properly protected and regulated, so that professional services are not 'diluted' by voluntary participation. He also develops the argument, which we discuss below, that Cameron's idea of the 'Big Society' was an essentially political manipulation of the good intentions that lie at the heart of voluntary action. This is not a new suggestion: different administrations for most of the post-1979 period have pursued policies which could be regarded as co-opting the voluntary sector, and some of the leftist MOP writing reflects on the fuzzy boundaries between the state and the voluntary sector; see for example, George Tyler's observation on politicians trying to take the credit for voluntary action:

> '*Politicians love to give voluntary workers a pat on the back, and then claim the credit for their hard work!*' (*Unpaid Work* (1996), aged 66)

Views on voluntarism, social care, and the welfare state in 1996

The 1996 *Unpaid Work* directive asks the question 'Does a society with voluntary workers show it is a caring society?' – the same question used in the 1981 and 1991 NSVs. Several writers, who do not explicitly describe their political affiliations, responded; all were committed long-term volunteers, and the majority were highly educated and from comfortable middle-class backgrounds.

A subset of these writers argued in 1996 that there was a need for voluntarism, and that intervention from the state should be limited. This includes Margaret Shaw who was working as a voluntary advisor at the Citizens' Advice Bureau (CAB), and was very active in charitable fundraising for other organisations. Margaret opposed the encroachment of the state:

> '*If the state takes over too much, there is also the tendency to expect "somebody" to solve all problems. Non-voluntary "caring" agencies can become very bureaucratic and its workers career-minded, those in need can be the losers then.*' (*Unpaid Work* (1996), aged 66)

She does not expand on her comment on the expectation that all problems will get solved by the state, so we remain unclear whether these expectations might be held by welfare recipients, or by volunteers and voluntary sector organisations, leading them to withdraw from providing services. Given her role as a CAB adviser, where she has contact with people in need, this brevity is a little frustrating. However, the second sentence quoted suggests she believes that there is something distinctive about the ethos of voluntary organisations and their delivery of 'care' when compared with large, professional 'for-profit' organisations. Linda Pope argues that public resources are not unlimited, but even if that were not the case:

> '*I believe we need to help each other, it's just being civilized... You can't pay a Scout Master it takes dedication and vocation to do these sorts of things.*' (*Unpaid Work* (1996), aged 62)

Like several other writers, this respondent is referencing the distinctive qualities of voluntary action. Linda Pope's voluntary action is undertaken primarily through the Catholic Church. Her argument that voluntarism and helping others are both obligatory and vocational, and relate to community efficacy, seem to be mediated by her religious beliefs and the religious context of her volunteering experience.

Alice Dickens has also undertaken church-based volunteering, but her volunteering biography also includes a large range of formal and informal activities over a 25-year period. Her argument for the need for voluntary work is an economic one, but she also argues that there are wider societal benefits:

> '*Providing services that the welfare state couldn't afford, however much it felt they were necessary, is an important part of voluntary work. While there are people prepared to make sure those services can be offered, at least some percentage of society cares.*' (*Unpaid Work* (1996), aged 54)

Her argument is that voluntarism should supplement the welfare state. Claire Cooper, who had volunteered as a Samaritan, a counsellor, and an active writer in letter-writing campaigns run by organisations like Amnesty International, offers a more complex viewpoint. She argues for the value of volunteering in enabling community efficacy and promoting the formation of social capital, but maintains that the state should support civic engagement.

> '*if everything were done by the state or a similar body it would diminish people's sense of oneness with others. I believe that people need, first by being granted respect themselves, and for themselves, to develop respect and caring for others.*
>
> *In turn, the voluntary societies need respect and support from the State, to enable them to function well and to encourage participation.*' (*Unpaid Work* (1996), aged 71)

This is a positive vision of awareness and respect for voluntary action, which contrasts sharply with the unreflective attacks on charity (high salaries, political connections, campaigning) that have been witnessed in more recent times. She also argues (as does Gordon Page) that '*the meeting of basic needs should not depend on charitable organisations, nor should the State exploit voluntary labour in order to save money*' (*Unpaid Work* (1996), aged 71).

This view goes further than those of Margaret Shaw, Linda Pope and Alice Dickens, but is supported by the religious Liberal Democrat writer, Roger King, who argues that volunteers are plugging:

> '*gaps in everyday life caused by the withdrawal of Government activity. My wife feels that at the Hospital she and all the Red Cross volunteers are in fact doing people out of jobs. There is a full-time need which the State is too mean to pay for – it would rather have a lot of people on State benefits, when they could gain dignity by actually earning their livelihood.*' (*Unpaid Work* (1996), aged 75)

This view has some resonance with those expressed by those of the more left-wing writers described above, and their views on how volunteers undercut those at the bottom of the labour market. However, Roger King provides a subtler critique, with its emphasis on the dignity of paid employment, and on the politically-inspired withdrawal of the state (seen as '*too mean to pay for*' services which it should be providing).

Claire Cooper and Roger King's views are closer to those of two, more politicised, writers, Annabel Green and Carole Barker.

Annabel Green's voluntary behaviour comprises a mixture of voluntary activity and activism, including a succession of activities relating to her children and their education, teaching adult literacy, and some involvement in an (unnamed) political party. She writes a passionate diatribe about how the state should do more for those in need, complaining that the government is '*all too keen to palm off as much as they can*' onto the voluntary sector. She gives the example of restrictions on benefits to asylum seekers, as a result of which:

> '*an enormous extra burden has been placed on church groups and charities helping the homeless, to keep these poor people from starving. I just heard this morning on the news that the government want to put more social service provision into the voluntary sector. It makes me very angry.*
>
> *A society with voluntary workers does show that it is a caring society, but far fewer of them should be necessary. Many voluntary posts are ones which carry enormous responsibility, require rigorous training and deserve a salary.*' (*Unpaid Work* (1996), aged 44)

She does not name the political party that she volunteers for, but her views do not suggest that she was a supporter of the then Conservative administration. Her views concur with those of Carole Barker, who describes having been involved in positions on school governing bodies, village committees, a parish council and her branch of the teacher's union, NASUWT. She argues that voluntary work '*encourages the state to do less and less for its citizens*', with the result that many people were falling:

> '*through safety nets once put there to look after their welfare and it's left to volunteers to pick up the pieces. The government's view is that people should stand on their own feet and if they can't, then it's not the government's responsibility to look after them. There is an army of unsung heroes who ask for nothing...and it's quite right that this should be so, but many people are helping out where the state ought to be taking responsibility.*' (*Unpaid Work* (1996), aged 46)

Carole provides the example of a local elderly man, caring for a wife with Alzheimer's disease, who was unable to access any statutory help or care, and was reliant on the help of neighbours in providing personal care for his wife. She agrees that neighbourhood support is desirable up to a point:

> '*but not when someone needs specialist care and nursing. It may save the country a fortune to have all these unpaid workers doing what the state should be doing, but I can't believe that this is what the general population wants.*' (*Unpaid Work* (1996), aged 46)

Caroline Lawson, whose views are not political, but are informed by her experience of ME and involvement in a support group for people with that condition, felt 'very strongly' that there were pressures to provide 'basic necessities' which should be:

> '*the responsibility of the state. It is outrageous that the quality of many people's lives is entirely dependent upon a small number of caring individuals who give up their time freely, and that whether a person receives the help or care or support that is required frequently depends on the availability of a suitably motivated individual or organization in the locality.*' (*Unpaid Work* (1996), aged 31)

The implied critique of 'philanthropic insufficiency' (Salamon, 1987) – the inability of voluntary action to generate a sufficiency of resources and to match them with the pattern of needs – is very strong here. Like most of this cohort of writers who have commented on the relationship between the welfare state and voluntary effort, Caroline's views are informed by her personal experience, both as a recipient and provider of support.

These different writers provide some coherent but disparate arguments for voluntary action, but also suggest the need to establish clear lines of demarcation between voluntary initiative and statutory responsibility, as well as the need to avoid undercutting the position of those occupying low-paid and insecure positions in the labour market. The more politicised writers muster more passionate arguments for the welfare state to do more for those in need, and not rely on neighbours and volunteers to step in when the state should be providing services. However, none of these accounts relate the problems of unmet need which they are describing to specific policies or legislative actions, although they do loosely refer to unmet needs for the provision of health and social care, often through the experiences of relatives or neighbours. It would not be surprising if individuals focused, in their directive responses, on their immediate experiences rather than on the complex policy and legislative environment for social care during the

1980s and 1990s, but it does limit our ability to relate the attitudes of individuals to the changing political and policy context for voluntary action.

Views on voluntarism, social care, and the welfare state in 2012

The 2012 *'Big Society'* directive was issued two years into the period of office of the Conservative–Lib-Dem coalition. As discussed in Chapter Two, New Labour had substantially increased public funding for welfare services, pursued active policies to promote regeneration in disadvantaged areas, training and child development, and pushed for an expansion of the voluntary sector's role in service delivery. In the wake of the 2008 world financial crisis, the mood switched dramatically: the Coalition government introduced the Big Society project, against the sombre backdrop of swingeing public spending cuts. In our analysis of responses to the 2012 *'Big Society'* directive, we have looked for shifts or continuities in the attitudes of the writers who discussed their views on the role of the voluntary sector and the welfare state in 1996 (note that Claire Cooper and Carole Barker did not respond to the 2012 *'Big Society'* directive).

Margaret Shaw was 81 when she responded to this directive. Still active in fundraising, and still providing informal help and care to friends, she expresses the view that there is a need for state intervention in elderly care:

> *'Some things, I think, need to be organised by the State. I'm thinking especially about social services' provision to some of my more elderly friends when they are discharged from hospital.'* (*The 'Big Society'* (2012))

This is not necessarily a change in her view on state intervention in the voluntary sector; indeed in 1996 she had argued against government encroachment on the delivery of voluntary care services. Rather it is an argument for strong statutory involvement in the delivery of care to elderly people, based on her recent awareness of the needs of elderly, infirm and housebound friends. This is not the view of Linda Pope, who states categorically:

> *'All my neighbours who went into homes paid for their care. Families MUST accept responsibility for their relatives.'* (*The 'Big Society'* (2012), aged 77)

Linda describes how she is no longer formally volunteering through the Catholic Church because of poor health, but is still providing extensive informal help to friends and neighbours. Like Margaret Shaw, her account is informed by her own experiences and involvement with elderly friends and neighbours, but unlike Margaret she sees the responsibility for care resting within the private sphere of the family. There seems to have been little change in her view since she discussed the issue of social care in 1996.

Alice Dickens describes continuing to be actively engaged in formal and informal activities in 2012, including long-term involvement in her local hospice, a commitment dating from the early 1980s. In 1996, she opined that voluntary action should provide services over and above what the state could afford to provide – seeing the voluntary sector, in terms which have a long history (see Webb and Webb, 1911), as an *'extension ladder'*. In 2012, her focus on state intervention in the voluntary sector was different. She argues for greater regulation of social care provision in particular fields of activity:

> '*Where professional-standard skills and abilities are needed…there should be an over-arching authority, either state or private, to ensure those standards are maintained but there is a place for voluntary help within those systems.*' (*The 'Big Society'* (2012), aged 69)

Alice's involvement in hospice care may have exposed her to New Labour's involvement in setting standards and increasing professionalisation in the delivery of health and social care. Her view has some resonance with left-wing writer, Gordon Page, who argues against the dilution of the professional and regulated delivery of health and social care services by voluntary effort. However, Alice also contends that regulation can be obstructive:

> '*I feel that a state-run hospice would not have the flexibility to operate to meet the need as seen at any given time. The prize example of a service which should never be run by the state and which relies heavily on volunteers is the RNLI. We always say a state lifeboat would be tied to the quay by red tape while sailors drowned.*'

The argument being made here is not that the state is failing to provide for its citizens, rather it is a consideration of the uniqueness of organisations run by voluntary action, which can provide flexibility and independence where the state cannot. Nevertheless, she argues, voluntary organisations still need some form of regulation.

Annabel Green, a more politicised writer, had much to say in 2012; her rhetoric echoed the concerns of the left-wing writers discussed above, on the relationship between the Big Society and cuts, and the replacement of paid jobs by volunteers. She remains a committed supporter of voluntary initiative, but:

> '*it should be a supplement in a country that provides good health care, social services, community services etc manned by professional well-paid staff.*'

Her commitment is to voluntary action that builds upon the secure foundations of a functioning welfare state funded by taxation. Looking back at the views of writers expressed in 1996, her views are not far removed from those of Caroline Lawson, the writer with ME, despite the gap of 16 years between these two pieces of writing.

The various views described above, relate primarily to the place of voluntarism in the provision of health and social care. Not all the writers discussed hold the same views. Linda Pope emphasises the responsibility of family and community to provide for those in need, whereas Annabel Green argues that the state should provide core health and social care services. There are also differing degrees of views on the levels of state involvement required. These views seem to be informed by cultural, religious and political backgrounds, and personal experience of need – this includes the needs of writers who are increasing in age, and the needs of their parents and peers. However, we do not find comments from these respondents that display an understanding of the voluntary sector, government policy and legislation over the last 30 years, or of developments in the voluntary sector. Individuals are able to comment on policy when aware of its impacts on friends, neighbours or communities, but none seem to refer to specific elements of policy that have influenced voluntary action and the voluntary sector. To what extent is that also true of the Big Society initiative?

Responses to the idea of the Big Society

David Cameron's vision of the Big Society has been the subject of much discussion, concentrating on what it tells us about Conservative party policy relating to the role of the state, how it shaped the Coalition's social policies (see, for example, Ware, 2012; Bochel, 2011; and Alcock, 2010), and how it had an impact on the voluntary sector (see Macmillan,

2013). Perhaps never outside wartime has a British government issued such a clarion call for an expansion of voluntary effort. Seven years on, the absence of a dramatic shift in levels of engagement (Chapter Four) arguably tells us all we need to know about the public's response to that call. Nevertheless, the understandings held by Mass Observers of the Big Society remain relevant. If we see the Big Society as a specific case of a more general point – of governments asking their electorate to contribute more to society – then the responses from writers on this issue capture statements about individuals' reactions to such a call, their capacities to do more, and their beliefs about the potential impact of this change in policy.

We do not add to existing extensive interrogation of the meaning of the 'Big Society'. We organise our discussion in the following way. First, we explore respondents' awareness of the context: the Big Society agenda in general. Then we consider their reaction to the idea.

Awareness, attitudes and reactions

Our directive on the Big Society, issued in the spring of 2012, sought observers' awareness and attitudes to the Big Society agenda, descriptions of their communities' capacity to respond to the Big Society initiative, views on responsibility for public service provision and the balance between statutory, voluntary and private initiative in the welfare state. The directive was launched at a relatively early stage in the Coalition government's austerity programme; thus we have little sense of the impact of public funding reductions in respondents' communities.

The 2012 'Big Society' directive received almost 200 responses. Here we focus primarily on a sample of 100 of these responses, which we use to provide a sense of the frequency with which the MOP writers express particular views. Where we quote from a writer who is not one of the 38 respondents whom we have followed over time, we refer to them by their Mass Observation identity number (see Chapter Three), rather than create a pseudonym for someone who may only be quoted on one occasion.

The analysis of these 100 responses took place in 2012, before this longitudinal study began (see Lindsey and Bulloch, 2013). Of our sample of 38 serial writers used for our more recent longitudinal study, 23 responded to the 2012 'Big Society' directive, but only 13 of those 23 responses featured in the original analysis of 100 responses undertaken in 2012. For the purposes of this more recent longitudinal study we included the responses of all 23 of our sample of 38 serial writers who responded to the 2012 *'Big Society'* directive (thus, ten additional responses were considered), using different analytic criteria to those deployed in 2012. There were, however, crossovers in these criteria. This means that although most of the discussion focuses on findings from our analysis of the original sample of 100, where there are analytical overlaps, we sometimes comment on findings from the 110 responses that were analysed in total.

Two-thirds of the original sample of 100 writers were female; there was a somewhat skewed age distribution, with more people in middle to late age; just over half of the sample was over retirement age. The sample was distributed more or less evenly across the country with the highest proportions living in the South East of England, closely followed by the West Midlands, North West England and the East of England, though the West Midlands was somewhat over-represented in relation to its population. A third of the sample mentioned their children in their writings; around three-fifths of writers did not indicate whether or not they had children – though note that the directive did not specifically ask about their family life. About three-quarters of observers did not mention any religious affiliation; as far as it was possible to tell, the remainder appeared to be of a Christian denomination. Few observers were explicit in their support for a specific political party, yet many writers made statements that suggested their political affiliations. It is not possible to classify all the observers accurately on the basis of these statements.

Awareness of the Big Society

Surveys of public opinion revealed low levels of awareness of the Big Society among the public. Even among those who were aware of it, barely one third felt that they had some comprehension of what it meant (Ipsos MORI, 2010, quoted in Defty, 2011, 73). Ferragina and Arrigoni (2017) used Google Trends data on internet searches to demonstrate that, other than at specific times, such as the 2010 General Election and one or more 're-launches' of the idea by the Prime Minister, public interest was patchy and limited. In contrast with Defty's findings, responses to our directive show that a higher proportion of MOP writers were aware of the Big Society than was the case for the population as a whole. They were also very sceptical about it, perhaps to a greater extent than survey respondents. This elevated awareness is probably because the sample can be thought of as an engaged group of individuals by virtue of their writing for the MOP. Engaged individuals tend to be more highly educated (Musick and Wilson, 2008), which in turn is associated with political efficacy and interest. One reason for this scepticism was that they felt taken for granted. Forty-nine writers felt that the community engagement for which the Prime Minister was calling was already taking place, and criticised Cameron's 'big idea' for failing to acknowledge such efforts; the concept:

> '*was small minded in failing to acknowledge (and support financially) the enormous amount of voluntary work already being provided in, by and for communities right across the country.*' (C3603, male, aged 68)

Attitudes to and understanding of the Big Society

Of the original 100 writers whose responses were analysed, 71 expressed views on the Big Society. Eight writers were ambivalent, eight were entirely positive and 55 were negative. Twelve writers (including some of those who were, on balance, ambivalent) demonstrated some positive attitudes, arguing that a reduction in bureaucracy and government inefficiency would be welcome, that the Big Society agenda might bring people together to help each other and strengthen communities, and that it would increase the likelihood of individuals and communities taking more responsibility for their own needs.

We might regard people who regularly respond to MOP directives as being reasonably well-informed and engaged, but our analysis found that the Big Society message had not registered widely. Some writers reported total lack of understanding laced with suspicion of the underlying politics. The following (from one our 38 writers) constituted the totality of one response, which we have also used as the epigraph to Chapter One:

> '*I haven't got a clue what it means. Nobody I've spoken to don't know either. If it's about our PM saying we're all in this together, it's a laugh.*' (Gillian Reddy, aged 67)

In similar vein, David Gardiner immediately dismissed the notion as '*a Dave Cameron PM thing, so without meaning*' – referencing Cameron's attempt ('call me Dave') to downplay his upper-class origins. Over one-third of those responding from our sample of 38 writers whom we have tracked through a series of directives (and by implication, therefore, the most engaged with MO) struggled to understand the idea. Respondent Sarah Thomas thought it a '*strange saying as it does not explain anything*'; for Gordon Page, it was '*hardly a policy with a budget, more a loose concept*'; Margaret Shaw felt that it was '*too woolly to be a good political phrase*'. Others regarded it as '*facile and glib*' (Annabel Green), '*fabricated*' (Emily Major), '*vacuous ... pointless and meaningless*' (Derek Prior) and '*gimmicky*' (Linda Pope).

Referencing a more general disengagement with political rhetoric, Dianne Roberts stated that she tended to 'switch off' when she heard '*any of these stupid phrases, like that one and "affordable housing" and "sustainability". None of it actually means anything*'. From a different perspective Charles Wright felt it was irrelevant to the '*real concerns of ordinary people*', which he xenophobically described as '*the taking over of our country by alien cultures*' as a result of unchecked immigration which was '*importing poverty and criminality*'.

A political strategy and a cover for cuts

Some writers perceived the Big Society to be a political strategy designed to differentiate David Cameron and the Conservative Party from Margaret Thatcher and her governments (a theory that has been previously been written about by Ware (2012)). Approximately a quarter of all the writers analysed thought that the Big Society agenda was a political manoeuvre. Unconsciously echoing Ware's work, Annabel Green suggested it was a ' *"New" Conservative antidote to Margaret Thatcher's infamous dictum: "There's no such thing as society"*', but she also regarded it as '*Hypocritical government propaganda – hoping to get things done for free or on the cheap*'. Roger King thought that the underlying motives were to make a political splash: '*big ... the chap making it must be full of ideas as to what it is going to bring forth*'. However, in practice, Cameron declared indifference as to the outcomes; there was clearly no top-down blueprint for this initiative, and the idea remained ill-defined.

Some writers speculated that the aim was to gain popularity by minimising the social distance between Cameron and his Cabinet colleagues, on the one hand, and ordinary people on the other. Illustrative reactions, from people with divergent political views, were the following. Frank Driver, a lifelong union and Labour activist, described it as '*a meaningless Tory stunt dreamed up by an old Etonian millionaire with no need or intention to participate*'; Charles Wright, a deeply right-wing contributor, wrote in populist vein of people '*existing on a higher plane than the rest of us*'. Catherine Neil's comment about '*Etonians who may have the old school tie but have never lived on a council estate*' was making a similar point, though her political affiliation was not clear.

A related reaction was that the Big Society idea served as a rhetorical cloak for substantial public spending cuts. This took various forms: a '*Tory stunt to get people working for nothing*' (George Tyler) with volunteering becoming '*the norm – no payment needed – good for the country*' (Maria Dyer); '*part of the thinking is that now so many people are unemployed, due to huge Govt. cutbacks, etc., they need to be kept busy*' (June Foster). Others saw it as part of a strategy to weaken organised labour through welfare cuts and a growth in casualisation and internships: for Gordon Page, there was '*nothing very big about this kind of society*'. This respondent objected strongly to central and local government relinquishing their proper responsibilities as employers and providers of professional services '*in favour of a rush to save money while loudly proclaiming the facile virtues of the Big Society*'. For Frank Driver, it was a '*cop out and a camouflage*' for funding cuts. He exemplified this with regard to local museum services, which in his area were now entirely run by volunteers.

The utility of this discussion is as follows. We can all agree that whatever else the Big Society was about, it constituted an appeal for greater voluntary action. The responses of individuals who are actively engaged in volunteering – indeed have been engaged in many forms over decades – are relevant to an understanding of the limits of such appeals. Collectively, there is evidence that the public was confused about the nature of the project, concerned that it was neither novel not distinctive, and opposed to what they interpreted as its underlying political motivations. It is not unreasonable that governments may, from time to time, ask their citizens to do more, but these responses suggest that citizens required an explanation of the underlying policy framework, and what was envisaged, and to what ends, since they were clearly resisting exhortations to do more. But what of the capacities of individuals and communities to engage?

Engagement and capacity: willingness to do more

As described in Chapter Four, our sample of 38 MOP writers have been engaged in a variety of formal and informal voluntary activities, ranging from unpaid help to family members to unpaid overtime for what is otherwise paid work in the third sector or public sector. The 2012 '*Big Society*' directive specifically asked individuals about whether they provide informal help or care (an under-researched aspect of volunteering (Ellis Paine, 2007)). Of the 100 responses analysed, many included descriptions of the multitude of ways in which these writers support others, and of initiatives outside of formally organised environments. Those describing their informal volunteering demonstrated personal relationships with the beneficiaries of their volunteering, as we would expect from Granovetter's theoretical accounts about the strength of social ties (1973; 1983). Causally, the engagement is a result of the relationship. Possibly as a result of the strength of their strong social ties, writers more frequently discussed having to curtail formal volunteering activity in favour of informal activity, as opposed to the other way around.

Voluntary action is not a morally neutral issue in western society. Volunteering is socially constructed to be a good thing, so some respondents seemed to feel under pressure to defend their commitment (or otherwise) to voluntary action, in some cases providing reasons for why they do not do more. We found transition stories that described previous volunteering contributions, contextualising current levels of engagement. Several observers highlighted the moral imperative they felt to volunteer.

'No. Sometimes I wish I did – as an experience, as something I don't do for gain or experience. Just to give. It seems a noble thing. It's a source of shame I don't.' (W4467, male, aged 37)

'[He] asked me whether I had ever worked with volunteers. Then: had I ever volunteered myself? I said that I hadn't. I felt a flicker of guilty annoyance at having been asked, and thought I detected a flicker of judgement on his face in return.' (B3227, male, aged 45)

Do these individuals, however, have capacity to do more? Defty (2011) found that there was general support for 'the principle of greater involvement in the delivery of services and more local control', but much less evidence that respondents 'were personally interested in getting involved in their local community' (p 74). Asking people about their interest in becoming involved in voluntary work is an uncertain process. Individuals are likely to offer socially desirable responses, especially to questions which ask them about their future intentions. However, we might expect MOP writers to be less likely to reflect the low levels of interest described by Defty. These individuals already volunteer for a writing project and thus can be thought of as 'engaged citizens'.

Individual capacities

The 2012 *'Big Society'* directive asked individuals whether they felt they could do more voluntary work, or whether they were already doing as much as they could. Of those from the original sample of 100 that commented directly (n. 58), the majority (n. 50) indicated that they do not have the capacity to do more. A little over a half (n. 27) indicated that they were already engaged, but could not take on anything further; a smaller proportion (n. 23) indicated that they were currently not engaged in voluntary work. Of those writers currently volunteering, but stating that they have no capacity for additional work, some identified being too stretched by their informal caring commitments. As Helen Cook commented, politicians are *'ignorant of real life as lived by most ordinary people'*. Informal voluntary work, undertaken because of strong social ties, was prioritised above formal volunteering.

Other writers indicated that current commitments to formal volunteering meant that they had no time to take on anything further (n. 14). Some respondents discussed the impact of age and infirmity on their capacity to volunteer (n. 14); some elderly observers were struggling with existing commitments, and were reducing their formal and informal volunteering (n. 7). This might involve replacing donations of time with monetary donations to causes that they support, a phenomenon noted in other chapters in this book by writers like Roger King. Those observers who stated that they were not volunteering at the time of the directive, and did not have the capacity to do so in the near future, did not identify what they perceived voluntary work to consist of. In some narratives, writers stated that they are not engaged in voluntary work, but appear to be undertaking informal activity by providing help to friends and family, or are in fact engaged in formal volunteering. An example is Alice Dickens, who denied she is a volunteer, but then recounted a number of ad hoc, frequent commitments, some of which individually do not absorb great amounts of time (staffing a bookstall to support her church) but which nevertheless would be recognised as formal volunteering. However, though feeling that she ought to be doing more, she declared that she doesn't have the capacity.

A small proportion of observers were very categorical about their motivations for not engaging in formal voluntary work. These reasons included what Brodie et al (2011) describe as a lack of 'practical resources' (p 40): being exhausted by paid work, or by looking after homes, children or family members (n. 9); being ill (n. 2); being too old (n. 7); and being disabled (n. 2). A small number had made a *conscious* decision not to take on formal volunteering roles (n. 3). As we note in Chapter Seven, retirement can be a trigger for disengagement. One retired headmaster remarked:

> '*I was a teacher and head-teacher for thirty-four years. I've stood on the touchline during countless football matches; many of them in the rain. I've seen more netball matches, cross-country runs, athletic meetings and swimming galas than most sports commentators. Christmas Fairs, Nativity Plays, Summer Fairs, Car Boot Sales by the dozen etc, etc, etc. Many of these I have organised. My days of volunteering for anything are over.*' (B4318, male, aged 69)

It is interesting that B4318 perceived his unpaid work as a teacher to be voluntary work. This sentiment of having already contributed to society through and beyond paid employment was echoed in a small number of other scripts, where writers mentioned having to give unpaid overtime to their jobs (whether in the public or private sectors) and feeling unable or unwilling to volunteer in their so-called 'spare time'.

Some observers stated that they are not 'the joining type'; others were put off by bureaucracy ('*You have to be CRB checked[2] before you can arrange flowers*' (Catherine Neil)), by age limits, or by hearsay or experience of power struggles in formal organisations. A small number of observers confessed to not wanting to volunteer, raising the issue of choice and personal selfishness:

> '*Anyway, all this is becoming a bit of a smokescreen of my own. I don't do voluntary work because I don't want to. I'm selfish, perhaps, and lack the impulse to give back to the community. Or am I like the majority of people who can't be bothered or who have many other things with which to occupy their limited free time?*' (B3227, male, aged 45)

In summary, among this engaged sample of 100 writers, there was little capacity or desire to take on more unpaid work. Only a small proportion, 8 per cent, of the writers felt that they could do more. However, this raises an outstanding question: how does the response of this sample of engaged individuals compare with the broader population? National surveys have asked whether respondents would like to spend more time helping groups, clubs or organisations, and typically around one-third of respondents say that they would. For those who have reported formal volunteering in the previous 12 months, the proportion is nearer one half. A number of our respondents are older, and often experiencing illness or disability which might affect capacity. The framing of the questions may also account for these responses. By asking individuals about whether they felt they were doing the 'maximum they can', we may have provoked a negative reaction compared to an open-ended question about whether people would like to do more. However, our findings cast some doubt on whether a *willingness* to do more can, in practice, be taken to signal that there is the *capacity* to do more.

Community capacity

Writers were asked whether the places in which they lived have the capacity to meet the communities' needs. When exploring this, we were aware of discussions, in the voluntary sector and elsewhere, of the differential impacts of ongoing and potential future public expenditure reductions on disadvantaged areas. Of the total of 110 written scripts analysed, 59 writers responded directly to this question. Most framed their responses in the light of what they knew of the individuals who make up these communities, and the type of activities in which their communities had engaged previously. Some urged realism:

> '*communities can affect useful changes when individuals act together with a sense of specific purpose with a concrete objective in mind; but this is usually very dependent on a few key people doing most of the organising and the rest as "moral support". I don't think that many communities could successfully sustain more than a few initiatives for more than a relatively short time.*' (R4526, male, aged 52)

There was certainly awareness of the socioeconomic circumstances of different communities. One respondent remarked upon the concentration in his area of '*pensioners with good health and a high disposable income. They are of independent means and no longer need to work*' (W4812, male, aged 45). In such contexts it was felt that voluntary action could easily be sustained, and writers described places in which volunteering and voluntary organisations played a big part in community life. Thus, Helen Cook characterised the market town in eastern England where she lived as an exemplar of the Big Society, referring to no fewer than 13 separate voluntary organisations in her response. Charles Wright thought that certain types of community could take on greater responsibilities if the government got out of the way. He saw this as simply a reversion to '*how it used to be before* [their] *responsibilities* [had been] *eroded by excessive legislation from successive governments'*. This respondent had introduced his writing by equating the Big Society with large-scale organisation and centralisation. He linked his general scepticism about the welfare state to a nostalgic vision of a former country:

> '*those old attributes once seen as 'Englishness' still survive in districts such as ours* [including] *... independence and respectability. So, I think it true to say, barring further damaging legislation, we could survive more of central government's withdrawal of support.'*

While not sharing his political perspective, others made similarly nostalgic comments, seeing the Big Society as a reasonable characterisation of how small communities operated before the welfare state, a state of affairs that is '*not, I think, possible now*' (Helen Cook), or something that was '*very far from most of the present society*' (June Foster).

Others pointed to challenges in places where 'community wealth' (Keohane et al, 2011) was lacking, as in an ex-mining town, which was characterised as a community in which people were not able to:

> '*pull together to make things happen. There's a kind of fatigue that's come with being economically downtrodden, a fatalism. People don't seem to have much confidence and rely on others to make a stand.'* (W3994, female, aged 40)

These comments echo Lindsey's (2013) research into voluntary action in two contrasting communities: the skills, energy, confidence and connections needed to take up the Big Society's opportunities were well in evidence in an area of affluence, but singularly lacking in a very disadvantaged neighbourhood a few miles away. The possibility that greater voluntarism might have regressive effects was also raised, in relation to the proposals of the Localism Act to give communities greater control of planning issues. One respondent (H3070) railed against the in-migration of well-off retirees who then manipulated the local planning system to '*keep house prices as high as possible*'. George Tyler expressed concerns that the same provisions might provide '*significant potential for populist and possibly transient ideas impacting on local policy*'.

An important theme of Ware (2012) is the decline of communities as a base for organisation. Few of our MO writers positively eulogised their communities. Several longstanding respondents lamented the decline of the strong social networks which they had built up when arriving in relatively new communities, such as overspill residential developments to which people moved from London in the 1950s and 1960s. There was also awareness of wider social changes consequent upon changes in the organisation of production. Sylvia Taylor lamented the slow decline of the social networks, including clubs, built upon a Ford vehicle assembly plant, networks which had provided support to ex-employees in retirement. H4553 recounted the demise of the strong manufacturing base of the community in which he had grown up in West Yorkshire. The consequences of this were '*the accelerated departure from the townships of most of the young people*' and an increase in commuting times for those remaining in work which, in an insight which Putnam (2000) would acknowledge, left them '*far less time and energy to give to community-focussed activities*'.

Some expressed forthright views on the need for continued infrastructural support from local government: George Tyler suggested that communities do not '*have enough power to manage their own needs*' without that support, and he was not the only writer to raise questions about how the financial costs of Big Society voluntarism might be met. Finally, the context in which policies were being implemented was something which exercised various writers. In the short term, Frank Driver felt that the funding pressures on local authorities were working against the grain of the Big Society: his local authority was coping with austerity by selling off open spaces, play areas and community facilities. These facilities, in the new town where he lived, had been established by the state, with public support for neighbourhood groups based in community halls built with public money. There was also a recognition that the scope for voluntary initiative was being squeezed by processes of centralisation of services of all kinds, and forces which were beyond the powers of community groups to control – such as major road schemes. Thus, there were laments for a lost community. Environments which facilitated engagement were being squeezed by market forces ('*the market has taken over*' (Sarah Thomas)).

Conclusion

There is no systematic and coherent body of evidence on attitudes to voluntary action for the 30-year period in which we are interested, although occasional surveys confirm a widespread belief in the virtues of voluntarism and its wider social benefits. The value of the MOP material is that it taps into the issues identified by engaged individuals, some of whom have track records of voluntary action extending over several decades. Their views are consequently to be taken seriously.

First, their evidence highlights challenges which will remain important if the shrinkage of the state continues, and if, consequently, more is demanded of volunteers. The evidence provided in this chapter, and in the book, offers a realistic understanding of what people currently do in terms of voluntary action. Many writers have described what might be regarded as formal volunteering – through organisations – but this was juggled alongside numerous other informal commitments as well as family responsibilities for unpaid care. While some of this undoubtedly reflects the fact that MOP writers are getting older, a persistent theme of this book has been that, when asked about voluntary action, respondents are immediately prompted to describe caring relationships and informal neighbouring. An implication is that if social need increases as a result of government spending cuts, individuals may prioritise responsibilities resulting from strong ties over those resulting from weaker ties; in other words, they are likely to engage in 'hunkering down', to use Putnam's (2007) terminology, rather than becoming engaged in wider community initiatives.

Second, we found a strong sense of where the boundary should lie between statutory responsibility and voluntary initiative. There is a positive sense that people can contribute, and that it is important that they are able to do so. This is counterbalanced, however, with scepticism about dilutions of professional services in the public sector, and strong criticism of the relationship between greater reliance on volunteers, austerity, and undermining the dignity of paid labour through the use of volunteers to undercut the position of the lowest paid members of society.

For these reasons, third, we found scepticism about capacities to take on further commitments. This is true both at the individual level, where we found individuals believing that they are so stretched already that they cannot take on further roles, and where they believe that they have already contributed above and beyond the call of duty. Community-level impacts are also highlighted. Respondents certainly described contexts in which voluntarism had attained some successes. Even in this restricted sample, however, there was also evidence that there are communities rich in networks of voluntary organisations which will carry on as before; whereas in others there is a sense of exhaustion. While policy debate has emphasised charity 'hotspots and deserts', the inferences drawn from this (CSJ, 2014) seem to be that the problems of poor areas lie in the failures of their residents to form enough voluntary organisations. Instead, we would emphasise the realities of everyday lives in disadvantaged areas, wherein the challenges of getting by squeeze the scope for community engagement, as touched upon by several of our respondents, which make it unlikely that voluntary initiative alone can make up for the shrinkage of the state.

Finally, MOP writing shows that the basis upon which appeals are made for greater voluntary effort is crucial. This group were extremely sceptical, both about the meaning of Cameron's policies and the context in which they were being implemented. For such policies to capture the imagination, clarity and honesty about the core message are crucial.

Notes
1   This may be a reference to the directive having been commissioned by a postgraduate researcher.
2   Now the Disclosure and Barring Service.

NINE

Conclusions

Overview

We opened this book with a quote from a Mass Observation Project (MOP) writer to the effect that the sheer scale of voluntary effort in Britain was so large that it would surprise 'even the Prime Minister'. Many efforts have indeed been made to quantify this effort but what is even more important, we argue, is to understand the personal stories behind the aggregate statistics. We believe that the volume and quality of material from our group of MOP writers provides unparalleled insight into people's journeys into and through voluntary action, the nature of their contributions, their reasons for becoming involved, and their attitudes to the place of voluntary action. The material presented in Chapters Four to Eight provides highly novel insights into how voluntary action has changed (or not) in the period covered by this book.

In writing this book we were interested in the extent of continuity and change in voluntary action. The quantitative evidence is clear: our work on survey datasets covering the period from the early 1980s onwards amply demonstrates underlying stability (Chapter Four). Although no individual social survey has been implemented consistently over the period which we have studied, there is consistency within individual surveys over time, in terms of the proportions of the adult population who are engaged in voluntary action, so we feel justified in this claim.

This raises the question of whether, given that the policy environment in the past three decades has been supportive, we might expect to have seen a significant increase in volunteering. Since the late 1970s there has been a consensus regarding the virtues of voluntary action, although specific reasons for supporting it, and the extent of practical steps to do so, have varied. Political discourses have ranged from base imperatives of economic necessity and naive anti-statism, to loftier impulses, such as the desire to inculcate civic virtues, or to promote individual wellbeing and the formation of social capital. Governments and advocates of the voluntary sector have placed different emphases on these arguments at different points in time (Chapter Two); although there has been

217

plenty of supportive rhetoric, there has not been one consistent policy framework in support of voluntary action. Of course, changing social, economic and political circumstances account for some of the variations in administrations' focus on voluntarism and the voluntary sector; for example, the management of mass unemployment in the 1980s, and the imposition of austerity policies after 2010, placed the voluntary sector and voluntary action centre-stage at these time-points. Thus, one answer to the question of stability is that in the absence of consistent policy we should not be surprised that little has changed.

That, of course, presumes that government policy could be expected to have a detectable effect on voluntary action given that individuals were living through what, by any standards, were several decades of turbulent socioeconomic change. Early in her term of office, Margaret Thatcher expressed the optimistic view that 'earlier retirement, shorter working hours, altered attitudes and aspirations…[would] mean that the range and number of volunteers is growing the whole time'.[1] In practice, the post-1979 years witnessed the collapse of manufacturing, consequent mass unemployment, and periods of recession, followed by a long economic boom in the late 1990s, ending in the crash of 2008. By any standards such far-reaching changes would be expected to have influenced the capacity of individuals to engage in their communities.

On the other hand, the period also witnessed sustained expansion of higher education. Since a core finding of the volunteering literature is that highly educated individuals are more likely to engage, the expansion of the proportion of the population who have higher qualifications ought to have been associated with an increase in the aggregate rate of volunteering. The period also saw considerable growth of the resources available to the voluntary sector, but with volunteering levels remaining fairly stable, that expansion seems to have been achieved largely through a steady increase in the sector's paid workforce.

In practice, the stability of volunteering rates is the net result of all these changes. Depending on one's point of view, this might be seen positively or negatively. Engagement has held up in tough economic circumstances because of a supportive policy environment and an expansion of education; alternatively, the benign effects of those supportive influences have been kept in check by economic realities (the most visible consequence of which is the recession-induced decline of informal volunteering in disadvantaged communities: Lim and Laurence, 2015).

As we see in Chapter Five, there has also been broad stability in the groups supported and in the activities being carried out by volunteers.

Again, this has both positive and negative implications. When it comes to the groups and organisations assisted by volunteers, there is consistency in the rankings: sport, hobbies and recreation, religious groups, children's education and youth activities have remained at the top of the list. Participation in groups associated with adult education has attracted larger proportions of volunteers (but note that the questionnaires for the Citizenship Survey (CS) and Community Life Survey (CLS) ask about groups related to education for adults, leaving open the possibility that respondents answer with reference to university societies and clubs; thus, these surveys could in part be capturing greater participation in university education). These developments provide ample confirmation of the importance of 'serious leisure' in voluntary action. There also seems to have been growth in the proportion of volunteers engaged in environmental groups. Over time, however, the proportion of individuals who say that they are giving help to groups working in the health/welfare/disability fields, or working with the elderly, has slipped down the order. Although this may relate to an increase in funded and paid work within this part of the sector (which we cannot explore with the available data), it may also suggest that meeting basic social needs through voluntary action will become more challenging, particularly within an ageing society.

As for the precise activities being carried out, a striking finding from data on the tasks carried out by individuals is the decline in the proportion who report being involved in fundraising. We assume this to be a function of novel ways of raising funds which take advantage of digital technologies: but it would also be a welcome development if it released volunteer time for other activities. It is worth pointing out, in the context of discussion of the types of activities undertaken by volunteers, that in searching for continuity over time we are constrained by surveys which have used categorisations first devised some decades ago. Some elements of voluntarism have only recently been incorporated into surveys (befriending and mentoring) and it goes without saying that long-established surveys are not going to pick up novel forms of engagement, for example those enabled by digital technologies. We do, however, note that some MOP writers discuss their relationship with digital technologies and engagement (Chapters Five and Six).

Understanding these developments requires more context and depth than is available through survey data on individuals. This is where the MOP material comes into its own on a number of fronts (Chapter Three). First, MOP disrupts the neat categories – such as formal and informal volunteering – used in social surveys to characterise voluntary action. Instead discussion of current volunteering and recall of past volunteering is at times contested and questioned, and contextualised within the fabric of writers' everyday lives (Chapter Five). When asked about unpaid work, strong familial and social ties prompted accounts of caring for relatives, and of support provided for neighbours. Respondents were uncertain about whether what they did counted as volunteering; some described actions which plainly benefited their own family directly (and which therefore might not fall within internationally recognised definitions of volunteering); and gave accounts of extensive involvement in leisure activities, which may, or may not, have included the giving of unpaid help to organisations (Chapters Four and Five). Demonstrating the limits of social surveys, we know of at least one MOP respondent (Sylvia Taylor) who did not report, in the directives most closely related to voluntary action, a commitment, extending over half of her lifetime, to the establishment and running of a community centre – though she did describe this elsewhere. This is by any standards, a level of engagement that would place her at the upper end of the 'civic core' (Chapter Five; see also Mohan and Bulloch, 2012).

Does it matter whether, if asked in a social survey, individuals would be able to distinguish between formal and informal volunteering? Most of the MOP writers whose responses we have used in this study are highly engaged individuals who, on the whole, have extensive histories of engagement in both types of activity. They have contributed complex mixes of voluntary activity, playing significant roles in existing institutions and in initiating new ones. They have often been central to their communities and indeed are over-represented when it comes to committee and other formal roles. For all this commitment, though, we emphasise that a key message from these writers is the prominence of, and priority given, to caring roles arising from strong social and family ties.

Where would we place these respondents, then, in relation to debates about 'dominant paradigms' of voluntary action (Chapter One)? Much of what these writers do is clearly formal volunteering through organisations, and might be interpreted as altruistic, but there is also a great deal of serious leisure in evidence. However, much voluntary effort is less easily categorised, and the MOP material doesn't always shed light on the organisational context in which activities take place. Where the material has some limitations is in relation to campaigning and activism. The phrasing of the directives encompassed a wide range of groups but the directives consulted were less explicit in relation to seeking information about protest and activism. Nevertheless, the proportion of respondents who described political engagement of various kinds and involvement in tenants' organisations (actions which might be regarded as part of the 'civil society' paradigm of voluntary action; see Chapter One) was higher than the national average. The directives selected for this study[2] are also relatively silent on participation in ad hoc events (protests and claims-making of various kinds) by organised groups, a form of participation which does not necessarily involve sustained commitment or organisational membership by the individuals who take part in it, but which Sampson et al (2005) regard as a growing feature of community life. Commentators such as Lichterman and Eliasoph (2014) and Evers and von Essen (forthcoming) rightly emphasise the importance of a broader conception of civic action, focused on deliberation and coordinated actions to effect social change. We agree with this emphasis, and are of the view that the commissioning of an MOP directive on these issues might provide scholars of civic action with some scope to explore the dimensions of these type of engagement.

What about motivation? *Ex ante* statements of motive, providing access to what individuals thought at the time they took a decision to volunteer, are impossible to access either through survey data or MOP material. Generalisations on motivations are hazardous; Leat (1983) is surely right to say that the psychoanalyst's couch may never be far away in this territory. It may be more defensible to say that what is in evidence are influences – parental, workplace, place of worship, community – which interact in contingent ways with the personal circumstances (at home, at work, social networks), values, identity and personality of volunteers (Chapter Six).

While individuals may rationalise the benefits they experience from voluntary action, in terms of personal validation and self-esteem, therapy, or career, ultimately seeking an explanation of prior motivations from respondents is extremely challenging. Instead, focusing on *when* in their lifecourse people volunteer, and *how* the roles and domains in which they choose to volunteer fit their life circumstances, skills and personality may offer more insight for both academic and practitioner purposes.

Given the relationship between motivations to volunteer, and changing life circumstances, separating motivations (Chapter Six) from trajectories through volunteering (Chapter Seven) is analytically challenging. A change in circumstances – for example a new job, with its attendant changes in social networks – may be associated with a change to the way in which opportunity is structured, whereby individuals may be asked to volunteer, or have their arms twisted to do so. A longitudinal perspective does suggest, in fact, that there are very few people who pass through their lives without any engagement at all, and that the level of engagement is much higher than cross-sectional surveys indicate. In the British Household Panel Survey (BHPS) the percentage of the population who volunteer in at least one wave of the survey, over a 15-year period, is at least twice the level found in any single year of the survey (Chapter Seven). The challenge, here, is retaining volunteers, converting intermittent engagement into long-term commitments to one organisation or individual, or for those who prefer change, to a variety of organisations or people. Volunteering trajectories, however, are complex: one person's commencement may be another's curtailment, exemplified by the retirement decisions of some of our respondents. Some engage, some withdraw, challenging the focus of Davis-Smith and Gay (2005) and Hogg (2016) on retirement as a trigger for engagement. However, decisions to commence, or cease, engagement can take place at any point of the lifecourse. From the accounts of a small number of our respondents, we might also raise questions about how much choice they had in the matter. Consider the view of one respondent that there was a normative expectation that someone in his position ought to take leadership roles, or others recounting how they were initially 'persuaded' to lead an activity, which they later described in terms of coercion, and even, in one case, being volunteered for a committee role. We also note that where some individuals seem to be almost coerced into volunteering during their lifecourse, they are likely to look for opportunities to disengage, which may present themselves as a result of lifecourse changes, such as moving house or changing jobs.

These motivations and trajectories are complex, and not easily subject to management or intervention; it cannot be presumed that people will take up a call to volunteer. To shed light on how they respond when asked to do more, we need an understanding of their attitudes to voluntary action as well as their attitudes to, and capacity for, greater involvement (Chapter Eight). We found that MOP writers had strong objections to being called to action to support basic public services. There also seemed to be little sign of awareness of what is going on in the wider voluntary sector – we did not find evidence that respondents comment spontaneously on issues such as charity salaries or dependence on public funding, two issues which were salient at the time of the 2012 'Big Society' directive. Respondents did, however, have a clear sense of the importance of clarity about the balance between statutory and private responsibility; they expressed strong views about being asked to make up for deficiencies in public services. If being summoned to serve they wanted assurances that they were not acquiescing with a job substitution policy, or an economy drive. Such sentiments were expressed equally strongly in the 1996 *Unpaid Work* and 2012 *The 'Big Society'* directives.

There is also evidence that writers were unpersuaded by the Big Society rhetoric of the Coalition government; vociferously sceptical about the underlying motivation and practicality of the proposals; and in some cases, were frankly weary, and forcefully articulated a sense of exhaustion and inability to contribute further. We read of individuals with extensive life histories of volunteering vigorously rejecting appeals to do more, and others questioning why the government did not acknowledge the sheer volume of voluntary work already taking place. Widening the argument to community capacities, there was recognition that high expectations of voluntary action might be reasonable in certain prosperous middle-class contexts, but certainly not in others, beaten down by large-scale unemployment. The message here is that appeals for greater voluntary initiative must be crafted in such a way as to take the public with them.

Future scenarios

As noted at the beginning of this book, the MOP writers whose testimonies are used in this book cannot provide a comprehensive picture of voluntary action: they are highly engaged, certainly, and they may be thought of as representative of *active* citizens, with a particular emphasis on those who came to adulthood from the 1940s through to the 1960s. Even within the observers, some write more extensively and with a greater degree of reflection than others, though this is not to deny the force of Gillian Reddy's blunt expostulation that '*it's a laugh*', if the Big Society was David Cameron's way of saying '*we're all in this together*' (see Chapter Eight). Thus, there are some voices we do not hear.[3] We acknowledge that the Mass Observation Archive (MOA) is seeking to recruit groups who hitherto have been less involved in the writing project (including writers who are younger, male, from ethnic minorities, from the north of England and from the devolved countries of the UK and/or who are more disadvantaged). This ought to provide a broader spectrum of insights in the future. Future directives could also probe the meaning of emerging forms of volunteering and social action in more depth. Social science will always struggle to keep up with the protean character of voluntary action and we need work on emerging developments like 'micro-volunteering', which is attracting some attention at present.[4]

So what does the future hold? The International Labour Organisation (ILO, 2011, 1) has referred to voluntary action as a genuinely 'renewable resource' for social development. The evidence of this book suggests that levels of engagement in volunteering are stable, but this may not be enough to cope with greater calls on volunteers. As the state continues to shrink, important public services will be relinquished; new activities will come into being such as free schools; and volunteers will be essential to relieve the burden on overstretched services. To the extent that the volunteering resource is relatively finite – at least in the short term – all these developments will increase competition for volunteers.

This raises the question of what practical steps, if any, might be taken to increase the numbers of volunteers. As things currently stand there are two policy emphases. One is the introduction of 'nudging' – changing the behavioural choice architecture to promote pro-social behaviour. Experiments in this regard do not, so far, appear to have resulted in significant increases in volunteering (John et al, 2011). The second is a greater emphasis on youth volunteering, exemplified by initiatives such as National Citizens' Service for young people, or the #iwill campaign to increase levels of 'social action' among those aged 10–20.[5] These very recent developments do not feature in responses from our observers. However, we may speculate as to how they might respond. Generally, in relation to nudging, we believe that they would highlight lack of capacity on the part of individuals, and also of communities; they would question the motives of those doing the nudging; they would not rule out voluntary engagement in public services but would be aware of where the limits should lie. In relation to youth volunteering, we imagine that they would welcome the principle of providing opportunities for constructive engagement, but express scepticism about how much might be achieved by such initiatives, bearing in mind the difficult economic circumstances currently facing young people.

Of course, these are quite specific initiatives. A strong message from the material presented in this book about the place of voluntary action in people's lives is that we need to think of policy in a wider frame of reference, since engagement is influenced in ways which are not confined to incentives or initiatives targeted at particular groups. First, when governments talk of volunteering, what is not always acknowledged is whether demands for greater voluntary action are compatible with the growing burden of unpaid care as the population ages. It was striking, in reading the MOP material, to see the emphasis on care for family and relatives, and the way this was prioritised by our respondents. Projecting this forward, the difficulties being faced by the care system in Britain, with severe problems of market failure in the private sector, and austerity in the public sector, must inevitably throw a greater burden onto families. From our evidence, this will almost certainly have ramifications for the availability of volunteers.

Second, consider some of the barriers that currently prevent the accommodation of voluntary action into everyday lives. Labour markets characterised by zero-hours contracts do not provide the social networks that bring people together, nor do they offer the 'orderly careers' which Wilensky (1961) characterised as underpinning social participation in the USA nearly 60 years ago; indeed, our writers document the changes to the labour market, and the notion of 'jobs for life' and 'full employment for all' (Beveridge, 1944) over the 30 years in which they are writing. Wilensky was particularly concerned at non-engagement among men in the more 'chaotic' sections of the labour market. Those observations seem remarkably prescient given the expansion of various forms of insecure employment, such as zero-hours contracts and, most recently, the 'gig economy'. These developments do not favour regular commitment to voluntary action.

Other markets and institutional arrangements also constrain participation. In relation to housing markets, there is likely to be higher levels of turnover of the population in communities: owner-occupation is off-limits to growing numbers of people, who are living in private rented accommodation with limited security of tenure, while welfare reforms push people out of high-cost locations while increasing commuting distances. In practical terms length of residence is known to be associated with higher engagement; present arrangements work against it for growing numbers of people. Welfare conditionality requires individuals to be able to accept work at very short notice. More generally, when planning for new residential developments, spaces for associational life are conspicuously absent, other than the occasional gym or café. At a time of huge social, economic and political change, what is needed is policy that enables the building of strong and weak ties in educational, cultural, residential and work-based communities for all age-groups. These various communities do not provide the basis for social organisation that they once did (Ware, 2012). There is an additional geographical factor to consider: in circumstances characterised by increased levels of socio-spatial segregation, our MOP writers show awareness that greater voluntary action might work well for some neighbourhoods but not in others. The localist rhetoric and policies of the present government are likely to benefit rich, stable communities, not poorer communities characterised by considerable population turnover.

The challenge is to create the economic circumstances which make similar levels of engagement possible for all, and ultimately this involves ensuring freedoms from the various social evils which William Beveridge recognised a lifetime ago. Beveridge was noted for his emphasis on managing the economy in such a way as to promote full employment in order to give people economic security (Beveridge, 1944); but he subsequently wrote *Voluntary Action* (1948) because he believed voluntarism was essential to a free society. Others have evoked the virtues of voluntarism while believing that there was no role for the state in creating the conditions in which people would engage in voluntary action. Nearly 30 years ago, Michael Ignatieff (1989) criticised the Conservatives' 'active citizen' rhetoric in precisely those terms: 'Conservatives believe the polity exists to maximise freedom but do not believe the polity should provide the means to enable all citizens to be free.' Present and future governments would do well to take this on board.

We think expectations of voluntary action should, therefore, be tempered with realism. Significant proportions of the population – a clear majority, on the basis of most available survey data – are already engaged, to some degree (that is, if one aggregates formal and informal volunteering together). Considering their descriptions of their routes into volunteering, the activities which they carry out, and their motivations for engagement, we are, however, sceptical about whether citizens in general can be drawn into greater levels of engagement. The economic circumstances facing many young people in particular, and those on the margins of the job market in general, add weight to this scepticism.

What might make our respondents step up to the plate? In 2012, many writers wrote about the economic crisis, the public spending cuts, and the impact of cuts on their local services. These descriptions contain a guarded sense of a Britain in crisis. Coalition rhetoric relating to the economic crisis and public spending cuts, such as 'broad shoulders', or 'we're all in this together' easily meld with the somewhat militaristic language employed by Cameron in his 'Call to Arms' (2010)[6] to join the Big Society. Perhaps unsurprisingly, this rhetoric was echoed in the writing of the observers, with a small number writing that their first thoughts relating to the Big Society were 'the Second World War' or 'the spirit of the Blitz', a notional time of national solidarity and 'pulling together'. For example:

> '*In a way it seems to be a throwback to the way things were (or were said to be) during the war, the "we're all in this together" mentality, the idea that everyone will pull together for the common good. I think that in a real crisis this is still so, in fact when I was talking to my husband just now about what the concept means, he remarked "you'd need an absolute disaster these days, for the idea to work". I think that is so. This country does have problems, especially financial, but the fact is that there is no one problem that faces everybody in the way that a war or a natural disaster would.*'
> (F3409, female, aged 64)

The voluntary sector will always bring forth new initiatives in response to need – consider foodbanks, even if the fact that they are so heavily used is hardly a sign of social progress. But an expansion of voluntary effort across the board requires, as this last extract suggests, a compelling narrative that is not based on sudden crisis or necessity.

There are nevertheless grounds for hope here. The stability of voluntary action is certainly one. The sheer scale of effort is another, with the Office for National Statistics (ONS, 2017) estimating the value of formal volunteering at some £23 billion. Economic aggregates do not always make the case, however. No one reading the accounts given by the MOP writers could fail to be impressed by the evidence of the willingness of individuals, in the right circumstances, to engage with causes in ways which fitted with their daily lives, often over many decades. Therefore, we finish with illustrations from the lives of our volunteers. They include the union activist joining up with Avaaz at the age of 78 in the belief that it offered a congenial home for someone of his political inclinations; the socialist who didn't believe in voluntary action but nevertheless made informal volunteering almost a routine part of his daily life; the 91-year-old retired executive acknowledging that his days of formal volunteering were impaired by declining mobility but still contributing, like other elderly MOP writers, wherever he could, replacing donations of time with donations of money; the individuals who thought that they could 'cut out the middleman, and do it for themselves'; those whose journeys had taken them through tentative steps of establishing playgroups for their offspring, and leading eventually to chairing significant local organisations. These individuals became involved for a variety of reasons, often specific to circumstances in their own lives or communities, rather than (as far as we can judge) in response to demands for greater citizen engagement. They were generally able to integrate their voluntary commitments with their daily lives, though some maintained those commitments in the face of many competing pressures. Voluntary action can be a renewable resource, as the ILO (2011) suggests; but it needs nurturing, and working with the grain of people's everyday lives, and that involves more than nudging and National Citizen Service. Ultimately it is about creating the conditions in which citizens have the autonomy and resources to provide a secure basis for engagement, and that is a much larger project.

Notes

1 Margaret Thatcher, speech to the Women's Royal Voluntary Service National Conference ('Facing the new challenge'), 19 January 1981, www.margaretthatcher. org/document/104551.
2 There are no directives that ask directly about activism. Had we analysed directives on general elections or, for example, climate change (2011) or human rights (2013) this might have provided more insights on activism.
3 All 38 writers have contributed to our understanding of voluntary action. Their responses have been considered, analysed and counted. However, there are 3 three writers whose writing has not been quoted or specifically discussed in the final draft of this book: Karen Vickers, Sandra Walker and Rebecca Young.
4 For example, see Sellick, V., 'The rise of the armchair volunteer', http://www. nesta.org.uk/2017-predictions/rise-armchair-volunteerhttp://www.nesta.org. uk/2017-predictions/rise-armchair-volunteer, noting that apart from providing some interesting examples, this piece does not offer any evidence as to the scale of such 'micro-volunteering'.
5 http://www.ncsyes.co.uk/http://www.ncsyes.co.uk/; http://www.iwill.org.uk/ http://www.iwill.org.uk/
6 David Cameron D., 2010, 'Transcript of a speech by the Prime Minister on the Big Society,' delivered in Liverpool, 19 July 2010, http://www.number10.gov.uk/ news/big-society-speech/

Appendix: Anonymised list of writers

Writer pseudonym[1]	M/F	Year born	Responses	Occupational history	Education & additional info	Where living	Who living with
Jim Banks	M	1926	10 responses 1990–2010	1940–43 retail work; 1943–45 conscripted as Bevin boy; 1945–48 army; 1949–75 accountancy dept, then company accountant; 1975 redundancy; 1975–81 various company accountant jobs; 1981 redundancy; 1982–90 senior administrator; 1990 redundancy	Father dies when writer is 12; leaves school at 14; 1944 City and Guilds certificates in Accountancy & Business; 1955–56 wife ill TB; 1991 moves to SW; 1997 wife dies; 1999 remarries	South East until 1991 then South West	Spouse until ˉ997; 1997–99 widowed, alone; 1999 new spouse
Carole Barker	F	1950	9 responses, 1995–2010	1968–72 HE; 1973–81 teacher; 1981–84 homemaker; 1984–95 supply teaching; 1995–2007 teacher; 2007 retires but a bit of locum work	1968–71 BA Biblical Studies; 1972 PGCE. Anti-conservative. Was local president of NASWUT	West Midlands	Spouse & child; 2004 just spouse
Pauline Bennett	F	1941	12 responses, 1981–2010	1958–79 journalist; 1970–82 mature student; 1983–92 market research; 1992–97 self-employ counsellor; 1997 retires	1970s/1980s mature H.; Lib Dem supporter. Married three times; several house-moves while writing for MOP	North West	Spouse

Writer pseudonym[1]	M/F	Year born	Responses	Occupational history	Education & additional info	Where living	Who living with
Pamela Clark	F	1951	5 responses 1995–2006	1970–73 HE; 1973–78 teacher; 1978–83 homemaker; 1983–87 secretarial work; 1987–unknown date accounts clerk	1970–73 teacher training; 1980s night school to gain secretarial qualifications; 1994 ill health; 2001 OU course; 2007 deceased	Yorks & Humber	Spouse & children
Helen Cook	F	1923	15 responses, 1981–2012	1942 retail work; 1942–65 marries farmer, homemaker; 1965–67 divorces, various housekeeper/cook jobs; 1967–86 marries employer who is writer and lecturer, home-maker and step-mother; 1986 runs B&B; 1993 p/t cook; 1994 retires	Leaves grammar school aged 16, no quals; 1965 divorces, sends youngest child to boarding school; 1967 remarries; 1986 widowed; 1994 possibly in relationship; atheist	East	Spouse & children 1942–65 youngest at boarding school; divorces; 1967–86 with 2nd husband and step-children; 1986 widowed; 1994 possibly living with male friend
Claire Cooper	F	1925	8 responses, 1995–2010	1943–45 unqualified teacher; 1945–46 lab technician; 1946–57 home-maker; 1957–61 lab assistant; 1961–68 in-service training as social worker; 1968–70 HE; 1970–81 social worker then social work director; 1981 early retirement because of stress	1943 leaves school at 18; 1946 starts to lose hearing; 1960 wears hearing aid; 1968–70 mature HE cert in social work; 2010 stops writing – poor health prognosis; left wing but 'politically lazy'	South East	Spouse; widowed between 2006 & 2008; alone

Writer pseudonym[1]	M/F	Year born	Responses	Occupational history	Education & additional info	Where living	Who living with
Alice Dickens	F	1942	14 responses, 1983–2012	1961–64 HE; 1964–76 journalist; 1976–78 mental health problems and freelance work; 1978–2007 journalist part-time; 2007 retires	HE; 1964 has to return home to care for school-aged brother after mother dies; 1976–8 post-natal depression; 1978 father retires, cares for granddaughter; 1983 nurses father, father dies; strong relationship with neighbours	North East	Spouse & child until mid-late 1950s, then just spouse
Frank Driver	M	1934	15 responses, 1981–2012	1949–52 trainee mechanic; 1952–55 army; 1955–61 HGV driver then transport manager; 1961–83 HGV driver then night depot supervisor; 1983 made redundant; 1983–97 HGV driver; 1997 medical retirement	Turns down grammar school for technical school, then leaves school at 15; 1956 reservist Suez crisis; Trade Unionist & tenant's representative; member of Labour Party; 1996 resigns from Labour Party; 2000 re-joins LP; family homeless several times; wife has rheumatoid arthritis; 1998 wife dies; atheist	South East	Spouse & children until 1980s; 1998 widowed; alone

Writer pseudonym[1]	M/F	Year born	Responses	Occupational history	Education & additional info	Where living	Who living with
Maria Dyer	F	1947	13 responses, 1984–2012	1965–71 apprentice hair-dresser with mother; 1971–76 hair-dresser different salon; 1976–78 lecturer – hair-dressing; 1979–82 various health problems; 1982–85 teaching; 1985 redundant; 1986–87 Community Programme Scheme; 1987–91 teaching, then ill; 1990 retires	O levels, leaves school at 18; poor relationship with mother; 1979 brother dies, experiences post-natal depression; Magistrate; 1990 retires; 1991 pneumonia, back problems, and ME	North West	Spouse & child until early 1990s, then just spouse
June Foster	F	1938	11 responses, 1984–2012	1954–57 library assistant; 1957–74 homemaker; 1974–78 cook; 1980–83 mature student; 1985 onwards child-minds for children; carer for grandchildren when retired	O levels, leaves school at 16; 1980s mature A levels and HE; 1980s fosters a child; spouse engineering manager; 2010s cares for grandchildren after son-in-law profoundly disabled	South East then 1973 West Midlands	Spouse & children; spouse

Writer pseudonym[1]	M/F	Year born	Responses	Occupational history	Education & additional info	Where living	Who living with
David Gardiner	M	1933	14 responses, 1983–2012	1952–57 architecture student; 1957–8 architect's asst; 1958–60 Nat Service; 1960–92 architect's asst; 1992 made redundant; 1992–98 gardener & draughtsman; 1998 retires	HE studied architecture, dispute over final exams, failed; Labour Party supporter; 1992 made redundant, gets by with odd jobs	South East	Spouse & children until 1980s, then just spouse
Angela Goode	F	1953	8 responses, 1984–2010	1971–73 degree in French, Psychol & Econs; 1973–77 manager trainee retail; 1977 leaves work to have children; by 1990 p/t work as retail supervisor	HE; Hare Krishna	South West	Spouse & children; 2010 child still living with writer
Peter Grainger	M	1927	6 responses 1984–2010	1947–mid-1950s RAF; 1950s agricultural college; 1956–87 farmer; 1987 retires.	Leaves school at 18; 1950s agricultural college; 1995 mature HE diploma in social science; 2010 leaves MOP because of poor health	South East	Spouse
Annabel Green	F	1952	10 responses 1990–2012	1969 au pair; 1970–73 Eng & History degree; 1974–83 librarian; 1983–2002 homemaker; 2002 p/t basic skills tutor	HE; Early 2000s – Basic Skills training; Spouse computer programmer; 2008 spouse retires	South East	Spouse and children – date children leave unknown

Writer pseudonym[1]	M/F	Year born	Responses	Occupational history	Education & additional info	Where living	Who living with
Stephen Johnson	M	1942	11 responses, 1990–2012	1958–64 short term jobs; 1964–99 starts as a clerk for a national newspaper, ends as senior executive; 1999 retires	Grammar School. O Levels Mother had MS when writer was a child. Identifies publicly as single, but living with same-sex partner	South East	Partner
Roger King	M	1921	11 responses, 1990–2012	1939–46 Army Captain; 1947–54 logging overseas; 1954–56 ill TB; 1956–82, Company Secretary, ends as international group pensions advisor; 1982 retires.	Scholarship grammar school; 'Commercial' 6th Form; RSA correspondence; 1954–56 TB; 1959 mature chartered secretary qualification; Lib Dem supporter, strong religious faith	North West 1956–82, then South East	Spouse and children until late 1970s (one child at boarding school), then just spouse
Caroline Lawson	F	1965	5 responses, 1996–2010	1984–85 retail work; 1985–89 degree German & Law; 1990–91 trained as solicitor; 1991 health problems, disabled & unemployed	HE & trained solicitor; 1991 ME. 2001 best friend died	West Midlands, then 1990 Yorks & Humb	1992–97 shared house; 1997 alone
Susan Leonard	F	1952	8 responses, 1984–2008	1969–71 teacher training; 1972–75 teacher; 1975–84 home-maker; 1984 onwards special needs teacher	HE; 1984–88 extra-marital affair; 1988 divorces, remarries; 1992 discovers older half-brother; Labour supporter but anti-Blair	North West	Spouse and child; splits from spouse; new spouse & step-children until mid-1990s, then just spouse

Row 1 Emily Major, F, 1974, "5 responses, 2004–12", occupational: "1992–95 HE then TEFL; 1996–99 travelling & teaching English; 2000–06 Compliance Assist Manager for hedge fund; 2006–08 hedge fund manager; 2008 marries, not working", education: "Boarding school; HE; 1995 TEFL course; 2001–02 sister sick; 2008 Sierra Leone visit", where living: "Africa South East", who living: "Spouse; 2010 spouse and child"

Row 2 Louise Masters, F, 1937, "14 responses, 1981–2012", occupational: "1951–98 various jobs in service or as cleaner; 1998 retires.", education: "Leaves school at 14 to go into service", where: "South East", who: "Spouse & children; spouse; widowed; alone"

Row 3 Catherine Neil, F, 1938, "13 responses, 1984–2012", occupational: "Various jobs; unemployed for 3 years in 1980s; 1986–95 tourist office; 1995 retires; then cares for grandchildren", education: "Grammar school; O levels. Strong religious faith – Catholic. Spouse dockyard fitter, then various other jobs", where: "South East", who: "Spouse & children until late 1980s, then just spouse"

Row 4 Gordon Page, M, 1944, "8 responses, 1995–2012", occupational: "1963–66 HE; 1987–91 BBC film editor; 1991 vol redundancy; 1991–96 freelance editor; 1996 difficulty with freelance work; by 2006 has retired", education: "HE. Green and left-wing views", where: "West Scotland", who: "Spouse and children; spouse"

Row 5 Donna Payne, F, 1952, "8 responses, 1981–97", occupational: "1968 p/t copy typing, leaves; 1968–96 unemployed, and carer for mother; 1996 onwards unemployed & disabled", education: "Poor attender at school, leaves at 16. Lives in extreme disadvantage. 2007 leaves MOP because of poor health", where: "South East", who: "Until 1996 lives with mother, then lives alone"

Writer pseudonym[1]	M/F	Year born	Responses	Occupational history	Education & additional info	Where living	Who living with
Emily Major	F	1974	5 responses, 2004–12	1992–95 HE then TEFL; 1996–99 travelling & teaching English; 2000–06 Compliance Assist Manager for hedge fund; 2006–08 hedge fund manager; 2008 marries, not working	Boarding school; HE; 1995 TEFL course; 2001–02 sister sick; 2008 Sierra Leone visit	Africa South East	Spouse; 2010 spouse and child
Louise Masters	F	1937	14 responses, 1981–2012	1951–98 various jobs in service or as cleaner; 1998 retires.	Leaves school at 14 to go into service	South East	Spouse & children; spouse; widowed; alone
Catherine Neil	F	1938	13 responses, 1984–2012	Various jobs; unemployed for 3 years in 1980s; 1986–95 tourist office; 1995 retires; then cares for grandchildren	Grammar school; O levels. Strong religious faith – Catholic. Spouse dockyard fitter, then various other jobs	South East	Spouse & children until late 1980s, then just spouse
Gordon Page	M	1944	8 responses, 1995–2012	1963–66 HE; 1987–91 BBC film editor; 1991 vol redundancy; 1991–96 freelance editor; 1996 difficulty with freelance work; by 2006 has retired	HE. Green and left-wing views	West Scotland	Spouse and children; spouse
Donna Payne	F	1952	8 responses, 1981–97	1968 p/t copy typing, leaves; 1968–96 unemployed, and carer for mother; 1996 onwards unemployed & disabled	Poor attender at school, leaves at 16. Lives in extreme disadvantage. 2007 leaves MOP because of poor health	South East	Until 1996 lives with mother, then lives alone

Writer pseudonym[1]	M/F	Year born	Responses	Occupational history	Education & additional info	Where living	Who living with
Linda Pope	F	1934	13 responses, 1983–2012	1950–53 copy typist; 1953 onwards, cares for step-children, then own child; home-maker	Grammar school; School Certificate; strong religious faith – Catholic; when aged 18 married high-ranking policeman, 21 years older	South East	Spouse & children, until 1970s, then spouse; widowed 2000; lives alone
Derek Prior	M	1929	9 responses, 1995–2012	1946–47 articled clerk; 1946–49 trainee librarian; 1949–51 Nat Service; 1951–62 librarian; 1963–66 theology degree; 1967 post-grad; 1968–91 ordained, parish priest; retires 1991	Father lorry driver; Grammar school, school certificate, leaves at 16; 1946–52 various library assoc exams; 1963–67 mature HE; Socialist, dislikes New Labour	North East	Spouse & children; 1980s just spouse
Gillian Reddy	F	1945	5 responses 1996–2012	1960–61 retail work; 1961–69 factory work; 1969–2005 factory work; retires 2005	Leaves school at 15, no quals; sister has cancer, brother has MS	East	Spouse
Diane Roberts	F	1943	12 responses, 1984–2012	1960–69 various book-keeping jobs; 1969 onwards, homemaker; 2000 retires	A level and vocational; spouse engineering manager; supporter of Margaret Thatcher	South East	Spouse & children until 1990s, then just spouse

Writer pseudonym[1]	M/F	Year born	Responses	Occupational history	Education & additional info	Where living	Who living with
Denise Rose	F	1952	11 responses, 1981–2008	1968–69 trainee florist; 1970–77 various unskilled jobs; 1977–81 unemployed; 1981–84 unskilled retail; 1984–88 florist, then manageress; 1988 onwards florist manageress	Leaves school at 16; 2008 becomes great grandmother. Daughter has mental health problems. Husband is strong Labour party supporter	South East	Spouse & children, by 2004 just spouse
Beverley Scott	F	1957	12 responses, 1983–2012	1976–79 HE; 1979–83 teacher; 1983–84 unemployed mental health problems then MSC scheme; 1984–87 unemployed mental-health problems; 1987–93 p/t library assistant; 1993–96 various short-term jobs; 1996–2009 locum teacher; 2009 retires	HE; 1983–87 depression and agoraphobia	Tayside, Scotland	Spouse
Sylvia Taylor	F	1930	13 responses, 1981–2010	1944–50 dress-maker; 1950–54 home-maker; 1954–67 dress-making at home; 1968–85 retail work, then manageress; 1985 made redundant; 1985–90 retail work; 1990 retires, then home-maker and carer for parents.	Leaves school at 14, no quals	South East	Spouse

Writer pseudonym[1]	M/F	Year born	Responses	Occupational history	Education & additional info	Where living	Who living with
Sarah Thomas	F	1926	14 responses, 1981–2012	1941–44 various jobs while also caring for mother and brothers; 1944–47 Land Army; 1947–51 various jobs; 1951–67 home-maker; 1967–71 various jobs; 1971 late pregnancy; 1974–91 battery farm-worker; 1991 retires	Welsh, moved to England in 1937. Mother severe mental health problems & violent. Left school at 14, no quals. Marries but not happy in marriage, 6 children; Husband is a factory worker, unemployed in 1980s. 1986 husband dies; Left-wing views	South West	Spouse & children until 1986; widowed, lives with younger child until 1990s; alone
George Tyler	M	1930	12 responses, 1990–2012	1946–49 apprentice mechanic; 1949–54 army corporal; 1954–72 different jobs as mechanic; 1972–89 mechanic then transport superintendent for council; 1989 made redundant; 1989–92 garden centre work; 1992 made redundant; 1995 retires	Evacuated in war, education interrupted, technical school; 1956 disabled brother commits suicide. 1979 son dies. Children marry but split up. Granddaughter born profoundly disabled	South East	Spouse & children until 1980s, then spouse only

Writer pseudonym[1]	M/F	Year born	Responses	Occupational history	Education & additional info	Where living	Who living with
Karen Vickers	F	1955	13 responses, 1984–2012	Short term jobs; homemaker; 1990 works for short-time with a voluntary agency; then unemployed	O levels; born N Ireland, father protestant clergyman, class differences between family and rest of community. 1974 married, moves to Scotland; 1978 separates/divorces & returns to N Ireland. Daughter with unspecified disability	1955–74 N Ireland; 1974–78 Scotland; 1978 then N Ireland	Spouse until 1978, then just 2 children, then children & parents; parents die; lives with adult daughter
Sandra Walker	F	1959	4 responses 1995–2004	1977–79 travelling & vol work; 1979–80 HE; 1981 unemployed; 1982–85 various short term unskilled jobs; 1985 onwards home-maker & home-educator	A levels; 1979–80 HE, then drops out; 1985 first child born; home-schools; 2004 describes herself as single housewife	1979 NE; 1980 NW; 1985 North Scotland	Spouse & children; split from spouse; children

Writer pseudonym[1]	M/F	Year born	Responses	Occupational history	Education & additional info	Where living	Who living with
Jack Wilkins	M	1926	8 responses 1983–2006	1940–45 various factory jobs; 1945–47 army; 1947–48 factory job; 1948–78 building work; 1978–80 redundancy, unemployed; 1980–81 retail work causes ill-health; 1981 onwards unemployed	1940 schooling ends, when 14, due to war; 1948 financially supporting retired parents. Mid-1990s son has mental health problems & dies	South East	Spouse & child
Charles Wright	M	1922	12 responses 1990–2012	1936–41 painter decorator; 1941–46 RAF; 1946–53 painter decorator; 1953–61 runs own painter-decorator business; 1961–77, buys and runs hardware business; 1977 business difficulties – sells up and retires	Born to a very poor family; leaves school at 14, no quals. Former Labour supporter then Conservative supporter, very right-wing views. 1971 best friend dies. Has an affair. Wife dies between 1997–2004	South East	Spouse & children until early 1970s, then just spouse; widowed; alone
Rebecca Young	F	1975	5 responses, 2006–12	1995–98 BSc theology & sociology; 1997–2001 p/t retail; 1999 post-grad diploma heritage management; 2001–02 PGCE; 2002 teacher	1995–2002 HE; 2002 leaves home, finds it difficult to settle into new community	South East	Alone

Note: 1 To find out more about these writers please contact the Mass Observation Archive.

References

6, P. and Kendall, J. (1997) *The Contract Culture in Public Services*. Aldershot: Ashgate.

6, P. and Leat, D. (1997) *Inventing the voluntary sector by committee*: From Wolfenden to Deakin, *Non-Profit Studies*, 1(2), 33–46.

Abrams, P., Abrams, S., Humphrey, R. and Snaith, R. (1989) *Neighbourhood Care and Social Policy*. London: Department of Health.

Alcock, P. (2010) Building the Big Society: A new policy environment for the third sector in England, *Voluntary Sector Review* 1, 379–89.

Alcock, P. (2011) Voluntary action, New Labour and the 'third sector', in M. Hilton and J. McKay (eds) *The Ages of Voluntarism: How we got to the Big Society*. Oxford: Oxford University Press, pp 158–79.

Alcock, P. and Kendall, J. (2011) Constituting the Third Sector: Processes of decontestation and contention under the UK Labour governments in England, *Voluntas*, 22, 450–69.

Alcock, P., Kendall, J. and Parry, J. (2012) From the third sector to the Big Society: Consensus or contention in the 2010 UK General Election, *Voluntary Sector Review*, 3(3), 347–63.

Almond, G. and Verba, S. (1963) *The Civic Culture: Political Attitudes and Democracy in Five Nations*. Princeton, NJ: Princeton University Press.

Andreoni, J. (1990) Impure altruism and donations to public goods: A theory of warm glow giving, *The Economic Journal*, 100, 464–77

Aspinall, P.J. (2009) *Research report 37: Estimating the size and composition of the lesbian, gay, and bisexual population in Britain*. Manchester: Equality and Human Rights Commission.

Bal, M. (1999) Introduction, in M. Bal, J. Crewe and L. Spitzer (eds) *Acts of Memory: Cultural Recall in the Present*. Hanover, NH: Dartmouth College and the University Press of New England.

Barber, M. (2008) *Instruction to Deliver*. London: Methuen.

Barnett, S. and Saxon-Harrold, S. (1992) Interim report: Charitable giving, in R. Jowell, L. Brook, G. Prior, B. Taylor (eds) *British Social Attitudes: The 9th Report*, Aldershot: Dartmouth, pp 195–208.

Bennett, M. (2013) *Volunteering and Giving in England: A Multilevel Study of 313 Neighbourhoods*, www.sp2.upenn.edu/wp-content/uploads/2014/07/socialimpactfellows_Bennett.pdf

Bennett, M., Bulloch, S. and Mohan, J. (2012) Age trends in civic engagement in the UK. Evidence to House of Lords Committee on Public Service and Demographic Change.

Bennett, T. (1983) Texts, discourses and reading formations, in P. Rice and P. Waugh (eds) *Modern Literary Theory: A Reader*. London: Edward Arnold.

Beveridge, W. (1944) *Full Employment in a Free Society*. London: George Allen and Unwin.

Beveridge, W. (1948) *Voluntary Action: A Report on Methods of Social Advance*. Woking: Allen and Unwin.

Beveridge, W. and Wells, A. (eds) (1949) *The Evidence for Voluntary Action*. London: George Allen and Unwin.

Binder, M. and Freytag, A. (2013) Volunteering, subjective well-being and public policy, *Journal of Economic Psychology*, 34(1), 97–119.

Blackstone, T. and Plowden, W. (1988) *Inside the Think Tank: Advising the Cabinet 1971–83*. London: Heinemann.

Blair, T. (1998) *The Third Way: New Politics for the New Century*. London: Fabian Society.

Blair, T. (1999) Speech to *National Council for Voluntary Organisations, Annual Conference*, February.

Blond, P. (2010) *Red Tory: How Left and Right have Broken Britain and How We Can Fix It*. London: Faber and Faber.

Bochel, C (2011) The Conservatives and the governance of social policy, in H. Bochel (ed) *The Conservative Party and Social Policy*. Bristol: Policy Press, pp 251–68.

Bolton, V. (2016) *Volunteering and Political Engagement: An Empirical Investigation*. Unpublished PhD Thesis, University of Southampton.

Bourdieu P. (1984) *Distinction: A Social Critique of the Judgement of Taste* (trans. R. Nice). London and New York: Routledge.

Brenton, M. (1985a) *The Voluntary Sector in British Social Services*. Harlow: Longman.

Brenton, M. (1985b) Privatisation and voluntary sector social services, in M. Brenton, and C. Jones (eds) *The Yearbook of Social Policy in Britain, 1984–5*. London: Routledge and Kegan Paul, 174–92.

Brodie, E., Hughes, T., Jochum, V., Miller, S., Ockenden, N. and Warburton, D. (2011) *Pathways through Participation: What Creates and Sustains Active Citizenship?* London: NCVO, IVR, involve and Big Lottery.

Brookfield, K., Parry, J. and Bolton, V. (2014) 'Fifty at fifty: Long term patterns of participation and volunteering among the 1958 NCDS cohort at age 50, *Third Sector Research Centre (TSRC) Working Paper* 119, Birmingham: TSRC, University of Birmingham, www.birmingham.ac.uk/generic/tsrc/documents/tsrc/working-papers/working-paper-119.pdf

Brookfield, K., Parry, J. and Bolton, V. (forthcoming) Lifelong nonparticipation amongst the NCDS cohort. Under review.

Bryman, C. (2008) Why do researchers integrate/mesh/blend/mix/merge/fuse quantitative and qualitative research?, in M.M. Bergman (ed) *Advances in Mixed-Methods Research*. London: Sage, pp 87–100.

Bulloch, S. and Rivers, C. (2011) *CAQDAS: Contributor to Social Science Knowledge*? Southampton: National Centre for Research Methods, http://eprints.ncrm.ac.uk/1781/1/Bulloch%26Rivers_2011MethodsNews_Spring.pdf

Bulmer, M. (ed) (1986) *Neighbours: The Work of Philip Abrams*. Cambridge: Cambridge University Press.

Buonfino, A. and Hilder, P. (2006) *Neighbouring in Contemporary Britain*. York: Joseph Rowntree Foundation.

Cabinet Office (2011) *Giving White Paper*. Cm. 8084. London: HMSO.

Cabinet Office (2015) Social action – harnessing the potential, *A discussion paper*, www.gov.uk/government/uploads/system/uploads/attachment_data/file/439105/Social_Action_-_Harnessing_the_Potential_updated_June_2015.pdf

Calder, A. (1969) *The People's War: Britain 1939–45*. London: Jonathan Cape.

Chaney, P. (2014) Multi-level systems and the electoral politics of welfare pluralism: Exploring third-sector policy in UK Westminster and regional elections 1945–2011, *Voluntas*, 25(3), pp 585–611.

Civil Exchange (various dates) *The Big Society Audit*, www.civilexchange.org.uk

Clark, T. with Heath, A. (2014) *Hard Times: The Divisive Toll of the Economic Slump*. New Haven, CT: Yale University Press.

Clarke, J. (2014) 'Community', in D. Nonini (ed) *The Companion to Urban Anthropology*. Oxford: Wiley-Blackwell, pp 45–64.

Clary, E., Snyder, M. and Stukas, A. (1996) 'Volunteers' motivations: Findings from a national survey, *Nonprofit and Voluntary Sector Quarterly*, 25, 485–505.

Clifford, D., Geyne Rajme, F. and Mohan, J. (2013) Variations between organisations and localities in government funding of third sector activity: Evidence from the National Survey of Third Sector Organisations in England, *Urban Studies*, 50(5), 959–76.

Clifford, D. (2017) Charitable organisations, the great recession and the age of austerity: longitudinal evidence for England and Wales, *Journal of Social Policy*, 46(1), 1–30.

Cnaan, R., Handy, F. and Wadsworth, M. (1996) Defining who is a volunteer: conceptual and methodological considerations, *Nonprofit and Voluntary Sector Quarterly*, 25, 364–83.

Commission on the Future of the Voluntary Sector (1996) *Meeting the Challenge of Change: Voluntary Action in the 21st Century* (chair: Nicholas Deakin). London: National Council for Voluntary Organisations (NCVO).

Commission on the Future of Volunteering (2008) *Report of the Commission on the Future of Volunteering and Manifesto for Change* (chair: J. Neuberger). London: The Commission on the Future of Volunteering and Volunteering England.

Committee of Public Accounts (2017) 46th report, 2016–17: National Citizen Service, *House of Commons Paper* HC 955, https://publications. parliament.uk/pa/cm201617/cmselect/cmpubacc/955/955.pdf

Cowley, E., McKenzie, T., Pharoah, C. and Smith, S. (2011) *The New State of Donation: Three Decades of Household Giving to Charity, 1978–2008*, www.cgap.org.uk/uploads/reports/The%20new%20 state%20of%20donation.pdf

Crow, G., Allan, G. and Summers, M. (2002) Neither busybodies nor bodies: Managing proximity and distance in neighbourly relations, *Sociology*, 36(1), 127–45.

CSJ (Centre for Social Justice) (2014) *Social Solutions: Enabling Grassroots Charities to Tackle Poverty*. London: CSJ.

Curtice, J. and Heath, O. (2009) Do people want choice and diversity of provision in public services?, in A. Park, J. Curtice, K. Thomson, M. Phillips and E. Clery (eds) (2009) *British Social Attitudes: The 25th Report*. London: Sage.

Davis-Smith, J. and Gay, P. (2005) *Active Ageing in Active Communities: Volunteering and the Transition to Retirement*. York: Joseph Rowntree Foundation.

DCLG (Department for Communities and Local Government) (2008) *National Indicators for Local Authorities and Local Authority Partnerships: Handbook of Definitions*, http://webarchive.nationalarchives.gov. uk/20120920031457/http://www.communities.gov.uk/documents/ localgovernment/pdf/735112.pdf

DCMS (Department for Culture, Media and Sport) (2016) *2016 to 2017 Community Life Survey Questionnaire*, www.gov.uk/government/ publications/2016-to-2017-community-life-survey-questionnaire

De Vaus, D. (2002) *Surveys in Social Research*. London: Routledge.

De Wit, A., Bekkers, R., Karamat Ali, D. and Verkaik, D. (2015) *Welfare Impacts of Participation*. Deliverable 3.3 of the project: 'Impact of the Third Sector as Social Innovation' (ITSSOIN), European Commission – 7th Framework Programme, Brussels: European Commission, DG Research, http://itssoin.eu/site/wp-content/uploads/2015/09/ ITSSOIN_D3_3_The-Impact-of-Participation.pdf

Deakin, N. and Davis-Smith, J. (2011) Labour, charity and voluntary action: The myth of hostility, in M. Hilton and J. McKay (eds) *The Ages of Voluntarism: How we Got to the Big Society*. Oxford: Oxford University Press, pp 69–93.

Defty, A. (2011) The Conservatives, social policy and public opinion, in H. Bochel (ed) *The Conservative Party and Social Policy*. Bristol: Policy Press, pp 61–76.

Driver, S. (2011) Welfare reform and coalition politics in the age of austerity, in M. Beech and S. Lee *(eds) The Cameron–Clegg Government: Coalition Politics in an Age of Austerity*. Basingstoke: Palgrave Macmillan, pp 105–17.

Egerton, M. and Mullan, K. (2008) Being a pretty good citizen: An analysis and monetary valuation of formal and informal voluntary work by gender and educational attainment, *British Journal of Sociology*, 59, 145–64.

Eikenberry, A. and Nickel, P. (2016) Knowing and governing: The mapping of the nonprofit and voluntary sector as statecraft, *Voluntas*, 27, 392–408.

Eliasoph, N. (2011) *Making Volunteers: Civic Life After Welfare's End*. Princeton, NJ: Princeton University Press.

Eliasoph, N. (2012) *The Politics of Volunteering*. Cambridge: Polity Press.

Ellis Paine, A., McKay, S. and Moro, D. (2013) *Does volunteering improve employability? Insights from the British Household Panel Survey and beyond*, *Voluntary Sector Review*, 4(3), 355–76.

Evers, A. and von Essen, J. (forthcoming) Volunteering and Civic Action – boundaries blurring, boundaries redrawn.

Ferragina, E. and Arrigoni, A. (2017) The rise and fall of social capital: Requiem for a theory?, *Political Studies Review*, 15(3), 355–67.

Finlayson, G. (1994) *Citizen, State and Social Welfare in Britain, 1830–1990*. Oxford: Clarendon.

Forrest, R. and Kearns, A. (2001) Social cohesion, social capital and the neighbourhood, *Urban Studies*, 38(1), 2125–43.

Geyne Rajme, F. and Smith, P. (2011) Modelling 'volunteering types' in the UK, *Third Sector Research Centre (TSRC) Seminar* and unpublished paper, Southampton: TSRC.

Giddens, A. (1998) *The Third Way*. Cambridge: Polity.

Giving Campaign (2004) *A Blueprint for Giving*. London: Giving Campaign.

Gladstone, F. (1979) *Voluntary Action in a Changing World*. London: Bedford Square Press.

Glasby, J. (2011) The Conservative party and community care, in H. Bochel (ed) *The Conservative Party and Social Policy*. Bristol: Policy Press.

Glennerster, H. (2007) *British Social Policy: 1945 to the Present* (3rd edn). Oxford: Blackwell.

Glucksmann, M. (2005) Shifting boundaries and interconnections: Extending the 'total social organization of labour', in L. Pettinger, J. Perry, R. Taylor and M. Glucksmann (eds) *A New Sociology of Work*. Oxford: Wiley-Blackwell, pp 19–36.

Goddard, E. (1992) *Voluntary work, Office of Population Censuses and Surveys (OPCS) Series GHS 23A*, London: OPCS.

Granovetter, M. (1973) The strength of weak ties, *American Journal of Sociology*, 78, 1360–80.

Granovetter, M. (1983) The strength of weak ties: A network theory revisited, *Sociological Theory* 1, 203–33

Groves, R.M., Fowler Jr., F.J., Couper, M.K., Lepkowski, J.M., Singer, E. and Tourangeau, R. (2004) *Survey Methodology*. Hoboken, NJ: Wiley.

Hall, P. (1999) 'Social capital in Britain', *British Journal of Political Science*, 29, 417–61.

Hardill, I. and Baines, S. (2011) *Enterprising Care? Unpaid Voluntary Action in the 21st Century*. Bristol: Policy Press.

Harflett, N (2015) 'Bringing them with personal interests': The role of cultural capital in explaining who volunteers, *Voluntary Sector Review*, 6, 3–19.

Harris, R. and Seldon, A. (1979) *Overruled on Welfare*. London: Institute of Economic Affairs.

Hatch, S. (1980) *Outside the State: Voluntary Organisations in Three English Towns*. London: Croom Helm.

Hatch, S. and Sherrott, R. (1983) Patterns of volunteering, in S. Hatch (ed) *Volunteers: Patterns, Meanings and Motives*. Berkhamsted: The Volunteer Centre.

Henriksen, L., Koch-Nielsen, I. and Rosdahl, D. (2008) Formal and informal volunteering in a Nordic context: The case of Denmark, *Journal of Civil Society*, 4, 3, 193–209.

Hilton, M. and McKay, J. (eds) *The Ages of Voluntarism: How We Got to the Big Society*. Oxford: Oxford University Press.

Hilton, M., Mouhot, J.-F., Crowson, N. and McKay, J. (2012) *A Historical Guide to NGOs in Britain: Charities, Civil Society and the Voluntary Sector since 1945*. Basingstoke: Palgrave

Hinton, J. (2013) *The Mass Observers: A History 1937–49*. Oxford: Oxford University Press.

Hinton, J. (2016) *Seven Lives from Mass Observation*. Oxford: Oxford University Press.

HM Government (2011) *Open Public Services White Paper*. Cm. 8145. London: HMSO.

HM Treasury (2002) *The Role of the Voluntary and Community Sector in Service Delivery: A Cross Cutting Review*. London, HM Treasury.

HM Treasury (2007) *The Future Role of the Third Sector in Social and Economic Regeneration: Final Report* (Cm. 7189). London: HMSO.

Hogg, E. (2016) Constant, serial and trigger volunteers: Volunteering across the lifecourse and into old age, *Voluntary Sector Review*, 7(2), 169–190.

Home Office (2005a) *A Generous Society: Next Steps on Charitable Giving in England*. London: Home Office.

Home Office (2005b) *Volunteering Compact Code of Good Practice*. London: Home Office.

Humble, S (1982) *Voluntary Action in the 1980s: A Summary of the Findings of a National Survey*. Berkhamsted: Volunteer Centre.

Hustinx, L. (2001) Individualisation and new styles of youth volunteering: An empirical investigation, *Voluntary Action*, 3(2), 47–55.

Hustinx, L. and Lammertyn, F. (2003) Collective and reflexive styles of volunteering: A sociological modernization perspective, *Voluntas*, 14 (2), 167–87.

Hustinx, L., Cnaan, R. and Handy, F. (2010) 'Navigating theories of volunteering: A hybrid map for a complex phenomenon, *Journal for the Theory of Social Behaviour*, 40(4), 410–34.

Ignatieff, M. (1989) Caring just isn't enough, *New Statesman and Society*, 3 February.

ILO (International Labour Organisation) (2011) *Manual on the Measurement of Volunteer Work*. Geneva: ILO.

Ipsos Mori (2010) *Is the Coalition Government Bringing the Public With It?*, www.ipsos.com/ipsos-mori/en-uk/coalition-government-bringing-public-it

Jacobs, J. (1961) *The Death and Life of Great American Cities*. New York: Random House.

Jenkinson, C.E., Dickens, D., Jones, K., Thompson-Coon, J. et al (2013) Is volunteering a public health intervention? A systematic review and meta-analysis of the health and survival of volunteers, *BMC Public Health* (13), doi: 10.1186/1471-2458-13-773

John, P., Cotterill, S., Richardson, L., Moseley, A. et al (2011) *Nudge, Nudge, Think, Think: Experimenting with Ways to Change Civic Behaviour*. London: Bloomsbury.

Kamerade, D. (2011) An untapped pool of volunteers for the Big Society? Not enough social capital? Depends on how you measure it...', www.seek.salford.ac.uk/user/profile/publications/view.do?publicationNum=30209

Kamerade, D. (2017) Using metadata from the MO archive to inform our understanding of post-1981 writers' demographic characteristics, Presentation to the Mass Observation 80th Anniversary Conference, Brighton.

Kendall, J. (2003) *The Voluntary Sector in the UK.* Abingdon: Routledge.

Kendall, J. (2009) The UK: Ingredients in a hyperactive horizontal policy environment, in Kendall, J. (ed) *Handbook on Third Sector Policy in Europe.* Cheltenham: Edward Elgar, pp 67–94.

Kendall, J., Brookes, N., Mohan, J. and Yoon, Y. (forthcoming) The English voluntary sector: how volunteering and policy climate matter, *Journal of Social Policy.*

Keohane, N., Parker, S. and Ebanks, D. (2011) *Realising Community Wealth: Local Government and the Big Society.* London: The New Local Government Network.

Kramer, R. (1990) Change and continuity in British voluntary organisations, 1976–1988, *Voluntas*, 1, 33–60.

Kushner, A. (2004) *We Europeans: Mass Observation, 'Race' and British Identity in the Twentieth Century.* Aldershot: Ashgate.

Land, H. (2006) We sat down at the table of privilege and complained about the food, *Political Quarterly*, 77 (S1), 45–60.

Lane, J., Passey, A. and Saxon-Harrold, S. (1994) The resourcing of the charity sector: An overview of its income and expenditure, in S. Saxon-Harrold and J. Kendall (eds) *Researching the Voluntary Sector* (2nd edn). Tunbridge Wells: Charities Aid Foundation, pp 3–15.

Last, N. (2006) *Nella Last's war: The Second World War Diaries of 'Housewife, 49'.* London: Profile.

Lawless, P., Foden, M., Wilson, I. and Beatty, C. (2010) Understanding area-based regeneration: The new deal for communities in England, *Urban Studies*, 47, 257–75.

Laurence, J. and Lim, C. (2013) *'The Scars of Others Should Teach Us Caution': The Long-term Effects of Job 'Displacement' on Civic Participation over the Lifecourse.* Institute for Social Change, working paper 2013/02, available at hummedia.manchester.ac.uk/institutes/cmist/archive-publications/working-papers-isc/2013/JamesLaurenceHardshipandCivicParticipation.pdf.

Lawrence, R. (1983) Voluntary action: a stalking horse for the Right?, *Critical Social Policy*, 2(3), 14–30.

Layder, D. (1998) *Sociological Practice: Linking Theory and Social Research*. London: Sage.

Leat, D. (1983) Explaining volunteering: a sociological perspective, in S. Hatch (ed) *Volunteers. Patterns, Meanings and Motives*. Berkhamsted: Volunteer Centre, pp 51–61.

Leonard, P. (2010) *Expatriate Identities in Postcolonial Organisations: Working Whiteness*. Aldershot: Ashgate.

Leonard, P., Halford, S. and Bruce, K. (2016) 'The new degree'? Constructing internships in the Third Sector, *Sociology*, 50(2), 383–99.

Lewis, J. and Glennerster, H. (1996) *Implementing the New Community Care*. Buckingham: Open University Press.

Li, Y. (2015) The flow of soul: A sociological study of generosity in England and Wales, 2001–2011, in Y. Li (ed) *The Handbook of Research Methods and Applications on Social Capital*. Cheltenham: Edward Elgar, pp 40–59.

Lichterman, P. and Eliasoph, N. (2014) 'Civic action', *American Journal of Sociology*, 120, 798–863.

Lim, C. and Laurence, J. (2015) Doing good when times are bad: Volunteering behaviour in economic hard times, *British Journal of Sociology*, 66(2), 319–44.

Lindsey, R. (2004) Remembering Vukovar, forgetting Vukovar: Constructing national identity through the memory of catastrophe, in P. Grey and O. Kendrick (eds) *The Memory of Catastrophe*. Manchester: Manchester University Press, pp 190–204.

Lindsey, R. (2013) Exploring local hotspots and deserts: Investigating the local distribution of charitable resources, *Voluntary Sector Review*, 4, 95–116.

Lindsey, R. and Bulloch, S. (2013) What the public think of the 'Big Society': Mass Observers' views on individual and community capacity for civic engagement, *Third Sector Research Centre (TSRC) Working Paper* 95, Birmingham: TSRC, University of Birmingham, www.birmingham.ac.uk/generic/tsrc/documents/tsrc/working-papers/working-paper-95.pdf

Lindsey, R. and Bulloch, S. (2014) A sociologist's field notes to the Mass Observation Archive: A consideration of the challenges of 're-using' Mass Observation data in a longitudinal mixed-methods study, *Sociological Research Online* 19(3), doi: 10.5153/sro.3362

Lindsey, R., Metcalfe, E. and Edwards, R. (2015) Time in mixed method longitudinal research: Working across written narratives and large-scale panel survey data to investigate attitudes to volunteering, in N. Worth and I. Hardill (eds) *Researching the Lifecourse: Time, Space and Mobilities*. Bristol: Policy Press.

Low, N., Butt, S., Ellis Paine, A. and Davis-Smith, J. (2007) *Helping Out: A National Survey of Volunteering and Charitable Giving*. London: Office of the Third Sector, Cabinet Office.

Lynn, P. and Davis-Smith, J. (1992) *The 1991 National Survey of Voluntary Activity in the UK*. Berkhamsted: Volunteer Centre.

Lyons, M., Wijkstrom, P. and Clary, G. (1998) Comparative studies of volunteering: what is being studied?, *Voluntary Action*, 1(1), 45–54.

McCulloch, A. (2011) Volunteering as unpaid work or unpaid help: Differences in reports of voluntary activity, *Third Sector Research Centre (TSRC) Working Paper*, Southampton: TSRC, University of Southampton.

McCulloch, A. (2014) Cohort variations in the membership of voluntary associations in Great Britain, 1991–2007, *Sociology*, 48, 167–85.

McCulloch, A., Mohan, J. and Smith, P. (2012) Patterns of social capital, voluntary activity, and area deprivation in England. *Environment and Planning A*, 44(5), 1130–47.

Macduff, N. (2005) 'Societal changes and the rise of the episodic volunteer' in J. Brudney (ed) *Emerging Areas of Volunteering, ARNOVA Occasional Paper* 1 (2), 49–61, Indianapolis: ARNOVA.

Macmillan, R. (2013) Making sense of the Big Society: Perspectives from the third sector', *Third Sector Research Centre (TSRC) Working Paper* 90, Birmingham: TSRC, University of Birmingham, www.birmingham.ac.uk/generic/tsrc/documents/tsrc/working-papers/working-paper-90.pdf

Madge, C. and Harrisson, T. (1939) *Britain by Mass Observation*. Harmondsworth: Penguin.

Matheson, J. (1987) Voluntary work, *Office of Population Censuses and Surveys (OPCS) Series* GHS 17A, *London: OPCS*.

Mohan, J. and Breeze, B. (2016) *The Logic of Charity*. London: Palgrave Macmillan.

Mohan, J. and Bulloch, S. (2012) The idea of a 'civic core': What are the overlaps between charitable giving, volunteering, and civic participation in England and Wales?, *Third Sector Research Centre (TSRC) Working Paper* 73, Birmingham: TSRC, University of Birmingham, www.birmingham.ac.uk/generic/tsrc/documents/tsrc/working-papers/working-paper-73.pdf

Mohan, J. and Gorsky, M. (2001) *Don't Look Back? Voluntary and Charitable Finance of Hospital Care in Britain, Past and Present*. London: Office of Health Economics.

Mohan, J., Twigg, L., Jones, K. and Barnard, S. (2006) Volunteering, geography and welfare: A multilevel investigation of geographical variations in voluntary action, in C. Milligan and D. Conradson (eds) *Landscapes of Voluntarism: New Spaces of Health, Welfare and Governance.* Bristol: Policy Press.

Moore, S. (2008) *Ribbon Culture: Charity, Compassion and Public Awareness.* Basingstoke: Palgrave Macmillan

Morris, M. (1969) *Voluntary Work in the Welfare State.* London: Routledge and Kegan Paul.

Musick, M. and Wilson, J. (2008) *Volunteers: A Social Profile.* Bloomington, IN: Indiana University Press.

NCVO (National Council for Voluntary Organisations) (annual) *Almanac of Civil Society in the UK.* London: NCVO.

Neale, A.H.L. (2012) The Mass Observation writers: Who do we think they are?, Mass Observation Anniversaries Conference, 4–5 July, Brighton: University of Sussex.

Norman, J. (2010) *The Big Society: The Anatomy of the New Politics.* Buckingham: University of Buckingham Press.

ONS (Office for National Statistics) (2017) *Changes in the Value and Division of Unpaid Volunteering in the UK: 2000 to 2015,* www.ons.gov.uk/economy/nationalaccounts/satelliteaccounts/articles/changesinthevalueanddivisionofunpaidcareworkintheuk/2015#valuation-of-unpaid-formal-volunteering

OPCS (Office of Population Censuses and Surveys) (1983) *General Household Survey 1981,* London: HMSO.

Pahl, R. (1985) *Divisions of Labour.* Oxford: Blackwell.

Pahl, R. (2011) Review of Mike Savage, *Identities and Social Change Since 1940: The Politics of Method, Sociological Review,* 59(1), 165–76.

Parry, G., Moser, G. and Day, N. (1992) *Political Participation in Britain.* Cambridge: Cambridge University Press.

Parsons, S. (2013) Mass Observation: How to combine information with the British birth cohort studies, *Resource Report for Cohort and Longitudinal Studies Enhancement Resources.* London: Institute of Education.

Pensions Policy Institute (2017) *The Wellbeing, Health, Retirement and the Lifecourse Project,* London: Pensions Policy Institute, www.pensionspolicyinstitute.org.uk/publications/reports/the-wellbeing,-health,-retirement-and-the-lifecourse-project

Pollen, A. (2013) Research methodology in Mass Observation past and present: 'Scientifically, about as valuable as a chimpanzee's tea party at the zoo?', *History Workshop Journal,* 75 (1), 213–35.

Portelli, A. (1998) What makes oral history different, in R. Perks and A. Thomson (eds) *The Oral History Reader*. London: Routledge.

Power, A. (2012) *The 'Big Society' and Concentrated Neighbourhood Problems*. London: British Academy.

Putnam, R. (1995) Bowling alone: America's declining social capital, *Journal of Democracy*, 6, 65–78.

Putnam, R. (2000) *Bowling Alone: The Collapse and Revival of American Community*. New York: Simon and Schuster.

Putnam, R. (2007) *E pluribus unum*: diversity and community in the twenty-first century, *Scandinavian Political Studies*, 30, 137–74.

Putnam, R., Leonardi, R. and Nanetti, R. (1993) *Making Democracy Work: Civic Traditions in Modern Italy*. Princeton, NJ: Princeton University Press.

Raban, J. (2010) Cameron's Crank: Review of Blond, P. (2010) 'Red Tory', *London Review of Books*, 32(8), 22–3.

Reed, P. and Selbee, K. (2001) The Civic Core in Canada: Disproportionality in charitable giving, volunteering and civic participation. *Nonprofit and Voluntary Sector Quarterly*, 30(4), 761–80.

Roberts, J. and Devine, F. (2004) Social capital, pleasure and the contingency of participation. *Social Politics*, 11(2), 280–96.

Rochester, C. (2013) *Rediscovering Voluntary Action*. Basingstoke: Palgrave Macmillan.

Rochester, C., Ellis Paine, A., Howlett, S. and Zimmeck, M. (2010) *Volunteering in the 21st Century*. Basingstoke: Palgrave Macmillan.

Rooney, P., Steinberg, K. and Schervish, P. (2004) Methodology is destiny: The effects of survey prompts on reported levels of giving and volunteering, *Nonprofit and Voluntary Sector Quarterly*, 33(4), 628–54.

Rose-Ackerman, S. (1996) Altruism, non-profits, and economic theory, *Journal of Economic Literature*, 34, 701–28.

Rotolo, T. and Wilson, J. (2006) Substitute or complement? Spousal influence on volunteering, *Journal of Marriage and Family*, 68, 305–19.

Salamon, L. (1987) Of market failure, voluntary failure and third-party government: Toward a theory of government-nonprofit relations in the modern welfare state, *Nonprofit and Voluntary Sector Quarterly*, 16(1–2), 29–49.

Salamon, L., Sokolowski, W. and Haddock, S. (2011) Measuring the economic value of volunteer work globally: Concepts, estimates and a roadmap to the future, *Annals of Public and Cooperative Economics*, 82(3), 2217–52.

Sampson, R. (2012) *Great American City*. Chicago, IL: Chicago University Press.

Sampson, R.J., McAdam, D., MacIndoe, H. and Weffer-Elizondo, S. (2005) Civil society reconsidered: The durable nature and community structure of collective civic action, *American Journal of Sociology*, 111(3), 673–714.

Sauer, R. (2015) Does it pay for women to volunteer?, *International Economic Review*, 56, 537–64.

Savage, M. (2010) *Identities and Social Change in Britain since 1940: The Politics of Method*. Oxford: Oxford University Press.

Savage, M. (2011) Reply to Ray Pahl: Sociology and social change, *Sociological Review*, 59, 176–81.

Seddon, N. (2007) *Who Cares? How State Funding and Political Activism Change Charity*. London: Civitas.

Shaw, J. (1994) Transference and countertransference in the Mass-Observation Archive: An underexploited research resource, *Human Relations*, 47(11), 1391–408.

Sheard, J. (1995) From 'Lady Bountiful' to 'Active Citizen': Volunteering and the voluntary sector, in J. Davis-Smith, C. Rochester and R. Hedley (eds) *An Introduction to the Voluntary Sector*. London: Routledge, pp 114–27.

Sheridan, D. (1993) Writing to the archive: Mass-Observation as autobiography, *Sociology*, 27(1), 27–40.

Sheridan, D., Street, B. and Bloome, D. (2000) *Writing Ourselves: Mass Observation and Literary Practices*. New York: Hampton Press.

Sherrott, R. (1983) Fifty volunteers, in S. Hatch (ed) *Volunteers: Patterns, Meanings and Motives*. Berkhamsted: Volunteer Centre, pp 62–143.

Smith, D.H. (1997) The rest of the non-profit sector: Grassroots associations as the dark matter ignored in prevailing 'flat earth' maps of the sector, *Nonprofit and Voluntary Sector Quarterly*, 26, 114–31.

Snowden, C. (2012) *Sock Puppets: How the Government Lobbies Itself and Why*. London: Institute for Economic Affairs.

Spencer, N. (2016) *Doing Good: A Future for Christianity in the 21st Century*. London: Theos, www.theosthinktank.co.uk/cmsfiles/archive/files/Doing%20Good%205.pdf

Staetsky, L. and Mohan J. (2011) Individual voluntary participation in the United Kingdom: An overview of survey information, *Third Sector Research Centre (TSRC) Working Paper* 6, Birmingham: TSRC, University of Birmingham, www.birmingham.ac.uk/generic/tsrc/documents/tsrc/working-papers/working-paper-6.pdf

Stebbins, R. (1996) Volunteering: a serious leisure perspective, *Nonprofit and Voluntary Sector Quarterly*, 25, 211–24.

Stebbins, R. (2007) *Serious Leisure: A Perspective for our Times*. New Brunswick: Transaction Books.

Summerfield, P. (1985) Mass-Observation: Social research or social movement? *Journal of Contemporary History*, 20(3), 439–52.

Tabassum, F., Mohan, J. and Smith, P. (2016) Association of volunteering with mental well-being: A lifecourse analysis of a national population-based longitudinal study in the UK, *BMJ Open*, 6(8), http://bmjopen.bmj.com/content/6/8/e011327

Talarico, J.M. and Rubin, D.C. (2003) Confidence not consistency characterizes flashbulb memories, *Psychological Science* 14(5), 455–61.

Tarling, R. (2000) Statistics on the voluntary sector in the UK, *Journal of the Royal Statistical Society: Series A*, 163, 255–61.

Tashakkori, A. and Teddlie, C.B. (2008) Quality of inferences in mixed methods research: Calling for an integrative framework, in M.M. Bergman (ed) *Advances in Mixed-Methods Research*. London: Sage, pp 101–19.

Taylor, E. and Taylor-Gooby, P. (2015) Benefits and welfare: Long-term trends or short-term reactions? In Natcen (eds) *British Social Attitudes: The 32nd Report*, www.bsa.natcen.ac.uk/media/38977/bsa32_welfare.pdf

Taylor, M. (2011) Community organising and the Big Society: Is Saul Alinsky turning in his grave?, *Voluntary Sector Review*, 2, 257–64.

Taylor, R.F. (2004) Extending conceptual boundaries: Work, voluntary work and employment, *Work, Employment and Society*, 18(1), 29–46.

Taylor, R.F. (2005) Rethinking voluntary work, in L. Pettinger, J. Parry, R.F. Taylor, and M. Glucksmann (eds) *A New Sociology of Work?* Chichester: Wiley.

Taylor-Gooby, P. (2012) Root and branch restructuring to achieve major cuts: The social policy programme of the 2010 UK Coalition government. *Social Policy and Administration*, 46, 61–82.

Taylor-Gooby, P. and Stoker, G. (2011) The coalition programme: A new vision for Britain or politics as usual?, *Political Quarterly*, 82(1), 4–15.

Teasdale, S., Alcock, P. and Smith, G. (2012) Legislating for a big society? The case of the public services (social enterprise and social value) bill in England, *Public Money and Management*, 32, 201–8.

Van Tienen, M., Scheepers, P., Reitsma, J. and Schilderman, H. (2011) The role of religiosity for formal and informal volunteering in the Netherlands, *Voluntas*, 22(3), 365–89.

Timmins, N. (2001) *The Five Giants: A biography of the Welfare State*. London: Harper Collins.

Unell, J. (1979) *Voluntary Social Services: Financial Resources*. London: Bedford Square Press.

Warde, A., Tampubolon, G., Longhurst, B., Ray, K., Savage, M. and Tomlinson, M. (2003) Trends in social capital: Membership of associations in Great Britain, 1991–1998, *British Journal of Political Science*, 33(3), 515–25.

Ware, A. (2012) The Big Society and Conservative politics: Back to the future or forward to the past? *Political Quarterly*, 82(S1), 82–97.

Webb, S. and Webb, B. (1911) *The Prevention of Destitution*. London: Longman, Green and Co.

Wheatley, D. (with Hardill, I. and Bickerton, C.) (2017) *Time Well Spent: Subjective Well-being and the Organisation of Time*. New York: Rowman and Littlefield.

Wilensky, H. (1961) Orderly careers and social participation: The impact of work history on social integration in the middle mass, *American Sociological Review*, 26, 521–39.

Williams, C. (2003) Developing community involvement: Contrasting local and regional participatory cultures in Britain and their implications for policy, *Regional Studies*, 37, 531–41.

Wilson, J. (2012) Volunteerism research: A review essay, *Nonprofit and Voluntary Sector Quarterly*, 41, 176–212.

Wilson, J. and Musick, M. (1997) Who cares? Toward an integrated theory of volunteer work, *American Sociological Review*, 62, 694–713.

Wistow, G. (1992) Health, in D. Marsh and R. Rhodes (eds) *Implementing Thatcherite Policies*. Milton Keynes: Open University Press, pp 100–16.

Wolfenden Committee (1978) *The Future of Voluntary Organisations*. Report of the Wolfenden Committee. London: Croom Helm.

Wuthnow, R. (1991) *Acts of Compassion*. Princeton, NJ: Princeton University Press.

Zimmeck, M. (2010) Government and volunteering, in C. Rochester, A. Ellis Paine, S. Howlett and M. Zimmeck (eds) (2010) *Volunteering and Society in the 21st Century*. Basingstoke: Palgrave Macmillan, pp 84–102.

Index

Note: Page locators in *italics* refer to figures or tables. Personal names in *italics* refer to pseudonyms of writers for the Mass Observation Project.